That was Business, this is Personal

by the same author

Billy Connolly: The Authorised Version
Gullible's Travels

DUNCAN CAMPBELL

That was Business,
this is Personal

The Changing Faces of Professional Crime

Secker & Warburg   London

First published in Great Britain 1990
by Martin Secker & Warburg Limited
Michelin House,
81 Fulham Road,
London SW3 6RB

Copyright © 1990 by Duncan Campbell

A CIP catalogue record for this book
is available from the British Library.
ISBN 0 436 19990 4

The sources of quotations at chapter heads are as follows: Chapter 2, quoted by Bob Woffinden in *Miscarriages of Justice* (Hodder & Stoughton, 1989); Chapter 3, C. Jung, *Archetypes and Collective Unconscious* (Routledge & Kegan Paul, 1959); Chapter 4, David Mamet, *House of Games* (Screenplay, Methuen, 1988); Chapter 6, Reg and Ron Kray, ed. Fred Dineage, *Our Story* (Sidgwick & Jackson, 1988); Chapter 7, quoted by Robert Hughes in *The Fatal Shore* (Collins Harvill, 1987; Pan, 1988); Chapter 8, Paul Eddy, Sarah Walden and Hugo Sabogal, *The Cocaine Wars* (Century, 1988; Arrow, 1989); Chapter 9, from Jonathan Green, *Says Who* (Longman, 1989); Chapter 10, Graham Greene, *Brighton Rock* (Heinemann, 1938); Chapter 11, from *Says Who*; Chapter 13, from *Says Who*; Chapter 16, Evelyn Waugh, *Decline and Fall* (Methuen, 1928); Chapter 20, Gilbert Kelland, *Crime in London* (Grafton, 1987); James Baldwin, *Nobody Knows My Name* (Michael Joseph, 1965).

Photoset by Rowland Phototypesetting Limited
Bury St Edmunds, Suffolk
Printed in Great Britain by
Mackays of Chatham plc, Chatham, Kent

Contents

Acknowledgements

I would like to thank all the people
who agreed to be interviewed, without
whom there would not have been a book.
I would also like to thank the many others
who helped to put me in touch
with people and who gave advice.
They are mostly too shy to want
to be mentioned by name.

Introduction

On 4 August 1989, two smartly-dressed, self-assured men in their late fifties were told by Judge Robert Sanders at Snaresbrook Crown Court that 'you are both old enough and experienced enough to know exactly what you were doing and your motive was greed'. He jailed them for ten and seven years for cocaine dealing. In 1964 the same two men had listened politely while another judge, Mr Justice Edmund Davies, had told them that 'this is nothing less than a sordid crime of violence inspired by vast greed. The motive of greed is obvious.'

The two men, Tommy Wisbey and Jimmy Hussey, were Great Train Robbers. A quarter of a century had elapsed between those two stern addresses from the bench. Their first famous trial – catalogued in films, books, documentary and song – transported them into the aristocracy of crime. The judgement at Snaresbrook – a suburban court in Essex that looks more like a convalescent home than a hall of justice – was buried low on the inside pages of newspapers. No one was going to make a film called the Medium-sized Cocaine Deal.

In a way the case symbolised what had happened to professional crime in Britain during that twenty-five year period. It had changed: from teams of organised criminals in overalls grabbing large bundles of Bank of England notes, to quiet, besuited drug-dealers selling white powders from Latin America. But what had happened in between?

Before I started work on this book, I re-read *East End Underworld* by Raphael Samuel, a biography of one of the first Borstal boys, Arthur Harding, who was described by a local police inspector as one of the 'slipperiest characters in Brick Lane', and who had graduated from petty theft to protection racketeering.

What was remarkable about Harding's descriptions of professional crime in those pre-war days was their parochial, almost Dickensian quality – one of the main characters even had the sort of name that only an Ealing comedy would have given to a criminal: Dodger Mullins. Towards the end of the book Harding refers very obliquely to a family in the area whose inability to hold down a regular job was attributed by him to their gypsy stock.

The family was called the Krays and if the Arthurs and Dodgers were to represent a localised, unsophisticated brand of professional crime that drew little attention to itself, the Krays were to change all that.

The notion of the gangster – glad-handing, gun-wielding, charity-donating, club-owning – came from the United States. And although the Krays were as English as bus queues and Bovril, what they were re-creating, first in the East End and then, disastrously for them, in the West End, was just a slightly distorted mirror image of what people were then watching in the one-and-ninepennies. This was crime as show business. Their clubs and later their memoirs were littered with photos of stars such as George Raft and Judy Garland, heavyweight champions and hard-drinking crooners.

The Krays ushered in a new era which has acted as a paradigm for British crime ever since – the family firm with its loyal henchmen, its rackets, its usefully-placed allies in the legitimate world and its constant undertow of menace.

South of the Thames, the Richardson family, under Charlie Richardson, enjoyed a similar reputation. Again, the sums of money involved were small and the crime for which Charlie Richardson was eventually jailed for twenty-five years, in 1966, was grievous bodily harm, not murder. But, like the Krays, the Richardsons had a dark reputation. Although they said their violence was of the 'smack in the mouth' variety, they were alleged to have used electric shocks and pliers to deal with recalcitrants: Richardson protested that his victims 'didn't even need an aspirin'. The crime he was charged with seems minor compared with the time he was given but the sentence was, like that of the Krays, intended to discourage other such ambitious criminals.

The Age of the Gangster effectively ended in 1969 when Mr Justice Melford Stevenson jailed the Krays for thirty years saying: 'I am not going to waste words. In my view society has earned a rest from your activities.' The era may have been a brief period of criminal history, it may have had the tiniest of effects on the national economy, it may have been responsible for the deaths of only two or three men but the fact that the Krays have remained synonymous with crime and gangland more than twenty years later is evidence of their strange effect on the national psyche.

The other criminal icons of the age had been the Great Train Robbers who robbed the Glasgow–Euston train of £2,631,684 in August 1963. Their jail sentences of thirty years sent a message out about high-profile gangs and high-profile deeds. Colin Shindler, author of the screenplay *Buster*, the story of one of the robbers, Buster Edwards, was to write later in *The Times*: 'In 1963 crime was still a game. The savage sentences seemed to break its rules.'

And Mr Justice Edmund Davies dismissed any notions of Robin Hoodery generated by the bravado of the crime as he passed those sentences: 'Let us clear out of the way any romantic notions of daredevilry. This is nothing less than a sordid crime of violence inspired by vast greed . . . As to violence, anyone who has seen the nerve-shattered engine driver can have no doubt of the terrifying effect on law-abiding citizens of a concerted assault by masked and armed robbers in lonely darkness. To deal with this case leniently would be a positively evil thing.'

But although the heavy sentences did little to halt the increase of armed robbery, criminals did realise that such an audacious crime, involving so many people, was doomed: there were too many loose ends and the premium on finding the perpetrators was too high. A simpler method was straightforward, in-and-out armed robbery – of a security van, a bank or a sub post office. Guns were becoming more easily available. The Age of the Robber had begun.

The end of the sixties and the early seventies saw the emergence of the 'Face', the armed robber who worked in a small team, had little interest in controlling territory beyond a nice mansion house in Hertfordshire or Essex and took advantage of laxity, both of the arrangements of security firms and the morals of some police officers. They described themselves as 'at it', 'on the pavement'. The police called them 'blaggers'. They had little to do with the old family 'firms' and little interest in owning clubs and casinos like the Krays. 'Instant Cash' was the *nom de blag* of one such villain and it summed up the philosophy of his peers – sawn-off shotguns in a Wembley bank followed by a spell of sawn-off jeans on a Marbella beach.

The pickings were easy: 'Just like jumping over a sweetie counter,' one described it, 'and when the police came round for you, it was a relief because you could pay them off and that would be an end of it.'

Firearms were used increasingly. One theory, advanced straight-faced by some armed robbers, was that the gun was a humane introduction to the robber's equipment – gradually people learned not to tackle a gunman whereas before they had felt there was some chance of disarming a man wielding a club or iron bar, thus risking a fractured skull.

Sawn-off shotguns, Smith and Wesson .45s, Colts, Lugers were bought, passed on and hidden. The money rolled in. The random nature of the attacks, the loose structure of the teams involved – no identifiable 'gangs' as such – meant they were hard to track down. In any case, there was a marked reluctance to do so on the part of many of the police employed in the hunt. It was a period of deep cynicism and casual corruption at the Yard and the robbers knew it and exploited it. This period has since been described as the Fall of Scotland Yard and the fall was a long and heavy one.

The Age of the Robber stuttered to a halt through the seventies because of two developments: the arrival of the supergrass – the informer prepared to give evidence against his former associates – and the cleaning up of the Yard carried out in the wake of revelations of widespread corruption.

Bertie Smalls, a major bank robber, was arrested in 1972. In exchange for evidence against his former colleagues he was granted written immunity from the Director of Public Prosecutions and Scotland Yard. Grasses sprouted everywhere, even the most 'steadfast' robbers suddenly disappeared from view to re-emerge giving evidence against their erstwhile colleagues in exchange for a smaller sentence and a new identity.

Meanwhile Sir Robert Mark had taken over as Commissioner of the Metropolitan Police in 1972. He intimated that he was no longer prepared to tolerate the abuses of some of his middle-rank detectives and the subsequent clear-out led to hundreds of resignations in disgrace from the force, a score of prosecutions and an acknowledgement that something was rotten in the Yard. It was seen as the cleaning of the Augean stables.

However, the sweep did not totally remove corruption from the force. A few years later a further internal investigation, Operation Countryman, conducted by officers from the Dorset police, found evidence of further malpractice but was unable to stand up more than a handful of cases in court: the Dorset police found reluctance within the Met to cooperate – it is no accident that the emblem once suggested for the tie of the internal investigation squad at the Yard was a rat. In addition, juries are reluctant to convict an officer who has been involved in arresting dangerous criminals whatever the evidence of corruption against him might be. But the investigations sent a message out to the younger officers and police contributions to the Age of the Robber were already in decline.

By the end of the eighties, a further development had made the career even less attractive to the young criminal: robbers caught in the act were shot dead.

Here is how one elderly armed robber, Ronnie Easterbrook, described the death of his colleague and his own wounding on one armed raid: 'I knew it was a police trap. I thought to myself "Let's get killed". I stepped over Tony and I reached out and fired low in the general direction of the police. Being trained marksmen their return was simultaneous. I could see the smoke rising from their guns. I felt something like a punch hit my shoulder. Also the noise of the shots hitting the car. It sounded like someone had thrown a shovel of gravel over it. I remember being mildly surprised that I was still alive.'

What was more than mildly surprising was that in 1988 Ronald Easterbrook, a man in his late fifties, was taking part in an attempted armed robbery at the Bejam frozen food store in Woolwich, south London, at all. For Easterbrook represented a generation of criminals that had long since given up jumping over counters and leaping into getaway cars. Easterbrook was a throwback. His colleague, Tony Ash, who had twenty-one convictions, all for minor offences, was killed.

The wreath sent to the Camberwell funeral read: 'With sorrow and regret. May your executioners and Seamus Ray live long and suffer every day.' Ray was the informer.

The rules of firearms etiquette had indeed changed by the mid-eighties, when it became clear that the armed officers of Scotland Yard's PT17 Blue Beret unit would shoot to kill if they believed the robbers they were pursuing would shoot at them. The Ron Easterbrook case was one example. Another came in the spring of 1989 when Jimmy Farrell and Terry Dewsnap were shot dead after an abortive raid on a post office in South Harrow. To the police such deaths are an inevitable consequence of robbers going armed. They say that they need to catch the robbers red-handed to ensure a conviction and that if they raid their homes in anticipation of the crime and charge them with conspiracy to rob it is easier for the men to win an acquittal in court. The robbers' friends suggest that the police now allow the shoot-outs to happen rather than pre-empt them with an arrest because they know there is little public concern over such deaths.

As the Age of the Robber ended, the Age of the Dealer began. Drugs had been an expanding market from the sixties but the dealers tended to be a mixture of former hippies, who had started as small dealers and realised there were larger sums to be made wholesaleing and setting up operations, and some new immigrants whose countries produced the raw materials so that the home-base contact was already made.

Then drugs started to enter prisons in a big way – smuggled in through girlfriends' kisses, dumped on prison playing fields by helpful friends on the outside, inserted in food packets and rolled up newspapers sent to the prison libraries. Inmates doing long stretches found that a quiet joint was preferable to the dubious attractions of illicit hooch made of rotting fruit in chamberpots.

At first there had been resistance to drug dealing – or at least hard drug dealing – amongst the professional criminal classes but they soon realised that here was a new way of making money that required no getaway car and ran less risk of informers. It had the added advantage that there was no victim running to the police. Some muscled in to existing markets, others helped create their own.

Many had come across cannabis in their sojourns in Spain and Morocco and cannabis was the simplest starting point. It had the advantage that it was a soft drug and disapproval of it was limited – magistrates and members of the legal profession now had children who smoked joints and did not jump off rooftops.

Then, in the mid-eighties attitudes to all drugs hardened and there was little distinction made between soft and hard. Twenty years after the great and the good – Brian Walden, Jonathan Aitken, Jonathan Miller, Humphrey Berkeley, George Melly and fifty-nine others – signed an advertisement in *The Times* in 1967 calling for the decriminalisation of marijuana, the law seemed less likely to change than ever. As it became clear that the penalties for importing the hard were little sterner than for the soft, the cost-conscious drug dealer shifted to cocaine and heroin and the lines between the heroin dealer and the cannabis dealer became blurred and obliterated.

Now the drugs trade remains an ever-expanding industry with a wide variety of people involved – the old professional villain, the young criminal who sees little point in the riskier activities of armed robbery, some members of the different immigrant groups which have links to drug-producing countries. The group attracting most attention by the end of the eighties, and provoking the setting up of a special squad, were called the Yardies, a word with a Jamaican origin which became a shorthand term for a black criminal in this country. The man in charge of the special squad, Detective Chief Superintendent Roy Ramm, told the *Observer* that they represented 'a complex matrix of much flatter pyramids than a traditional Mafia organisation. You might find someone who will be both trafficker and street dealer.' They are seen by the police as armed and ruthless, but their power and prevalence is treated with scepticism by most members of the black community who say that their existence has been exaggerated and that the term is now used simply to embrace anyone black and involved in crime.

The Yardies took over from the Chinese community's Triads as the chief bogey-figures among immigrant groups but although the latter have been involved both in violent crimes, usually involving their own community, and in criminal dealings in commodity futures, their network is regarded as a small one.

But the Age of the Dealer embraced more than just drugs. In tandem with the growth in narcotics dealing were the new bloodless crimes, based around the City, of insider dealing, VAT, computer and 'long firm' fraud – and a new internationalism.

The VAT frauds were simple in execution: gold would be legitimately bought abroad, flown surreptitiously into the United Kingdom, melted down and sold. VAT would be avoided. Again – no guns, no chases, few risks. VAT fraud represented the perfect job opportunity for middle-aged robbers wanting to retire from violent crime.

Computer fraud had a less obvious appeal since it required greater technique and expertise, but by the end of the eighties Scotland Yard's computer fraud squad were seeing the development of a variety of imaginative schemes that were netting their operators tens of millions of pounds. Computer hackers were able to transfer funds electronically or divert tiny sums from rounded off transactions into separate accounts. Hackers could also blackmail companies by threatening to put a 'virus' or 'logic bomb' into their computer system and thus paralyse its operations.

Imaginative use was being made of the new forms of computerised bank technology. In March 1989 came news of the Hole in the Wall wheeze whereby a supermarket chain was blackmailed by threats of food contamination into paying money into a bogus Halifax Building Society account. Then all the patient thieves had to do was use their card to get money from the cash dispenser. Hundreds of police around the country targeted cash dispensers in the hope of catching them but with no immediate success.

Expanding international businesses allowed for the development of the 'long firm' fraud – the setting up of a bogus company, acquiring vast credit over a long period and then vanishing. There was no shortage of City businessmen prepared to advise on the swift movement of the money. The international aspect of the business was illustrated in 1989 when detectives investigating the earlier shootings of two criminals, Brian 'Little Legs' Clifford and Paddy O'Nione, believed to be involved in long firm frauds, flew to Saudi Arabia to interview members of the Yemeni community there.

This international development in a traditionally chauvinistic profession worries the police as 1992 and the end of European barriers approaches. The Association of Chief Police Officers (ACPO) are already discussing how the breaking down of the restrictions will lead to increased possibilities for the smart criminal. The Trevi group of community ministers already cooperate on terrorist information and Interpol is expanding, but criminals have been observing the Department of Enterprise invocations to be ready for 1992 just as any other growing business has.

By the end of the eighties, the Commissioner of the Metropolitan police, Sir Peter Imbert, was calling for the creation of a national detective agency along the lines of the FBI, integrating the fifty-two existing police forces in the United Kingdom. In a keynote address to the Police Foundation Sir Peter mooted the new structure which would mean local forces surrendering some of their sovereignty and the customs burying some of their differences – which had surfaced particularly over drugs investigations – with the police.

The extent of the Age of the Dealer is illustrated by the detected – far less the undetected – growth of such activities. The latest annual figures (1987) showed that a total of 590 cases involving £1.8 billion had been investigated. The Fraud Squad reckoned that by the end of the eighties around £14 million a day was being swindled from firms in Britain by means of insider dealing, computer fraud and mortgage insurance theft. The bright boy who once might have robbed banks had exchanged the black shirt/white tie for the white collar/silk tie notion of crime. Education was paying off. And as the line between criminal fraud and sharp business practice – what Al Capone described as the 'legitimate racket' – became blurred, different people entered the profession. Drug dealing had seen members of the middle-classes become involved in professional crime in a large way; now they were joined by others with the same educational background in a world which had always been portrayed as exclusively working-class.

Charlie Richardson, he of a couple of ages back in criminal history, is now a City businessman, having served eighteen years of that twenty-five year sentence. He looks the part – smart, well-cut suit, neatly trimmed beard. He appeared in a Channel Four documentary in 1988 in which he drew the parallels between crime and the City. 'The City is much more crooked than anything I was ever involved in,' he said.

And as the City played its part in the new age of crime, so the latest technological accessories had their uses. Car phones and shortwave radios for drug dealers became *de rigeur*. Scanners, which can scan the frequencies used by customs and police and locate the place from where a transmission is coming, found a new market, selling for as little as £200 a time.

As the criminals have embraced new technology, so have the police. One of the greatest developments has been in 'genetic fingerprinting', or the 'DNA signature' whereby people can be traced by their blood, semen, saliva and tissues, in tests pioneered by Professor Alex Jeffreys of Leicester University. The increasing sophistication of the police computer, of new forms of identification of suspects, of the video camera have all shifted the odds towards detection in traditional cases but have yet to be applied so successfully to the Age of the Dealer crimes.

In a way what has happened to British crime parallels what has happened to British industry. The old family firms like the Krays – 'never knowingly undermined' – and the Richardsons have been replaced by multinationals of uncertain ownership, branches throughout the world, profits dispersed through myriad outlets. They have even worked in the same fields that were expanding profitably on the legitimate side: drugs and computer technology. The 1990s is seen as a boom time for them, with the exploitation of a recreational western culture that wants its luxuries and its drugs. The legitimate businesses will run alongside the illegitimate ones.

'Respect' is what the old gangsters used to want, the new gangsters are not remotely interested in respect. 'Respect' means attention and attention means inspection. Respect doesn't pay the boy's public school fees or the squash club membership. The last thing the new criminal wants is recognition in a north London club and the desire for discretion has meant a notable absence of 'Faces' on the scene. This is part of the reason that the Krays and Richardsons and the Great Train Robbers still loom so large. What subsequent professional criminals – as opposed to murderers like Peter Sutcliffe and Denis Nilsen – have achieved such notoriety? There are the crew on the Costa del Crime but they mostly belong to the Age of the Robber. Who else has penetrated the public imagination?

Possibly David Martin, who hanged himself in his prison cell in Parkhurst in 1984. But his fame sprang more from the circumstances of his capture than the nature of his crimes: David Martin, in a way, was a throwback too. He came to prominence when film technician Stephen Waldorf was shot in mistake for him in Bayswater and nearly died from his wounds. Martin, a north Londoner, used to steal cars from police stations, drive them to France and then phone the police to let them know that their car was in de Gaulle airport car park. He was reputed to have made his getaway from robberies dressed as a woman. At the time of the Waldorf shooting he was on the run, wanted for the wounding of a policeman. He was finally cornered on the track in the Belsize Park underground, tried at the Old Bailey and jailed in October for twenty-five years for attempted murder, grievous bodily harm, burglary and possession of weapons. He made it clear that he had no intention of serving a sentence that was identical to the one given Denis Nilsen for killing sixteen young men and he took his life on 13 March 1984.

His parents, who still live in a large estate near Manor House, north London, are deeply bitter both about their son's death and about the publicity that surrounded him. 'They are absolute pigs and scum,' was the gentlest thing that Joan Martin had to say about the people who wrote about her son. 'I was chased, pushed and shoved. They made things up, they told us they would put down what we told them and what appeared was lies. Nobody really knew what he was like. I would rather be David Martin's mother than any of their mothers.'

The relatives of most men convicted of crimes have roughly similar views of the press. Well, they would, wouldn't they, might be the first response, but if journalism is the first rough draft of history then crime journalism has a habit of being rougher than most.

Sometimes reports of crimes can read like an extended police briefing; the criminals one-dimensional figures. On the other hand, some of the books by ex-criminals seem self-pitying and partisan, the uncomfortable pieces of violence brushed quietly under the carpet.

Crime on screen often has the same one-dimensional character; the heroes either the tough-but-tender cops or the live-fast-die-young gangsters. An essay entitled 'The Gangster as Tragic Hero' by Robert Warshow which appeared in *Partisan Review* in 1948 put it thus: 'The gangster is the No to that great American Yes that is stamped so large over our official culture.' Carlos Clarens, in his book, *Crime in the Movies*, observes that 'a gangster pal was both a badge of sophistication and a way of asserting that all successful Americans met at the top.'

American films from *The Godfather* through to David Mamet's *Things Change* have managed to make the Mob almost loveable, a change noted by Jack Katz, a California sociologist, in *Seductions of Crime*, which looks at how our perceptions of crime have been moulded. Over here films featuring our own criminals – *McVicar, Buster*, both starring pop stars – have also been criticised; columnist Julie Burchill describes it as the 'modern muddle-class misapprehension that criminals are in some way the misguided elite of the working-class, too sensitive and entrepreneurial to settle for being factory fodder'.

But the continuing and ambivalent public fascination with crime remains. When a security guard at Heathrow airport apparently disappeared with £1 million worth of his employer's money in 1989 there was a sneaking 'good luck to him' about the reports of the crime. One barely reported case in 1988 sums up, perhaps, the bad-boy notion of crime which in some quarters has lent it the same sort of appeal as a career in football, boxing or pop music: nine men, mostly in their early twenties, were jailed at Bristol Crown Court for a series of robberies. What they enjoyed most, however, was waiting until the police arrived on the scene and then fleeing in turbo-charged Ford Escorts, sometimes even slowing down to let the police catch up with them before speeding off again, pausing only to deliver a laconic V-sign out of the window. 'They even cruised up and down outside stores they had robbed,' said Detective Inspector Graham Hatswell after the case. 'Then they would play cat and mouse with us.'

Which brings us to why some forms of crime are almost tolerated and excused while others provoke a public fury. In general, rightly or wrongly, it is not the professional criminal who attracts the greatest public opprobrium. It is the rapist and the child molester, the mugger, the house burglar who leaves his faeces on the carpet and the drunken thug who cause the gravest fear and concern. Professor Jock Young of Middlesex Polytechnic discovered in one area of London that he researched in the late eighties that the greatest concern was not crime but dog mess – mess left by dogs which had been bought because of fear of burglars and muggers.

Corporate crime, crime committed by organisations in pursuit of profit, remains mostly unexplored: it leaves no bullet holes and the bodies of its victims don't die on the pavement outside the bank but in less spectacular fashion, of industrial disease or carelessness. Its practitioners are not called Dodger or Little Legs, its methods are more difficult to investigate, punish or report.

Some thoughts occur. Firstly, and hardly an original notion, if crime is one of the great worries of people in this country, there seems remarkably little interest in either finding out its causes or in attempting any radical ways of dealing with it. There is little new research being carried out into the causes of crime and the rise of violent crime is now accepted to be as inevitable as the rise in house prices. Attempts to delve deeper into its roots are seen as either irrelevant or a regression to the much-ridiculed 'we are all guilty' mentality.

Secondly, as regards punishment, the main new direction for the nineties is the building of nearly twenty new prisons all with 'en suite' bathrooms, as though the tardy acknowledgement that people do not like carrying out their bodily functions in public is a major step forward. In the meantime, prisoners are taught few new skills, and are lucky if they are to get any education that might point them in a different direction. Almost everyone interviewed in this book – police, criminals, judge, prison officer – agrees that the penal system is a disgrace yet no Home Office minister has yet had the vision to try and deal with it. The result is an assembly line of crime churning out more criminals every year. Prison officers, many of whom resent their lowly status compared to police officers, and who are paid a menial wage for a menial job, lament the fact that they are now little more than lock-up merchants. New ways of deflecting avoidable crime are being explored now in France, different prison techniques are examined in Holland and West Germany. Yet the ideas seem largely ignored in the United Kingdom and if we glance abroad for inspiration it is across the Atlantic at the country with one of the most violent and active criminal societies in the world.

Thirdly, much of the information we have on crime is one-dimensional, portrayed in black and white, learned from the screen or the headline and with little relationship to reality. The mystification of crime helps no one.

What pervades the issue is a sense of hypocrisy: 'greed' is an entirely reprehensible motive for the train robber or cocaine dealer, yet greed has been granted a sort of jocular respectability elsewhere in society. One hundred and fifty officers may be dispatched to raid an inner-city party which will yield less drugs than the average charity ball, yet the same manpower will never be thrown against the subtler fraudsters.

Three court sentences in the last month of the eighties said much about public attitudes to what is defined as crime: one man was jailed for five years for helping to organise an Acid House party; another was sent to prison for three years for the manslaughter of an Asian shopkeeper, whose death he greeted with the words 'one less Paki'; and a Conservative Party Home Affairs Committee Chairman received a small fine for drunk driving, the day after one of his senior colleagues had outlined how many people were killed by drunks on the road each year.

What that does not address, of course, is that some people like crime. And they will carry on doing it. It is exciting. It is not nine to five. It offers an escape from the terror of the humdrum. It may no longer be 'romantic' – gangsters do not belong in an age of loft conversions and exercise bicycles – but you can make a damn good living from it if you're clever and we live in a world where increasingly you are what you own.

There are still the criminal gangs, not like the Krays but looser, de-regulated, diversified as befits the nineties, technologically sophisticated, with wider horizons than the south coast of Spain. And there are other 'gangs' involved with crime, in multi-million pound businesses. They too have their jargon and their heroes, their haunts and their pecking order and their rituals. But there is one major difference. They are legal. The police gang, the law gang, the prison gang, the caring professions gang and the crime press gang.

This book is about individuals from all those 'gangs' and what they think of each other. The people who appear in it are not 'typical' or meant to be.

They come from different worlds – the young bank robber from Crawley and the elderly judge from Hove, the black probation officer from Wolverhampton, and the Kray twins' fixer from the west coast of Scotland. But many strands unite them: almost all had found the job exciting whether it was robbery or detection, almost all did not tell people they met casually what they did – whether being a detective, criminal, probation officer or prison officer. Almost all felt that their lives when portrayed in the press or in television fiction were misrepresented. And almost all said that their calling – the crime, the police, the prison service, the press – made heavy demands on their private lives and among colleagues often led to the break-up of relationships and the bottle. Some had regrets, some felt that the journey had been worth the fears and the pressure. They are mostly men – crime and its detection remain still very much a boy's own activity, although there are now more women drug dealers than there ever were female bank robbers. Perhaps that chauvinism is best summed up in the words of the mother of one of the bank robbers who appears briefly in this book: when told of one of her wayward son's criminal exploits she would shake her head and say, 'He's a boy, isn't he, he's a boy,' much as if he'd been caught stealing apples or torn his shorts on a tree.

Most of us commit our little crimes – of dishonesty, threatening behaviour, malicious wounding – every day. Some of us take it further and move from the amateur to the professional. It is those people and the people whom they encounter in their lives that this book is about.

I

The Face

We rob banks.

Clyde Barrow,
Bonnie and Clyde

'When we were waiting for the verdict, it reminded me of those films when you're in a landing craft and you're heading towards the beach and you think, "Fuck this – when that flap goes down we're in shit street," but everyone still manages to laugh and joke. You laugh your bollocks off . . . nervous release of some kind I suppose. There was a lot of jesting, like you were going to the gallows. I think we'd all given up.

'The judge said to me, "Robert Alles King, you played for high stakes and you lost." I always remember that. "And you will go to prison for sixteen years." My brief kept saying I'd get fourteen. As I turned round to go downstairs all the briefs looked like a row of bedraggled crows and all the cozzers shrugged and tried to look sympathetic – as we'd been paying them off for years, that didn't surprise me.

'All the women, all the gangsters' molls, they were all done up to the nines and they were all crying. You've never seen such a ghastly sight in your whole life as these five or six women with mascara all down their chops and their wigs at an angle, all weeping. I just burst out laughing. It was like something out of Monty Python or a scene out of Kafka. I was in almost uncontrollable laughter like I was on drugs. The screws were going, "He's a right psychopath, he's a nutter. Sixteen years and laughs in the judge's face." It hit me the next morning though.'

For the next morning Robert Alles King woke up inside one of Her Majesty's prisons with a prospect that was more Kafka than Python. It was 1973 and one of London's most accomplished bank robbers had quite a few next mornings to contemplate the stakes he had played for.

'Kingy' is a talented mimic – Glaswegian, Greek Cypriot, Home Counties toff, Italian, middle-class social worker, he can do them all. The first one he learnt was his dad, a Scot who had come down to London in the thirties to find work as a postman while Mrs King worked as a cleaner. King's father fought in the Spanish Civil War, was a communist all his life and subscribed to the Left Book Club, though he never talked about his Spanish experiences – he was invalided out to Gibraltar with tuberculosis – to his family. One daughter became a GI bride and headed for America as a hopeful teenager. Robert Alles became the oldest brother. His mum wanted the best for this bright boy.

'We came from Upper Holloway but my mum thought the schools were a bit rough and would have a bad effect on me so she sent me to Crouch End.' It turned out to be the other way round. 'There was petty pilfering from shops, that sort of thing. There were no such things as O and A levels, they were unheard of. If you failed your eleven plus then that was it, you were factory fodder. If your dad had a good job, then you would leave and become a plumber's mate or a printer – that was regarded as a very prestigious sort of job. In our school, it was either the print, the meat trade or crime. If you had relatives in the print or at Smithfield or knew someone who had, you were all right.'

Bobby King had neither, but he did have a conscientious mother. 'She got me a job as an office boy at Lloyd's in Leadenhall Street because she thought that held out great opportunities for the future.' He was one of those boys with little red collars that ran around with messages. 'I hated it. All those underwriters – "Boy!" – clicking their fingers at you.' One Sunday, bored with having to go up to the Admiralty and fetch messages, he set off the air raid sirens on the roof. He was sacked on the spot. 'They went mental.'

He drifted in and out of jobs, apprentice fireman, railway worker, a mini supermarket, sweeping up leaves in the parks. 'I used to hang around this caff in Hornsey Rise.' There he met 'all the guys out of the flats who seemed to me much more attractive characters than the ones I went to work with, who were pretty dull, I felt, and naïve. I'm sure I was too. But these other kids and their older brothers – some had been in Borstal – I found much more attractive characters. They knew how the police operated, which I found a bit shocking.

'They used a different kind of language, a lot of working-class street slang. I think that was the first time I heard the expression "Old Bill". Their fathers had been in and out of jail and made a living receiving. It was illegal gambling schools, clubs, cars, pubs, that whole scene I found really attractive. And the clothes. It was just as Italian suits were coming in. They had this whole aura about them, always pulling birds and really attractive ones. I drifted into it quite consciously.'

Bobby King's first robbery took place at the top of Hornsey Road in north London. A friend had spotted people moving out of a flat above a pawn shop so they climbed up a drainpipe, went in through the roof and 'nicked everything that was nickable. £40 each we got. That was the start, having got away with it and got the buzz out of it.

'There was about four or five of us. I went down to Joseph's in Seven Sisters Road and bought this Italian suit for £15. Went to the hairdresser's and got a college boy haircut. Then the Hollywood Club, the local dance place, where we stood around looking sharp and talking out of the side of our mouths.'

By now his parents were beginning to realise that young Bobby was not exactly heading for a senior management post in the Prudential. For a start he didn't get up in the mornings, yet he seemed to have enough money to go drinking in the Holloway pubs and to buy sharp suits. He left home, moved in locally with friends, would return home, row, then move out again. And there was now alternative accommodation elsewhere.

'I was only sixteen when they had me in the Scrubs for burglary, house-breaking. I couldn't believe the food. I thought they were having a joke, like when you go to public school, or you go to the army for the first time; I thought this must be the initiation bit. But it was for real – goulash and porridge, really horrible potatoes with black spots in them and stalks of cabbages. Nowadays it's edible. It's boring but it's reasonably nutritious. You were locked up most of the time. They let you out a couple of hours a day to sew mail bags in the yard.'

Outside again, he was arrested for joyriding a Morris Minor that a friend had stolen and was sent for three months to an open prison for young offenders on the Isle of Sheppey. 'They had you pulling spuds and marching left right and centre and you lived in huts. The food was a lot better because you could nick eggs. Exactly the same day I got out, I came to Victoria Station, came up to Hornsey Rise and there were two friends and we went straight out and did a burglary in Highgate. We had a right touch, about a couple of hundred quid a piece. It still wasn't even midday of the day I got out of jail.'

His contemporaries were now choosing their different directions: some 'drifted back to straightness', taking jobs as plumbers or long distance lorry drivers. But the others were by now 'getting a bit of a smell at the whole prison culture'. And learning their profession.

'You can tell when a house is empty, simple things like the milk hasn't been taken in, windows are shut. We would go up to the door looking for some fictitious character if anyone answered. If nobody answered, I would creep round the back, shin up the drainpipe, boot the window in and nick valuables. Then sell them to the local fence, Benny, who reminded me of Blackbeard the Pirate. Slowly, through trial and error, we started going to look things up, get books on silver markings in the libraries. When you had some experience you could tell the difference between a diamond and a zircon and a piece of glass.'

Up in Hertfordshire to steal some phosphorous bronze fittings that he and a friend had heard about he was caught again. 'I got a thorough belting for escaping from the police. I legged it through the town of Ware with about five or six burly coppers chasing after me. I was quite fit. I flew. But I never knew where I was, I was lost. If I had been on Holloway Road I would have been sweet but I was out of my area. The magistrate sentenced me to another three months' YP.'

When he came out his loyal girlfriend was waiting for him. It was the glorious summer of 1959. He immediately left her to go to Jersey and spent the sunny months robbing hotel rooms. 'It was so cheap we only had to do one or two a week. It was like a mini Costa del Crime . . . You could just go around in shorts and beach shoes and a T-shirt, wander in and out of hotels at liberty.

'When I came back there was a petrol shortage on and I got nicked with another guy siphoning petrol. Pretty low-life stuff, this – I was skint. This time I went to Clerkenwell and the magistrate gave me six months. I had now done quite a lot of time in quite nasty jails.'

At the age of eighteen he married. 'I saw it as a way of having some sort of home and roots and somebody who wouldn't give me any shit. I regarded her as rather a doormat of a girl who would do anything I said.'

He was soon back thieving. 'It was more serious. We got nicked for burgling a house in Highgate. I got twelve months and I went to Lewes prison.'

Inside he met John McVicar, 'Chopper' Knight and David Quatromeni, three men who were already becoming 'faces' in the criminal world. Quatromeni was from the Angel, Islington, and had shot another criminal called Joey Oliver – 'it was getting into gangsterism and guns'. Knight was later to embark on bullion robberies, on one occasion sawing through the side of a bullion van in Kent, and McVicar had already decided he wanted to make money. 'Being a thief is a terrific life, but the trouble is they do put you in the nick for it,' as he was later to explain to the *Observer*. Bobby King had also decided on the terrificness of the life.

'A mate, Dave, and John and I used to talk about ways of getting money and we decided to go into armed robbery. We met up when I came out and went on several, not with guns, just with coshes. Small jewellers, terrorise the staff, grab everything in the showcases and leg it out to a stolen car. Very cowboyish – mostly territories that we knew. It was also so quick we didn't worry about disguises at first, but then that started coming in: overall, caps, glasses, cotton wool in your mouth and not calling each other by our right names, pretty basic stuff.' They soon had their own place in the criminal hierarchy of the sixties.

'The Krays and the Richardsons were the Firms. But they were gangsters, they didn't go out and get money like us. They got it by other means – protection and by having clubs where people like us spent all our money.

'The Richardsons were south London. But in the north and east it was the twins and another firm, the Nashes. We used to go over to west London because we had several feuds with them. We used to take the piss out of them because we regarded them as being very uncouth. They were all scrap metal dealers in Shepherd's Bush and Notting Hill. We used to like going over there because they had some really good clubs and there would be sort of club girls, girls who were on the game.'

It was a boom time for armed robbery. 'Always you were sniffing around and people were putting things up to you and you were looking at them. That would be during the day. We would go home dutifully in the evening and see our wives and then we would be out on the razzle most nights. Pubs and clubs, West End often. The Revolution, Le Val Bon, the Regency Club . . . the Rising Sun . . . the Spanish Patriot. We would drink vast amounts. There would always be girls there who worked the clubs. We thought we were getting a bit sophisticated so we would go to restaurants and order wine and have rather nice cars. It seemed really marvellous at the time. The group I was with didn't get on terribly well. McVicar wanted to be the boss and I used to take the piss out of him – he had all these very romantic ideas about crime. We began to drift apart.'

Then he met the man who was to shape his future, or a large slice of it – Bertie Smalls, a short squat robber who looked like Bob Hoskins in *The Long Good Friday*, but without the charm.

'He was a very quiet man, a rank Tory, very racist, white supremacist sort of stuff. He loved violence. He would talk in sort of prison underworld jargon. He couldn't handle straight company, he liked to be with "one of his own", an expression he used all the time. Very secretive. Very paranoid. He used to keep changing cars when there was no need to, but he rather liked that life-style I suspect. No interest in anything beyond crime and he was extremely ambitious. We had a drink one day with the guy who was acquitted on the Great Train Robbery and he loved that. We used to go into those pubs in Belgravia with all these chinless wonders in there and sit in little alcoves.'

During the daylight hours there were jewellers' shops and post offices to be robbed. It was a roller-coaster life.

'We'd be skint for a few weeks then we'd have loads of money and go barmy and not do anything for a while, go about clubbing it and buying clothes. Bertie was totally unknown. He came from Wood Green. So he and I and a couple of others were now into fairly heavy armed robberies that were getting heavier all the time. Housebreakers would come across guns in burglaries and would offer them for £20 or £30. We were waylaying cars that were coming back from banks picking up wages, wages offices, post offices.

'One post office it was just a question of me vaulting over the counter the minute after them delivering a great big gunny sack with all the postal orders, cash and stamps. If we could get away with it, leaping over counters, grabbing and running, we would do it. We would decide amongst ourselves who did what – very fucking democratic. More often than not I would drive. But because I was quite fit I was usually the one who would vault over the counter. This shock method meant that people didn't use to budge.

'We used to put salt instead of pellets in the shotgun cartridges. This meant that if one of those rugby-tackling types tried to stop us we could shoot and he would think he had been hit. The theory was it would give us time to get away and if we were caught it was less serious because we hadn't actually shot anyone. We were quite a liberal gang.

'I reckoned I'd finally made it when I was driving down the motorway in a Jag with The Doors on one of the first car tape players.

'Once we were pursued. A mate and I, and another guy, we knew a guy who was putting money in the safe-deposit box at the Nag's Head. He used to do it every night. It was jam packed with people, Saturday evening. I leapt on him and just grabbed it off him, he just had it tucked under his arm. He started screaming and hollering and cars chased us, taxis and ordinary cars. We couldn't get rid of them so we ended up piling into these flats and jumping over walls in different directions.'

When King became a father he made a brief effort to make money more conventionally, working with a friend who installed suspended ceilings. The money was reasonable, he could pay the rent and go out at weekends. But boredom set in and Bertie Smalls beckoned.

'By now he had moved on a few stages. There were four or five guys around Hoxton who were into pretty spectacular sort of robberies. They all had really nice cars and I had fuck all. The first one we did, I got about four grand, after about a week of being back with them. They liked me because I was quite game. People were freelancing a lot.' It was a change from knocking up false ceilings.

'I would lie in bed until about midday and then I would get up and wander up to a meeting pub. We would drift around in the afternoons down to the West End to clubs and then back to the pubs in the evening. A very appealing life. You didn't give any time for your wife or kids or family – just the occasional £50 conscience money. You didn't really keep in touch with friends inside except with Christmas cards, but when they came out, if they were liked, there would be a few hundred quid depending on the stage of finances.' And there were financial dealings to be done with the other side of the law in London.

'I was disqualified from driving, so if I got stopped and got a ticket I would phone up a few officers I knew at the local police station, make a meet and pay the going rate, £25, to get it put in the book that the licence had been duly shown. By now the local CID and the local villains all knew each other. In fact I can't remember one local CID who wasn't crooked. If I had a mate who'd been nicked on the manor I would go and see a copper I knew to see if he could have any help. They would go away and see what could be done. Everything from the minor to the serious.

'The biggest one I paid out was for Bertie Smalls. I got a message via Bertie Smalls' wife on this one. I knew I was sweet because I had all sorts of alibis. He had already sweetened the filth so I went down to visit him in Brixton and he told me the cozzer I wanted.

'I ended up meeting him in Tufnell Park. Two of them showed up in a Mini. A big dopey one driving and a right smart geezer who was an inspector. I had to give him two grand. I got in the back seat. Drove around up to Hampstead Heath and they were a bit cagey, a lot of small talk about how the Arsenal was getting on. Up to Highgate Village and I gave them the two grand, we went in a pub, had one beer and said see you later and that was it, done.

'Two days later my next job was to tell the solicitor that I would be at Marylebone magistrates' court. We went there and there was this rather sweet young graduate in law. He'd had a few dozen cases, but this was the first heavy scene he'd had. He was clearly nervous. But all the groundwork had been laid. He came out after the hearing he said, "My God, this is the easiest case I've ever had." He couldn't make it out. He had thought: desperado, fugitive, gun in car, copper got injured – there was a bit of a scuffle because Bertie Smalls had pushed this door in the copper's face and the copper got a couple of stitches in the eye. In court the policeman got up and said, "I could have fell in the scuffle." I think they were just after dough, I don't think they had anything on him. They knew he was at it, they both knew what each other was at but Bertie Smalls was only too pleased to put up a couple of grand and have an end to it. He got a fine and a conditional discharge if I remember rightly.'

The Faces were now aspiring to an altogether snappier way of life: 'I think we were quite contemptuous of the Krays' scene, although we sensibly kept that opinion to ourselves. By now we were much more interested in what we regarded as fairly sophisticated little country retreats down in Hertfordshire. Occasionally we would dodge off to the West End, one or two little clubs we knew that were frequented by bank robbers and pretty good hoisters, a group of Australians we knew. It was very comfy. No one else knew about it, the police didn't know. The West End was littered with places like that.

'We saw ourselves as gangsters and we loved going to see gangster films and reading about big robberies. We watched American films because we thought British gangster films were crap, and they always were – Richard Burton, Dirk Bogarde and Stanley Baker as cockney villains, for fuck sake! Cagney and George Raft were our heroes. And really good westerns, *The Wild Bunch*, these ageing villains robbing trains, we loved that.'

And like the Wild Bunch, the cowboys who didn't realise that their era was slipping away, they were making plans for a big one: Barclays Bank in Ilford.

'There were nine of us. The planning was five to six weeks. People had to go and look at it. I was about the fourth person asked on it. I went into the bank dressed in a suit and was writing a moody cheque out, looking like a travelling salesman, mingling. The security men brought these great big bags like mail bags and they got loaded onto a lift and went in. I was very dubious that it was money. We found out it came from Tesco's in Essex. A security driver who had been on that run, he had talked to a relative about it and he told a friend of a friend. He went down to see this fellow and he said, "Well, I want a drink out of it but I'm not in on it. I can tell you that they deliver every Monday and we don't even know how much it is. But it's a great big drop."

'The thing that confirmed it was they told me to look out for a little red Mini van that went to the bank about a couple of minutes before and sat there for a couple of minutes to reassure themselves that there was no suspicious characters about. And that's what made me think there must be some money about.

'We got the cars and vans and guns and we took a ladder in, a couple of us, as painters. It was my thing to whizz up the ladder and two of the others were to start a kerfuffle, stop the bank guards getting in there. They just dropped the money and ran. I put the ladder up against the bank, the guards legged it out the door, knocked a woman over. We got the blame for that. We grabbed a sack or two apiece. We had a white Transit van, so we slung the bags in and dived in after it, nobody really knew what was going on.

'We drove quarter of a mile – left, right, left, right, left, right to a side street then into other cars and everyone split. A couple of us had rented a flat in Essex where the money could be counted and I was to go home and wait for a phone call later that evening.

'I got the call and was told to go to a pub in Havering, the wilds of Essex. So I went out there. I was with my father-in-law in his car. He was a straight bloke, never knew a thing. I said I had to pick some stuff up, and would he like to run me out there because he knew I was disqualified and I'd give him a drink. We met at eight or nine on a dark evening. I had these two potato sacks with my money in it and the money for two of the others. I had sixty thousand quid on me. In the pub car park we moved them from one boot to another, highly unsuspicious, the children running around, a dog, my father-in-law.'

King, however, was becoming disillusioned with Bertie Smalls.

'These bank robberies were now getting less and less sophisticated because Smalls was now with a sort of wild bunch from Ealing. Animals really, morons, could hardly string a sentence together, pretty game but really unbright. Smalls had fallen out with a lot of people. By now I was with another firm doing small secure robberies that would get us a couple of grand apiece, using our knowledge and finding things that were fairly easy. I was very unimpressed with the people that Smalls was with, and so I declined to work with them.' As a sideline, Bobby King had a drinking club which he had bought from Smalls, that catered chiefly for Irishmen. King's involvement in the club was safely hidden behind the 'wine committee' and it gave him a small income. He planned to buy a house and started looking at properties in Muswell Hill.

On 6 April 1973 Bertie Smalls turned Queen's Evidence. He became a police informer, a supergrass. Bobby King was one of his first victims.

'About two days before I got nicked, a mate said to me, 'That Bertie Smalls is going to grass all you lot up.' I didn't believe it. No chance. You used to hear this all the time, "He's a grass . . . that one's a grass . . . he's definitely a grass."

'I was in the divorce court and as I was going in I saw Inspector Alec Eist, who I knew, walking towards me with another copper. He said, "Hello, Bob, we want to see you." By now my antenna is blipping away but there's fuck all I can do because I'm in the court and all these other coppers have filtered in. I said to my counsel, "I think I'm about to be arrested." She said, "Of course you're not, they can't arrest you for divorce."

'As we get outside – wallop. "Robert King you are under arrest." Handcuffs on. The lawyer is standing there aghast: "Where are you taking him?" she asked. They just said, "Wembley. He knows why." And I said, in front of her, "I don't want to answer any questions unless my solicitor's present." They whisked me away and took me to Ealing police station.

'In the car my brainbox is ticking over like a lunatic, and Eist says, "Well, you know Bertie's done it to you." This was confirmation. I thought, "What the fuck can he say?" I said, "I don't want to answer any questions." Of course by the time it got to the Old Bailey it was, "Yes, I done it, copper. I know Bertie's a grass, but you'll have to prove it," words to that effect.

Bertie Smalls had implicated Bobby King in five serious robberies, the largest one for quarter of a million pounds. Although the evidence on which Smalls had himself been arrested, for a robbery in Palmer's Green, was quite weak, he decided to tell the police everything.

'I think he was beginning to go off his rocker with the life-style and the drink. The paranoia now was really setting in. It amused me in a way because he always used to say everyone was a grass. He was obsessed with who was and who wasn't a grass. I used to say, "It won't be long before you get round to me." For me personally grassing is a taboo that runs too deep, but who knows what happens to people. He set a sort of fashion – Charlie Lowe, Maurice O'Mahoney, Roger Denhardt, John Irish, Don Barrett, who was one of our lot.

'The police had leapt on my father-in-law and he cooperated with them although he didn't know what was in the bags. I had already split with my wife and they were thoroughly pissed off with me. Janice, my wife, had suffered every imaginable indignity at the hands of the police and her parents hated me for it. So Small's evidence, my verbals and my father-in-law's evidence amounted to corroboration and my conviction.'

Smalls' evidence to the Old Bailey jury was highly convincing. 'He was very self-effacing in court, one of the reasons I think we lost. There was me and five others on trial. After he had had six briefs going at him what had been revulsion, living on immoral earnings, poncing, was turning into sympathy. He was convincing. His memory was incredible, but that fitted for me – he paid much more attention to details because he loved it so much, whereas for me it was all a bit of a bore.'

Bobby King was sentenced to sixteen years, which was reduced on appeal to fifteen when Chief Justice Lawton ruled that a sixteen-year sentence should only be given when a robbery was 'exceptionally horrifying' to the public, and people had been shot or seriously injured during it. Nobody had been injured – except, perhaps, psychologically – during any of the robberies King had been charged with. Bobby King had meanwhile started his sentence.

'In prison a disillusionment and disgust with the whole scene had set it. There were only one or two guys who wouldn't talk constantly about this crime shit.' So King took another route that was just starting to be explored inside: the Open University degree. He passed his O and A levels and graduated in history and sociology, doing his studies first in Albany Prison on the Isle of Wight and then at Maidstone in Kent. He was allowed out from Maidstone during the daytime to research his honours thesis into the relationships between the Kent Quakers and local liberalism. 'I used to do work in the archives for a day out. I used to photocopy what I wanted and fuck off and have a bit of lunch and a few drinks. I would go down to Ashford to research the Quakers. The governor, who was a Methodist himself, used to give me a fiver for my lunch. The screws used to go mental. I was absolutely fascinated about getting into the history of ideas, it really opened my eyeballs to the history of ideologies. I used to go and talk to the governor about it. I used to go through all the old papers for my research and all of a sudden you've found something, it's a terrific feeling. And you begin to get a few clues, gain a few insights into why you are like you are.

'I remember when I had done about a year of my degree, and I had just learnt what the pecking order in society meant, coming in to my cell and saying to another bloke, "Hey fuck off my bed, I'm higher up in the pecking order than you." And he goes "Whaaat?" – looking at me as though I was cracking up. And I said, "Didn't you know there was this German bloke who studied the feeding habits of chickens and worked out a theory of how we all fitted into society?" My few mates in jail used to think, I'm sure, that I wasn't all there.

'I was lucky because I was fairly high up the pecking order, but I had to be careful how I spoke and didn't use words that appeared to be designed to belittle people who didn't have that vocabulary, except with some representatives of authority and some psycho morons. I used to get a buzz out of living dangerously and making my mates, my good mates, laugh at all the loonies. But they were quite proud of me really I like to think, they liked it. In Maidstone there were quite a few middle-class blokes, crooked accountants. There was one who had been chair of a football club, he had a private jet and a massive house and swimming pool, member of the Tory party and all this sort of stuff. I got a bit matey with him because I felt sorry for him. He kept putting his foot in it and getting bashed up because he didn't know the score.'

King studied and read and read and studied. Other prisoners painted: 'The pictures people paint inside are pretty predictable – keyholes and chains, the red robin sitting on the snow-covered prison window-bar and all that bollocks. It began to dawn on me there was a link between this crass sentimentality and violence as a way of life. I remember reading this paper about the Nazis and how their art was always this frightfully homey stuff, the whole idea of motherhood and niceness. At the same time they would sling a kid in the oven. It always makes me get very edgy when I see or hear very sentimental stuff. I think, "That's not a kick in the arse off being a loony Nazi," though that's probably a bit unfair on some sentimentalists.'

Fellow prisoners included Irish republicans and Jake Prescott of the Angry Brigade. 'I did twenty months on remand in Brixton in that special unit with the Price sisters [who were convicted of the Old Bailey bombing] on the floor above us. We used to talk to each other out the window. It's probably a dead sexist giveway but when I looked out of that window they looked like two little Sunday-school teachers. It was only a matter of weeks after the Old Bailey bombing that we were nicked.

'Nowadays I'm a sort of anaemic liberal if I'm cornered, I suppose. Loads of the people inside believed in capital punishment, provided it wasn't for what they'd done, and especially for nonces. They were pretty conservative. The ultimate for them would have been the house in the country and the children at private schools.'

He ended up doing seven and a half years, the bulk of it in Albany.

'I was never bored in prison. You can't be bored if you've got Blake and then whizzing off into Stendhal.' There were other more pressing problems: 'Fear – when there's a riot brewing or a strike I thought, "Fuck me, I've got to do my bit," torn between being yourself and what you know is the prevailing atmosphere. I could see how systems worked, ideologically. If I didn't sing the Marsellaise with enough gusto and connection, I was suspect; if I did, then the authorities would home in on me. You can't fucking win, only hope for a dishonourable draw.

'I didn't find missing women too much. I go through long periods of sexlessness. The woman I was going out with at the time, the missing was fantasising about being with her. Occasional wank and that's it for a while. It fucks you up when you come home because you would sit for hours and not want to communicate.

'They give you a Red Band when you're coming near the end of your time and they're worried you may get into a bit of skullduggery. The minute you get a Red Band you think, "They must be looking at me a little bit favourably," so you withdraw from some of your more obvious black marketeering.' His attitude to prison officers was changing anyway.

'When I was sixteen or seventeen I just hated screws. I would gladly have mown them down with machine guns, cut their toes off with hacksaw blades. I hated them mortally. The other prisoners used to love me because I was a great screw baiter and I used to wind them up. But as I got more and more into my last long sentence it started to dawn on me that they were like that towards me because I was like that towards them. I just got a lot less nasty. You could get sceptical and say that's because I was wangling for parole, but I don't think that was the real reason. I think it dawned on me that we were all the same in the same shit together. The Hate Factory, McVicar called it. Jimmy Boyle touched on it – we brutalise them and they brutalise us. So I started to come down a notch and they would come down a notch and in the end it would be Bob and Fred and "How's the missus today?" "Oh, murders I had last night . . ." and you would sit and listen. It's painful to realise the screw was in the same shit as you, just smelled a bit different, that's all. Some of them were, by any measure, decent blokes.

'Same with the police. You would come across a decent young copper, probably a youth club leader, he's going to wind up in the CID. Gone into the force for sound reasons but they get corrupted over a period.'

He emerged, older, greyer but without having become fat on institutional food or with the spark burnt out of his expression. 'My probation officer was a nice geezer, a Catholic from Belfast. It was quite clear that he and I were in tune with each other after half an hour. I was bang lucky to get him. Never used to hassle. I said to him right from the off, "I'm going to be your best client ever," because I knew in my heart of hearts there was no way I was going back. And I know they've heard all this shit before. We didn't play that game and everything worked out fine.'

He worked for a while in a wine bar and fell for a warm-hearted middle-class woman who worked there. However their life experiences and life expectations were poles apart. 'It was like having a walk-on part in *Mrs Dale's Diary*. But when we were alone she was a softness, an escape from the harsh.' Then he found a job with the Save the Children Fund in Lambeth working with young offenders on a pilot project that tried to demonstrate to offenders the effect of their actions on the victims.

'We managed to get a couple of victims and I went along and spoke to the people first and told them what we were trying to achieve and the kids were primed that they weren't going to get a cuff. It went really well. We did it about four or five times but Lambeth council, being what it was, took a bit of a dim view of this and thought it was bit pro-police, which was absolute nonsense. Me, pro-police?

'There used to be just me as the kids' advocate, a copper from the juvenile bureau that we knew very well, post-Scarman, nice sort of bloke, quite bright and he would be with the victim. And after a few weeks all parties concerned felt that this could be quite fruitful. What we were trying to say was that the kid, going through the ritual of the courts and solicitors, gets more and more distanced from the reality of his crime and how it affects people. But it got ridiculous sometimes. The victims would say the kid could pay them back by joining the army, something ridiculous like that. It wasn't meant to be punitive in that way, it was meant to be enlightening for all parties concerned.

'You used to get these fierce feminists in Lambeth, they would almost object to you being in the room. They would be so utterly liberal about any crime committed except rape. They would say, "It's all wrong, Bob, you getting fifteen years and blokes convicted of rape get six months suspended sentence." But they don't – there's guys in there doing twenty or thirty years for serious rapes. It's all part, it seems to me, of a blindness to reality. Most of my colleagues, who were extremely nice, decent people – the world would be a better place to live if there were more of them – were as silly as arseholes. I feel so guilty saying that, but their puritanism, their desire to create a working environment based on being "ideologically sound" used to remind me of prison, except that my colleagues in Lambeth used to shit themselves at the first sign of violence.'

Meanwhile he was bumping into the pieces of his past.

'I saw my parents-in-law. I was working in a children's home as a locum and I was standing at the bus stop with all these kids that I was taking to the swimming baths. My ex-in-laws looked so old and vulnerable and I thought, "God, to think that I could have killed them once!" They asked me what I was up to and said to come round for dinner, but there was no way I wanted to because it was just sort of dead. As long as they could see there was nothing at all they had to worry about, and that far from posing any threat to them I just felt deeply sorry for them, with a touch of anguish. And they dote on my kids.

'I saw Bertie Smalls once, which was very peculiar. It was about a couple of months after I had got out. I was going over to see my mum and dad and I was driving over Crouch End Broadway. He pulled up right in front of me at the traffic lights. He was unmistakable, especially as I'd been used to driving behind him in cars. I followed him. He pulled up on the bend in Park Road. I went past, did a U-turn and sat in the car and just watched. He was looking in a shop window, got back in his car and drove off – he didn't see me. I went to my mum and dad's and said, "I can't make it tonight," because I was feeling really weird. I had actually already made a clear decision with myself that there was nothing I was going to do, so I was exploring my own feelings. I was really quite pleased with myself that I'd driven off and hadn't had the slightest urge at all to have any sort of revenge.'

His two boys had grown up: 'I'm really pleased with them. Both work for the Council, designer dustmen, both do a bit of painting and decorating on the side, get a few quid and have their couple of stints in Greece and Italy every year. Perfectly normal and nice. They like the same class music as their old man. I must have ruined them when they were little. They dug one out the other day – *In the Court of the Crimson King*! I said, "that's a collector's item"!'

He has now qualified as a chef, seeking work amongst the big financial and banking houses. There is a flat in Highbury. The local pub. 'In the old days we enjoyed being recognized going into clubs. I know I still enjoy it now in a very different way. I do feel a twinge of delight that there is some sort of recognition there. But I soon put them right about it, that it was all sort of part of the past.

'Last Christmas I stayed with some really straight people who I had met. They didn't know anything about my background. The woman I was with, a friend, she said, "Do you want to mention it?" And I said not unless it comes up. It came up over dinner because they were talking about social work and I said I used to be very delinquent when I was a kid. They were articulate, working-class Tories. And they said, "Oh, you was in trouble with the law when you was a lad? . . . Most lads do." And I said, "Well, I ended up getting a very long prison sentence," and the mother said, "How long is long?" "Sixteen years." "What did you do?" "Robbing banks." "Oh, that's all right," the father said, "I knew some lads like that once up in Blackburn." I wished I'd kept my gob shut.

'I find it incredibly amusing the way one plays the other off for what seems to be their own ends, the prison-reform social-work thing. I am going to do a book about why middle-class people are so fascinated by bits of working-class rough like us. There's something weird here somewhere, why this fascination?

'When I was studying, my tutor used to keep asking, "What are you going to do with your degree, Bob?" I thought of some sort of teaching, social work, but in the end I know nothing about it because I've always lived on the streets and that is another world. After I came out I went to a Workers' Educational Association weekend in Cambridge and found myself thinking, "This is a sham." All the time I was sitting bolt upright and people were talking about Jane Austen and how their garden was coming along. And I had gone straight from one institution to another institution.'

2

The Daughter

We need to remember
that hanging is not
the only way in which
the law can take life.

Stephen Sedley,
London Review of Books

Kathy Bailey's father, Reg Dudley, was arrested in 1976 for the murders of two north London criminals, Billy Moseley and Micky Cornwall. Moseley had been killed in 1974, his body cut into pieces and dumped in the Thames. Pieces of his torso were washed up on the shore, to be discovered by bird-watchers and a group of boys playing before Sunday lunch. The finds gave the case its name – The Torso Murder. Micky Cornwall was shot in the back of the head and buried in a shallow grave in Hertfordshire. Dudley, his partner in the jewellery trade, Bob Maynard, his daughter Kathy and four other were charged in connection with the deaths. In some papers, they were called the 'Legal and General Gang' or 'Murder Incorporated'.

It was suggested that Moseley had been killed because he was having an affair with another criminal's wife and that he knew of the whereabouts of money owing to Dudley. He had, said the prosecution, been tortured. His friend, Micky Cornwall, then supposedly vowed revenge. So he too was killed. Kathy, who had had a brief affair with him, was accused of conspiracy to kidnap for supposedly luring Cornwall to his doom. The trial lasted 136 days, the longest murder trial ever heard at the Old Bailey, and finished in June 1977.

Reg Dudley and Bob Maynard were convicted of the murders and jailed for life with a recommendation that they serve a minimum of 15 years. Kathy was also convicted for conspiracy to cause grievous bodily harm and was given a suspended sentence; she had already spent some months in Holloway Prison awaiting trial.

Shortly after the verdicts were announced, a council cleaner found a large round object in the public lavatory at the end of Richmond Road, Islington. It was the slowly defrosting head of Billy Moseley. The finding had no effect on the verdict or the subsequent appeal.

So Reg Dudley stayed inside, where he was in his daughter's earliest memories of him.

'I remember him coming home from prison and me asking him what block [of flats] he wanted – because we used to run up to strangers and ask them what block they wanted – and it was my own dad,' says Kathy. 'We used to live in Caledonian

Road at a place called The Crumbles, which was an old Victorian tenement block. I was six or seven and my father was in prison. I think kids used to tell people their dad was in hospital.'

Kathy now lives not far from the old Crumbles on a sprawling, austere Islington estate. She shares her flat with a large, sloppy dog called Honey, a slimmer one that was found pining in a pensioner's home four days after its owner had died and a cat with a wonky leg. There is a stream of visitors, some relatives, some friends, some on this side of the law, some on that. The six-year-old who was anxious to direct the visiting stranger has become a dark-haired, attractive woman whom people still seek out for advice.

If her father was 'in hospital' in those early days, her mother was around, a bright, sparky woman called Eileen, with a throaty chuckle and a drink problem. There was an older sister, Moira, and a collection of affectionate uncles and aunts who worked as decorators and in other equally respectable jobs. Reg followed his father's trade of petty crime when the chance of a career as a professional footballer with Arsenal came to nothing.

'There was a time when there was a lorry parked in the street full of old-fashioned grey gas stoves, lovely enamel painted panels. We took a load of them upstairs, me and my sister, and my dad asked what we were doing with them. And we said, "It's all right, the kids who were stripping the lorry off said the man said we could have them." It turned out they were my dad's panels – whether they were stolen or not, I don't know. All the kids were in to everything, but it wasn't considered naughty. I've got a vague recollection of visiting him somewhere and him giving me a load of those penny and halfpenny sweets.'

The family moved to Ramsgate, where Reg worked in an amusement arcade. But the marriage was stormy and soon Reg Dudley was jailed again.

'I was aware of the teachers spending extra time with me and I used to think it was because I was bright, but it might have been because my dad was in prison and they thought I needed help. After my father was sent away for grievous bodily harm, I was mollycoddled by a couple of teachers, who were very kind to me.'

Reg Dudley was a Division Two criminal. He had had regular jobs – at clubs and at the amusement arcade – but crime was his real livelihood and had been ever since the war when he began his career with small-scale ration book fiddles. He dealt in stolen and fake jewellery and as he got older hung out in Hatton Garden with Bob Maynard or went drinking with his other friend, Charlie Clarke, a Hornsey greengrocer.

'As an older child I remember frequent turnovers when the police would raid the house and search it. It was a regular occurrence. At one time it was every time something went missing in Hatton Garden. Mostly early in the morning, sometimes tea time, not so much the dawn raids they do nowadays. As little as two and up to ten or twenty policemen depending on what robbery they were going into, how big it was and what was involved. There was no animosity. It was the

"Come on, we know you're number one suspect, you know we've got to do our job" routine. I would make them a cup of tea.'

Kathy's older sister Moira met and married a Guyanan who worked in a gambling club and left home. Her mother was hitting the bottle, her father was constantly in trouble with the law. Kathy went to one of London's largest and most unruly comprehensives, Rising Hill, and learnt little: 'The teachers couldn't even keep control of the kids in school, let alone point them in the right direction.'

A good-looking teenager with long brown hair and a wicked smile, she began to mix with the local lads.

'The boys' main thing was stealing cars and that sort of thing. The funniest thing was my dad, who had been a criminal all his life, used to try and drum it into me that he didn't want me to mix with criminals. His father was a crook, but his two brothers were never that way inclined at all. I don't think they disapproved, there might even have been a bit of hero worship.'

It was the sixties. Thursday nights were spent at the Tottenham Royal, others at the local disco, the Downbeat. People left school at fifteen, the boys for the meat market and the print, the girls for shop work or office work if they could type. Kathy got a job as an invoice typist. And started going out with a trainee villain, Barry.

'It seems you can analyse the ones who turned out OK. Most of their parents were normal everyday working people. Those that did go astray were usually from a broken home or a home where a relative was a criminal. There were those that stood on the edge of the circle and dared the others to get on with it, but they would be missing when the police came along. Some were quick to get away or came to their senses younger. Two or three of them have gone on to be in crime for the rest of their lives. Two or three after Borstal went straight and a few of them have got on well in life, with their own businesses as publicans and things like that.'

Those who went to Borstal were admired. At the end of their sentences they were welcomed back as heroes. As they got older the homecoming ritual changed. 'If they had a done a proper prison sentence there would be some sort of gathering of people and most of the men attending would donate money to try and get them a better start this time out. That doesn't happen so much nowadays because there are so many going away, getting big sentences, so many hard luck stories.'

Kathy had graduated from seeing her dad inside to visiting boyfriends in young offenders' institutions. The young men were brought for their visits at double-march time. Kathy thought that if she ever had to do that she'd die. It did not have the same deterrent effect on her young man. He was one of those people who never knew when to stop.

'I think his mother told me when he was caught. I went along to the court. And when he was to be weighed off by the magistrate I got up and said I was to blame for his crime. It was the exact opposite! I used to beg him not to because I was crazy about him and couldn't bear the thought of him going away. But [in court] I said I wanted to go nice places and have nice things and it was my fault that he turned to crime. It was complete load of lies and it had no effect whatsoever. He certainly didn't thank me for it. I think he was embarrassed.'

Meanwhile Reg Dudley plied his trade. 'We were conscious of my dad being involved in jewellery. I never ever worried about him. I always had total confidence in him. I knew one or two of the people he worked with, but I was just Reggie's daughter.'

But the carefree life was about to end. Kathy married a young man called Johnny Dann, nicknamed 'Doughnut' because he had once worked in a bakery. The marriage was not a success. One night when he was out with a group of friends in a Wimpy Bar in the West End, there was a silly staring competition with another group of young men. Remarks were made on the lines of 'What's for afters?' 'I'll have you for afters.' There was a stabbing. A young man died. Kathy's childhood ended.

'I suddenly realised it wasn't kid's stuff. Someone had actually been killed. Although there had been couple of other incidents – someone had got beaten up outside the Downbeat – it wasn't anything really to do with me, it didn't touch me. Then you realise that someone has a wife and a mother and you think, "the waste of it all".' Although the marriage was over, Kathy did what she was to make a habit of and stood by her man. Women knew their place in those days.

'If there were fights in those days the girls would try and stop it or would run and hide if there were glasses flying. Nowadays with teenagers it's the girls that start the fight half the time. I can remember getting slapped a couple of times by a boyfriend but I had usually asked for it.'

She was nineteen, her husband inside and her marriage over. Her father had embarked on another sentence of five years for receiving stolen jewellery. Life was speeding up.

'I had started to drink in pubs by then and in the local pub I had met my first bank robber, which was what was called the big league in them days. They were men and were treated as men rather than boys and lived fast, flash.'

There were fancy restaurants where you could spend the average weekly wage on a bottle of wine before you headed off to see Danny La Rue perform. The robbers were in their pomp. 'They got away with quite a lot. They were a lot luckier, there was less security and there were a few bent police around who could be helpful to them.'

Kathy's father knew one of those policemen, Alec Eist. Alec did a lot of people favours. It upset some of his fellow officers but he operated quite happily for many years on the 'drinks' he was bought, before suffering a heart attack and heading for the big disciplinary hearing in the skies.

Kathy led the good life. 'Most of the wives were unaware of their husband's other life-styles. Bertie Smalls and Fred Sinfield, who both became famous supergrasses, had long-standing affairs that went on for years. Their mistresses were more possessive of them than their wives. I often wondered if these added pressures helped tip the balance when they decided to confess all.

'Of the robbers I knew, there were the thick ones and the bright ones: they didn't put forward any profound political views or ideas about anything but they were sharper and quicker witted. They all realised when it was far too late, when they were tucked up and ensconced in prison blankets doing twelve years or more. They suddenly realised what they could have done, that they did have the capability of working at something else, a straight job.

'The first time around there were no regrets because when they first got big sentences it made them higher up in the hierarchy. But the second lump has ruined most of them. They've lost their best years. The ones in their late forties know they can't go away again because they know they're going to be old cabbages when they come out.'

In those days the bank robbers were looked up to by some of the young men in the same way that they admired footballers and boxers. 'They were all riding the crest of the wave, everyone was in awe of them. But the younger generation now, they just call them ageing bank robbers. They are not impressed by them. They just think they're fools for having spent so much time inside. You still get a few young scatty ones who will try and do a security robbery, but they work two or three at a time instead of six or eight. But it's not long before most of them get caught so it's no longer considered an easy living.'

She was visiting her father regularly. He did his time with equanimity, playing football and badminton, painting. His tiles, delicate rural landscapes, decorate her flat. His oil paintings have been shown at Shell House in Victoria as part of the Arthur Koestler Prize exhibitions.

By her mid-twenties Kathy was going out with a Face, Ray Baron, an articulate young man who robbed banks. Her father had re-emerged and was back at work, still at the dodgier end of the jewellery trade.

'My dad stopped actively stealing and he was buying and selling. By now I had been married, divorced and was living with a bank robber. In my dad's field there weren't many doing what he could. There were no more clever safe breakers or burglar alarm people and I suppose that was one of the reasons he retired, because it was difficult to get in and out of places.'

But there were more glamorous options than north London could offer. In 1974 Kathy and two friends set off for Lloret de Mar, a resort in Spain, to run a club, the Captain's Arms. It was a disaster. As arms do, it folded.

'None of us had any idea. None of us could speak the language and it went bust after a few months. It turned out it had been on its last legs anyway.' But others followed that route, starting up restaurants and bars on the Costas.

Back in London the next year, Kathy and Reg Dudley were among the more than thirty people pulled in for questioning in connection with the Moseley and Cornwall murders. Reg Dudley treated the matter laconically; his dog had been taken in with him to the police station; 'Either charge him or let him go,' Dudley told the police. Kathy was taken to Holloway Prison.

'I don't think it dawned on me when we were charged, it didn't sink in. I was on the hospital wing in Holloway where you had mostly either junkies, murder charges or very sick people. We had one old bloke who came in to talk about Current Affairs and most of the girls would go along just to ask him if he had any fags and, if he didn't, they'd go away. I felt a bit sorry for him and mostly I used to sit and talk to him about my case. I used to see Janie Jones, too, because she was a "carrier", getting the food for her block. She always looked great: beautifully made up and with hair nicely done and wearing a fur coat. And I would see Anna Mendelsohn, one of the Angry Brigade, doing gardening.' She was given bail when the trial started.

Which is when our paths crossed. I was working at *Time Out* magazine in Kings Cross. It was a time when there had been much publicity over George Davis, a bank robber whom people claimed had been wrongly convicted. His friends, to draw attention to his case, chained themselves to Big Ben, drove a car at the gates of Buckingham Palace and, most spectacularly, dug up and poured oil on the Test pitch at Headingley, thus disrupting the Ashes match between England and Australia. Finally, amidst wild scenes of celebration, Davis was pardoned, released and greeted by his wife Rose who had worked tirelessly to prove his innocence. The euphoria was short-lived. Not long afterwards he was caught trying to rob the Bank of Cyprus on Seven Sisters Road, convicted and jailed again. Other campaigns to prove the innocence of men inside foundered on the reefs of public scepticism. But prior to this disillusionment there was a great journalistic interest in, not to say fashion for, miscarriages of justice. It was in that atmosphere that I was first told about the Torso Murder case by a petty villain who had gathered that there was something strange about this case and suggested we look into it.

How do you decide if a case is genuine or not? I have had one young man come into the office and tell me an utterly convincing tale, only for his father to come in apologetically the following day to explain that his son was a pathological liar and guilty of the crime. I have met one man in prison, protesting his innocence and explaining that a gun had been planted on him – the only weapons he had in his house, he said, were baseball bats for 'beating up coons'. Maybe he was innocent but life seemed too short to make it worth trying to find out. Equally, there were a number of cases where the evidence seemed planted or dubious but where the person concerned had got away with other similar crimes and the police just felt that his time had come. But this case was different.

I sat through the Torso Murder case in the Old Bailey. There was no forensic evidence linking the accused to the murders, there were alleged semi-admissions which the defendants denied and there was a supergrass, Tony Wild, claiming he had heard Dudley laughing about the head found in the public lavatory.

I started trying to track down the various relatives and friends of the dead and the accused and trying to piece together the case. From the very beginning there seemed to be no real connection between the two murders. There was no reason to believe that Dudley, hardly an Ayatollah on moral matters, would feel it was so out of order that Moseley was having an extra-marital affair that it should be necessary to kill him and cut him up. Nor did any of the hints that Moseley knew of crimes that Dudley might have committed seem to add up either. On top of that, Moseley was one of Bob Maynard's closest friends and, after the trial was over, his ashes rested on the Maynard family mantelpiece. No, Moseley's murderer seemed much more likely to have a more personal motive; it might even have been a beating-up which went further than intended and then required the gruesome dismemberment and cover-up.

Cornwall, who was known as the Laughing Bank Robber, was a bigger criminal than Moseley. The motive for his murder appeared to have more to do with a robbery than any plan to revenge his old friend's death. The names the press had given the 'gang' – 'Legal and General' and 'Murder Incorporated' – turned out to be based on little: Dudley and Maynard had come into a Hatton Garden pub one evening looking like two men in a Legal and General insurance commercial. 'Murder Incorporated' was a headline-writer's fantasy. The 'gang' – the seven accused – even included some people who had never met before their arrests. There was something very wrong about the case.

But the sheer length of the trial, Dudley's unsavoury past, the fact that most of the accused came from a criminal milieu, meant that there was little interest in it. I was often alone on the press bench. The trial rumbled on. The judgements came in and Dudley and Maynard were banished to the cells, protesting their innocence.

A few years later I met Tony Wild, the supergrass, and he told me cheerily that he had made up his evidence. The names of the men who were believed to have really carried out the killings floated around north London and the prison grapevine. There were high hopes of an appeal.

But the times of worrying about miscarriages of justice had passed. The BBC's *Rough Justice* programme, which took up such causes, was taken off the air for too diligently pursuing a case. The post-Davis scepticisms lingered. The graffiti – 'MDC [Maynard Dudley Clarke] Not Guilty Right' – remained but as Islington was gentrified the walls where the legend appeared were knocked down or cleaned and the men remained inside. They refused to admit their guilt and thus lost their chance for a shorter sentence and earlier release. Kathy Bailey organised marches and petitions and gave interviews and thought that something would turn up. It never quite did. People turned away.

'I wasn't aware of belonging to a criminal class until after the Maynard Dudley case. You are unaware that you're being brainwashed into it. For instance, it's normal when you meet people to be open and friendly, and the natural thing you ask someone is "What do you do for a living?" The way I was brought up was that you must never ask someone that. So conversation was always limited because you had to skirt around what might be embarrassing. It was a different language really. You can still see it now if you ask someone in that environment what they're doing; they'll look at you as if you're a policeman and all you're doing is trying to be friendly.'

But the murder trial taught some other lessons. 'We lost a lot of people that we thought of as friends over the case. I found a lot of people maybe even had it in their heads that it was true. I felt like a peculiarity for about five or six years. There was quite a lot of people thinking they were being nice by saying, "Well, your dad might have done it, but we know you couldn't possibly have done it." They thought they were being nice to me but they were upsetting me twice as much.'

Shortly after the murder trial Ray Baron was arrested and charged with armed robbery. Although he was eventually acquitted, he was re-arrested, went on the run, fled to Spain, returned and was recaptured. By this time he and Kathy had parted and Kathy had met and later married another man who had done time for armed robbery, a sunny north Londoner called David Bailey. They had a few years of marriage before there was another knock on the door.

'When my second husband got sent down, the barrister said it wasn't worth pleading mitigation because the judge was known as "Penal Pete". But I said, "Let me go in." The judge wasn't interested and I told him I had been told not to waste my time with him and then he started to listen. I said, "It's the women who suffer because we have to trek up and down the country and try to survive."'

In the meantime Kathy had branched out, trained as a masseuse – a straight one, doing Chinese massage for women only – and had worked for a vet, and in various pubs. 'Earlier on, you never thought of doing a mundane job but you used to think, wouldn't it be nice to have a little shop where I was my own boss, a nice boutique, a gift shop. But none of us had the sense to put some money away for that.'

The visits to her father continued and meant that having a regular job brought its own problems. Few London prisons have Sunday visiting; when travelling to country prisons in winter, Sunday train and bus services are either staggered or non-existent. So any regular job became irregular because of taking too many weekdays off for visits.

'I've been doing visits for more than ten years. To start with ninety-nine per cent were taken up with either discussing the appeal and when that failed the campaign and when that failed new ideas to try and get the case reopened. So even though it was over, you were still reliving it. It's only the last few years that we've accepted that we're not going to get any justice, that the bulk of the sentence is behind us anyway and the most of the conversation is about coming home – 1992 hopefully – or getting into a semi-open prison. It was a tremendous strain until we realised that we weren't going to get any justice. You always felt you weren't doing enough and you were trying to keep up a jolly attitude when you knew people didn't give a shit. I hated that. Now it's just tiredness. I'm prison-visit-weary.'

She is an expert on prison visiting: which minicabs meet which trains, which ferries coincide with which visiting times. The travel is expensive and although the Department of Social Security will help with travel payments, the bureaucracy means long delays while a prisoner may be waiting impatiently for a visit. 'So

I rely on handouts to get me on visits and periodically my dad will send me money.

'When you visit, the prison officers either treat you like it was their job and they just want to get you in and out as quickly as possible, or they make you wait outside in the cold before they open the gates, go through all the gear, search unnecessarily in things it would be impossible to smuggle anything. You can get a very nice officer working in Brixton or Wormwood Scrubs, then he gets transferred to Wandsworth and all of a sudden he takes on the same horrible hard-line attitude that Wandsworth is famous for.

'At Parkhurst you can have a couple of years of happy-go-lucky then an incident inside the prison or maybe next door at Albany, a riot or disruption, can cause them to clamp down – and the best way to punish the prisoners is to take it out on their visitors or relatives. Years ago I hated Parkhurst when I had to visit David or Ray Baron. It took ages to get there because of the slow ferries and trains. But when my father was moved there for a small operation recently it was a treat to go to the Isle of Wight and come back feeling not absolutely whacked out, meeting old friends on the ferry and having a drink and a laugh.'

While Reg Dudley has been inside, his wife, mother, sister and brother have died. 'I think my dad has handled it brilliantly, better than anyone I know. The last year I've felt it was time they moved him to a lower category prison where his brain could function better.'

Meanwhile, Kathy has watched the flash young blokes from the early seventies emerge from prison. 'Loads of people are completely changed when they come out. Their confidence is destroyed. They can be very bitter and not just hate the society that put them away but everyone else as well. I've seen a few that have got through their time by having a puff of weed and have come out more or less dependent on that. I can think of one who just cannot adapt. He lives in his little flat like he's still in a cell and cannot mix with anybody other than the people who were around him there.

'David is one of the few who has come out OK. Which is partly because he's got a sense of humour and partly because he has the ability to not let anything wind him up while he's away. Part of his philosophy is never worry about anything that you have no control over.'

Kathy doesn't try to hide her irregular past. 'If you want a niceish job where you're mixing with "straight" people they've got to be told about your family. I'm very careful about who I tell it to. I've done it on the train coming home from Dartmoor, which is something I never used to do. Someone asked me where I'd been and I said, "I've been to see my dad in prison." They wanted to know why he was in and I told them. The reaction wasn't bad, but it was more to do with the way I told them. People around me at the moment I think do believe me and I appreciate that. There are a few straight people you can tell who believe you, but it's better to get to know them first.

'With the other women visiting prison there was, at one stage, such a loving loyal wife attitude that I couldn't stand travelling with them. I couldn't bear listening to it. But the last five or six years I've realised there are some more like me – been married, divorced, had one or two boyfriends away, did their own thing, were their own people. I'm not a hardline feminist but I really believe sincerely in women's rights. I have got opinions and I have got something to say and I don't have to ask permission to say it any more.'

Even in the most chauvinistic of worlds, that of the women who wait for their men inside, the changes are happening. 'It is changing a lot now. Men can't expect the modern women to play this ridiculous role. The new generation won't take it. The ones whose mums have sat indoors baking and knitting for twenty years while their husbands were in prison might do it, but the others don't. Nobody gets condemned for not waiting any more. Most people say, "Thank God you had the sense!" In the old days it was thought of as disgusting, you'd be slagged off and ostracised.'

And the hard irony is that much of the supposition in the Torso Murder case was based on that old morality: that Dudley and Maynard would somehow disapprove so strongly of infidelity that they would take violent action, that Kathy would be in some way involved through her brief fling with Micky Cornwall. Perhaps if the case had been tried today, more than ten years on, it would have crumbled along with those old preconceptions.

'All my life I've detested violence, and yet you would never believe it to think of the life I've led. I hate violent people,' says Kathy. 'I don't even like verbally violent people.'

Her favourite book is Herman Wouk's *Don't Stop the Carnival*, which she has read four times. 'It's no great literary thing. It's about a bloke from New York who buys a rundown hotel in the Caribbean. Which is what I wanted to do! It's comic. A little bit of romance. Sadness.

'I went on a course at the City Lit so that I could write everything down that has happened, but then I realised how ignorant I was. I wanted to learn English first. But then when I do study English and use all those phrases it doesn't sound like me anyway.'

She lives alone now but remains on friendly terms with her husband. 'I'm glad I'm no longer attached to any acting criminal. I don't ever want to go through it again. For selfish reasons. I would rather be alone.'

She says it like Greta Garbo. But Greta Garbo didn't grin.

The case flutters only briefly into the news nowadays – young Bob Maynard stood in the European elections of 1985 to draw attention to the case, Reg Dudley was featured in a television programme about lifers. The trial itself, as we have noted, had only really attracted press attention at the opening and for the verdicts. It was while the jury was out that a number of the crime reporters re-emerged. Kathy's boyfriend of the time, Ray Baron, observed them as they arrived. 'There,' he said, as a figure in a black mac hoved into view, 'goes the Prince of Darkness.'

3

The Crime Reporter

With what pleasure we read newspaper
reports of crime! A true criminal becomes a
popular figure because he unburdens in no
small degree the consciences of his fellow
men, for now they know once more where evil
is to be found.

Carl Jung, *Archetypes and Collective
Unconscious*

'In the old days the crime reporters actually went to the scene of the crime. Body
was found. Missing girl, probably nude or raped. Day One is the body. Day Two,
hopefully they've identified her. Day Three, it's The Village Under Suspicion.
Day Four is The Finger of Suspicion Points at Me. It doesn't change too much
now. Then you'd finish up in court and you'd be doing deals for their life stories,
the background stories, the Who's Got the Mother story. Six or seven reporters.
One will say, "I've got the mother," "I've got the father," someone's got the
sister-in-law. Money would change hands.'

This is James Nicholson talking, the Prince of Darkness, a man who is almost
as much a part of the Old Bailey's cast of characters as the woman bearing the
scales of justice on the roof. Both are familiar figures to police and criminals, both
are slightly eccentric dressers. The nickname came from a black cape which he
wore from his early days reporting crime and it has stuck with him, throughout
careers with the *Daily Sketch*, *Daily Mail*, *Daily Express*, *Daily Star*, and the *People*.
He is the crime reporter's crime reporter – 'not as old as God's dog but I won't see
fifty-five again' – and we are in the snooker room of the Press Club off Ludgate
Circus with just a glass of Guinness and the green baize for company.

He was born in Batley, Yorkshire. 'I came from an ordinary working-class
family. My old man was a dry stone waller, you don't see many of those now. I
went to Batley technical college and learnt all about physics and chemistry, but
my teacher at the time said I had an imagination, said I could write things – not
very well as a writer, but I could put stories together and my imagination was
always there. I was sixteen, and there was a vacancy on the *News* in Batley. A
vacancy in the editorial staff – 'editorial' seemed a big word to me. I got a job as a
teaboy-cum-general-dogsbody.

'I was carrying proofs about the place for maybe a couple of months and
collecting paragraphs, go and see the local vicar sort of thing and then I finally got
the job of my life I suppose: I was made cemetery reporter.

'You had to go to the cemeteries every day and take a list of the dead. I would just collect names – for eighteen months. It was a remarkable experience. Don't forget in those days the war was on and you had limited rations. You only got one egg a week, and so on. It was great being a cemetery reporter because you went to every funeral and they were given special dispensation – ham teas. So I spent my time getting fit on these. And you would put all the names of the mourners in because that sold papers. People would give you cards at the end of the funeral with all the names on them. It was great.

'A lot of funny things happened in cemeteries, quite outrageous, unreportable things. I've seen people fighting at funerals. An undertaker fall down a hole, broke his nose. I saw them once bury a guy in half a grave of water. As the funeral cortege were coming towards the grave, the gravediggers were still putting in sawdust so it looked OK. There were only half a dozen mourners so it was obviously some layabout who had died. When they put him down, well he was given a mariner's funeral.

'After not very long I went around doing the obits, so you had to go and see the low life. There was not very much high life in Batley. It was the end of the world; the birds fly backwards away from Batley. You would go to the house and in many cases they wouldn't actually talk to you until you'd had a look at the dead. It would be the man or the woman or the daughter of the house and "doesn't he look lovely?" kind of thing. Meeting all those relatives actually trained you to deal with stress situations.'

The attitude to the press then was different. 'In those days everyone wanted their picture in the papers. You'd go to the funeral, get the names, ring the desk. You'd get six names, you'd do three and another reporter would do three and all those names mattered.

'It got me close to people. I did courts and I would write them for the weekend paper. So I was meeting policemen in those days and throughout my life I've been friendly with policemen. Over the years I've also become friendly with villains. The police know this. I've learnt to walk that narrow tightrope.

'The first time I was ever threatened I was working for *Batley News*. The fellow in the dock was one of the really heavy thugs. They described him in the court as a bully and the swine was waiting for me outside and said, "Don't put that in the paper." But of course it went in the paper – "Batley bully fined, threatened with prison." And he was about twenty-five and I was then about sixteen or seventeen and he chased me – never caught me. That was my first villain; eventually he did get a lot of time for beating somebody very violently.'

Court reports, the staple diet of most local papers, kept him busy, taking him to the assizes in Leeds and Wakefield and Huddersfield. You went by bus in those days, not in a BMW 633 CSI with a bleep and a car phone.

'I got the taste. I met policeman and solicitors. They wanted their name in the papers. There was no television in those days; you became famous by being in the papers.'

He did his shorthand at night-school, hitting 120–130 words a minute. When his National Service came around Nicholson volunteered for the RAF, was passed for the Fleet Air Arm and finished up on an air gunner's course. Then he returned to the meagre wage of the provincial press. By now he was learning the crime trade.

'I had my first murders, the first two were men I knew, local. The first was a guy who went to a dance in Dewsbury, picked up a girl, took her home, stripped her and strangled her. He was hanged. Hanging was very much in vogue in those days. The fellow was arrested in church. The second was a kid I knew from school, Jess Maymon. I saw him on the day he committed the murder. God, what a name from the past.

'I used to look with a kind of envy at the evening papers, the *Evening News*, *Evening Post*, *Telegraph* and *Argus*. They used to send their reporter down, usually a fellow of twenty-five or thirty, they were big wheels. In those days I used to copy what they said and put it in my story. It still goes on today. Plenty still lift the evening papers – "Are the evenings out?"'

Pickings were slim on the paper and the last straw was when his expenses chit for a bus fare to Huddersfield was queried. 'I had been working night and day and he didn't want me to put my four and five pence a week expenses in so I went to Blackpool, to an evening paper. My salary doubled.

'Blackpool being Blackpool there was a hell of a variety of court cases. Morning to night I'd sit in court. I had a runner then to take my copy back to the desk. By the time you're coming out of court you could read what you'd written in the morning. I had a village round, too, so one day a week I wouldn't do courts. I'd do "Round the villages with James Nicholson." I even had a logo with my thing on the page.'

The cast of characters in Jimmy Nicholson's reporting past come on stage unprompted. He has reminisced before and he is a pro. 'There was Louisa Merrifield, an ex-Salvation Armyist. Poisoned her landlady, Sarah Rickets, with rum and shoe polish. It was interesting because one of the famous people from Scotland Yard, Colin MacDougall, came to Blackpool to investigate under the instructions of the local chief this mysterious death of an old woman found in the bungalow who had, according to the doctor, been given arsenic. Apparently there's arsenic in the shoe polish.

'For thirteen days she was on the loose. I used to go out with this bloody woman at night. She accepted me because I was on the local paper. I got quite friendly with her. By this time the story was "Scotland Yard – Murder Squad". There was a Murder Squad in those days; they still say there is but there isn't, it's C1. It was big news: "Scotland Yard Probe Mystery Death". She was lording it.

'"I didn't kill her," she would say. While she was giving us cups of tea the cops were going round the garden with a mine detector looking for the poison, because they said she said she'd bought tins of poison.

'It was when I started drinking actually, during those thirteen days hanging around. We used to take her to the Clifton Hotel in Blackpool and she was a star. She'd sign autographs at two and sixpence a time. She was portly, in her forties, a Salvationist. You looked at her background. She'd lost three husbands. All suspect murders. She was hanged by Albert Pierrepoint.

'I got to know him quite well. He was a boxing referee and he used to come to Blackpool, but he never used to talk about the hangings. His buddy, Harry Allen, did. Harry enjoyed the press, he was a great friend of the press. Still is. He had a pub called The Happy Struggler. We named it the Happy Strangler. An instant quote was Harry.

'Anyway, on the Merrifield case, it was hilarious, those days. Once I was with Arnold Rosenfield, who was a famous crime reporter with the *News Chronicle*, then with *The Times*, sitting in a lounge. Arnold was a little Jewish guy, very interesting man. She said, "Would you like some tea?" and Arnold said, "I don't take tea." And she looked at him and said, "It's not bloody poisoned." That broke the atmosphere.'

The end of capital punishment took some of the edge out of the coverage of murder cases. Some old reporters even attribute to this the collapse of the London evening paper market – it used to boast three papers and a circulation three times that of today's *Standard* – saying that people were less interested in grabbing the paper with its trial verdicts once there was no possibility of an execution.

Jimmy Nicholson was in Blackpool for eight years covering crime – 'fish and chip murders' – and enjoying the life of the established local reporter: 'Passes to everything, all the shows. I was married. I didn't fancy coming away.'

But Fleet Street beckoned as Fleet Street did.

'I got a good exclusive from George Formby's funeral. George Formby left his money to a girl he got engaged to. He'd died and left his fortune to his sweetheart who was a teacher in Preston, much younger than him. All the jewels and all the money went to this girl, she was twenty-five or thirty. I got this exclusively from a lawyer at the funeral. It was a big front-page story. I was offered a job on the *Daily Sketch*. I went down one day and had interviews at the *Sketch*, the *Mirror* and the *Express*. I joined the *Sketch* and became a bylined crime reporter. I did the major stories for the next five years, culminating in the Moors Murders. It was great. If it was a big one I got it, child murders – quite a few of them were hanged in those days.

'I was on the Moors Murders from Day One to the day they were sentenced and I'm still covering it, I'm still involved in the Brady situation because there's still been two bodies not found. I actually saw Myra the day she first appeared. She was given bail for three days until Smith, the witness, said that there's more bodies up there. After that it started snowballing.

'I think she was bemused by it all at first. But as time went on it became obvious to everyone that she was the dominant one. She was the first to say hello to Brady in court when he came in. We were sitting next to her, a yard away, she was doodling. He just shut himself off. They were in love in those days, wanted to marry each other.

'Brady is the only guy who's ever taken me to the Press Council. In 1978 he wrote to them because I did a splash piece on him, used pictures that had never been used before. Myra with the dog, you've seen them many times since. It was in the *Express*. I said then that he was responsible for at least four of the murders. And he actually wrote to the Press Council complaining that this was trial by newspaper. Derek Jameson was my governor then. He called me upstairs and said, "You're in trouble. Better sit down and have a drink." I said, "Not at this time of the day." "You've been Press Councilled." I thought, "Who the hell?" "Brady."

'He wanted his day in court. He thought he would get out to put his case. So we had the first letter in his handwriting denying the murders. Derek said he was going to write back and say, "Dear Mr Brady, if you want to put your side of it, Mr Nicholson will come and see you at your convenience. Any time in the next thirty years." And we never heard anything else. He sent me a Christmas card with "Wish you were here" on it. He was in Parkhurst!

'They offered me a rise to come down to London after the Moors Murders. They don't do that now, they say you either come down or you're fired. I came down and I never looked back.' The Batley commoner became royalty.

'When I came to London I just slipped into black, I don't know why. It's respectable, I suppose. In the meantime the *Sketch* had given me a break from crime and sent me to cover the TT in the Isle of Man. Up there I did a piece about the covens which I sold to the BBC. The guy I interviewed there gave me a black mac, a cape type of thing, to illustrate the story and I never gave it back to him. I wore it when I came to Fleet Street. Lost it. Saw another one in Soho and bought it and that was pinched at the Old Bailey.

'In the north I used to wear the cape round my shoulders. If they ever release that documentary that Michael Parkinson produced on the Moors Murders, you'll see it. There's about an hour of me in it. When they were digging graves they used me as a vehicle. Sidney Bernstein [Chairman of Granada TV] stopped it from being shown, because people were still alive. It was macabre stuff. On that film it shows me wearing that damn coat.

'I used to turn up in it. At one of those sieges, Balcombe Street, the Commissioner there said, "That devil Nicholson is here." And someone said, "Not the devil, call him the Prince of Darkness." "Well, Prince of Darkness then . . . he's asking dopey questions at four o'clock in the morning saying he's got editions to catch when there are no papers." It went on from there.'

Indeed it did. Reporters starting out at the Old Bailey have the Prince pointed out to them – there he is hanging around for a quick word with a barrister outside Court 11, that coat, the slightly tinted glasses, the wispy dark hair, the persistence.

'I suppose I helped to create the bloody monster which I found in recent years has just grown round me. I don't wear it now . . . you saw me the other day and I was wearing silver-grey. At the Black Panther trial it got so bad I turned up in white one day. It was all fun.

'It's a bit weird to find yourself on the golf course and a judge says to you, "What did you do in that hole, Prince?" A lot of the high-ranking people call me Prince and it's become a bit of a burden. My reputation precedes me. A picture was taken of me at the top of the *Express* building with the Old Bailey in the background and lightning struck – it got all dark and the photographer caught it.

'I have had letters from all kinds of nuts claiming to be devil worshippers. One wrote and said, "You must come down, we have weekly meetings." I gave it to the *News of the World*.'

He met the Krays at the Esmeralda, the club they managed, or rather mismanaged. 'They thought they were untouchable. They were. It took two and a half years to nick them. Unless that barmaid had come forward and fingered them, said that Ronnie was at the Blind Beggar . . .

'I've seen Reggie in prison, but not for a couple of years because he seems to have been taken over by people who want to shape his career when he comes out. I usually get a Christmas card from him and the family. I only got to know the Krays since they were inside because I was friendly to their mother. I felt sorry for her, going three times a week visiting three sons. I would take the old man for a pint.

'When I first came down I spent a lot of months on that, days in sleazy clubs mixing with very dangerous men. The Richardsons were running parallel to them. There was a lot of animosity. Cornell was one of the men working for the Richardsons who refused to work with the Krays and called Ronnie a poof. That was what it was all about.

'I've got a lot of respect for Reg Kray. He dedicated himself to educating himself and he wanted to get out. I said once on a radio programme that they should let him out. There was all hell let loose. I got calls from policemen, saying, "Why did you say that, the man's a bastard?" I said, "Compare the Krays with what we see today." Kray says himself there are a lot of people in south London who say there would be a lot less trouble in their pubs if Kray was around. They would rather pay than have trouble.

'When I was doing the Krays I was with a photographer in the Blind Beggar at 7.30 one night when I was asked to take a last drink and leave. I was trying to get background on the shooting, months after. The governor was there, we had a Guinness and a gin and tonic. Suddenly at the end of the bar there appeared three huge guys in overcoats, like walking doors. The governor said they'd paid so I raised my glass, only half in acknowledgement. I went in the john and one of the guys was there. So I said, "Thanks for the drink, what are you having?" "Don't worry about that, son" – I think I was older than him – "make it your last." "Why?" "Because you're a reporter." I said, "All I'm trying to do is . . ." "I know what you're trying to do. Just leave."

'I told the photographer and he was up and ready for going. I said, "What can he do?" I ordered another one. The manager disappeared.

'Two of these guys walked up and said, "Look, we'll give you a chance to go. We don't want any trouble. Out." So I said, "It's 7.30 at night, what have I done wrong?"

'One guy got one arm, the other got the other. I walked like that with my feet about a foot from the ground. It was Chaplinesque. They dropped me on my feet. They said, "Across the road there's a pub and there's a drink waiting for you."

'Across the road was this Irish pub. We went in, I'm wearing black, the cape. Looking like a fugitive from Mothercare. The guy behind the bar said, "You're reporters. There's a Guinness for you. There's a gin and tonic for you. A guy just popped in and paid for it."

'At the end of the trial one of the guys got off and I went to a party with him at the Regency Club, where the stabbing of Jack "The Hat" McVitie was planned, and there were these three guys who threw us out of the pub. One said to me, "You know why we threw you out that night was because we had this guy coming in and he was the lynchpin of the Kray empire at that time."'

Those were the days when gangs were so identifiable that they almost wore blazers with the initials of their firm on the pocket. Times change.

'Gangland is not as it was in the sixties. The last gangs were certainly the Richardsons and the Krays, the Tibbses. These were all big firms, involved in protection rackets and armed robberies, but there aren't those kind of gangs now. Technological improvements in the police mean they're far more sophisticated now. You still find the small firms. The drug gangs are around now.'

The press gang of course is still intact. They have their own club, their own pecking order, too. The late Percy Hoskyns, the former *Daily Express* crime correspondent, who preceded James Nicholson as President of the Crime Reporter's Association, much loved in crime reporting circles, wrote of the Crime Reporters Association: 'a group of professional journalists who are to Scotland Yard what lobby journalists are to the House of Commons – an élite body who can be trusted with confidential information to be used to mutual advantage'.

In that 'mutual advantage' hangs a dilemma. In order to operate every crime reporter needs the cooperation of the police for the day-to-day ration of robbery and murder. And just as the prime minister's office can tip off favoured political correspondents who present things in a sympathetic way, so can Scotland Yard. The generation of crime news operates in various ways: before the end of a major trial journalists are invited to a press briefing with the officers who handled the case so that they can be given the background to the case. This will often include information that has not come out in court, either about the investigation or about the character of the accused. The fruits of these sessions then appear in the papers the day after the trials as 'backgrounders', complete with photos of the accused, the victims, the weapons or the haul involved. (The *Daily Telegraph* is renowned for its lurid court reports, which its editor, Max Hastings, has cheerfully acknowledged as 'in keeping with the long tradition of middle-class hypocrisy'.)

Often these may be totally accurate accounts, but there can also be a temptation on the part of the police to emphasise some details and gloss over others, just as every official spokesperson is tempted or even obliged to do.

By the end of the eighties a new fashion for taking journalists on drugs raids had developed. While the police could argue with some justification that this meant there was little chance of rough stuff or planting evidence, at the same time it places the journalist in an odd position. He or she has been coopted, as it were, for the operation and not unnaturally identifies with the chaps going over the top; this can lead to a lot of breathless, battle-ground prose, quite apart from the trickiness of the ethics involved.

Scotland Yard also holds monthly briefings at which the main crime issues of the time are sketched out for the assembled press. As with the lobby, correspondents have to observe the etiquette of the unattributable quote. The diligent ones check stuff, retain their scepticism, the others print what fits, safe in the knowledge that most people with criminal records cannot sue. Jimmy Nicholson has been a crime correspondent for many years but has retained a reputation for being the person who asks the awkward question at the briefings.

'We have a press office at Scotland Yard, where you can find out what's been happening overnight if you haven't already been belled. Usually if it's big you get a telephone call or a bleep. Then you check in to Scotland Yard. More often than not there was nothing to report overnight. Farcical. Twenty-six thousand policemen and nothing. Sometimes you'll have told them about a murder and it wouldn't be on the list.' So individual contacts have to be made.

'You would get a call from a friendly policeman who'd tell you that he's just going out on a murder. I've been on a case where they hadn't told the bureau, but I've been with a policeman when he was called out on a murder. "For Christ's sake, James, I've got to go. There's been a murder down so and so . . . give me an hour before you ring anybody." Then I would get my car and bugger off and follow them. If I'd been boozing I'd get a cab.

'There's never a quiet day. There's always something on the tapes to follow. For instance there's a murder in Brighton. They'd ring and say, "Get to Brighton." Get to Birmingham. Get to Ireland. Wherever there's a big one. Sieges. I say I've been to every siege since Troy. I said that once on TV and it's been repeated.

'If there's been a murder you go along and there'll be a press conference and you can get alongside them. Often you would get a body and you wouldn't even get a sex. "It's a girl, she's fourteen, fifteen." That kind of information would be fed back to you by a man who you'd established a relationship with at another do. That's the job of the crime reporter: get in with the people who matter.

'They would find the killer and your job is to get what he was like – the Michael Ryans of this world. You've got to get close to the mother and father. The local law might help you so you'd get that background. The committal would come along and you'd attend that. You can't publish the details if it's an old-fashioned one but you get all the details. If it's a new style paper committal then your job is to see who's handling it. Try and meet them in the local pub, ring them up and then establish another relationship on the ground that you're not going to use the information until after the trials.

'Then you have the trial and you've got to follow that through. Same with big inquests. Or the interesting rapes, like the Vicarage rape, follow it through from Day One.'

And while the crime press all know each other well, the ones who have been dealt a good hand by their police contacts learn to keep their cards close to their chests.

'You get wise to sharing information with other reporters. The first big case I was on was Hanratty. [James Hanratty was hanged for the A6 murder of Valerie Storie. Originally another man, Peter Alphon, had been arrested for it. Hanratty always protested his innocence and there have been a series of books and campaigns to clear his name.] They flew me to Ireland. When I got into the airport I met the head of the Irish police who I knew from when I covered murders in Dublin. I had a photographer, John Madden, with me and I suppose he was rather surprised I knew this big man. He said, "I suppose you're here about the Ryan case?" Yes. He said, "His name is not Ryan, it's Hanratty." So I said, "What about Alphon?" "They've had to let him go."

'This was dynamite. The photographer says, "God, what a story." The news editor was then Bert Pack and he hardly knew me because I was arriving from the north and I rang him and said, "James Nicholson. I understand they've got the wrong man." He said, "Bloody hell, a big story and we've got to send a nut like you over."

'I said, "Look, it's an incredible story but I got it from a man I know extremely well." He said, "Put it in copy."' I had a double Scotch. I don't drink Scotch. I thought, "Jesus, what have I done?"

'I had only put the phone down for ten minutes and they were back. Bert says, "You're on." What a story! Man Accused of Shooting Two Released. Seeking Another Man. Tom Sandrock, Johnny Johnson, all the old-fashioned crime guys, that madman from the *Sun*, an ex-fascist, are all there. No one in Dublin is talking. I'm in the Gresham Hotel, a palatial place, pillars and everything, washing my face in the gents. I look in the mirror and there's this bloke about six foot six. He said, "Are you James Nicholson?" I didn't stop, kept on washing my face. He said, "Well, James Nicholson, you've probably done something that'll put Bob Acott [the British policeman in charge] back on the beat." "Who says so?" "Well, I am Tom Sandrock, *Daily Telegraph* crime correspondent." I said, "How do you know what I've said?" He said, "Because your photographer has told me that . . ." "My photographer *what*!" "Your photographer said they're looking for another man." I said, "He'd no right to do that." He said, "Well, they're trying to keep it secret." I said – I'd had two Scotches – "Well, can we come to some arrangement?"

'The crime reporters mafia were upstairs trying to exclude me from the conference. But they didn't succeed.

'It went all round Ireland for seven or eight days. Wherever the police went we went. The trail went cold. Then flowers appeared from Liverpool sent by Hanratty to his mother. I flew to Liverpool. Been in bed two hours. The telephone. A voice said, "James, get your ass down to the police station" – only ass wasn't in the vernacular in those days; it was probably "Get yourself down pronto to the police station. We've got him."

'I drove down at about 5.15 a.m. Coming out of the police station was the man who phoned me, Stanley Parr, Deputy Chief Constable, a very good friend of mine. He said, "We've got him in there. His name is Hanratty."'

Jimmy Nicholson flips through the names of cases like a football fan recalling great matches of the past.

'The last big gang was the Brinks Mat. Most of them were locked up before we could get to them and we couldn't get the families. Way back Harry Roberts, who killed two policemen at Shepherds Bush, asked me to see him. As long as you don't glorify them it's all right. I certainly don't run to policemen and tell them what I'm doing and certainly I don't tell crooks what policemen are doing. I have a very good relationship with lawyers.

'In the early days it did require a lot of going to clubs. You make friends with policemen if you play golf. You get invited to farewell parties or resigning parties and they know we have a certain dispensation from the commissioner. They're told, "You can trust this reporter."'

There have been side-tracks away from the paths of the Yard and the Bailey and the incident room. Nicholson won £200 in compensation after he was hit with a bottle by a young man at a demonstration to find the 'Pig of the Month' – a reference to an unpopular west London policeman – in Trafalgar Square in the seventies. He made a citizen's arrest. 'I was wearing this blue mohair suit which was fashionable in those days. The blood came down. I'd had a few at lunchtime but I'm not a guy who gets stoned. I grabbed him and he goes, "I'm sorry, mister, I'm sorry." There was a front-page picture of me in the *UK Press Gazette*, a very big one. He got six months suspended.'

Conflicts are not always so cut and dried. Many defendants and their families hate reporters, distrust them and have reason to. Equally, victims of crime or the bereaved may have to wake from a pill-induced sleep to see an array of slightly overweight men in trenchcoats sitting eating bacon rolls and drinking tea from paper cups in cars outside their houses, cameras and notebooks at the ready.

'After a horrific murder people often want to talk to you, they can talk to an experienced journalist. If they're guilty, I've had people rehearse their story to me before they speak to the police. With many you can feel as though you're intruding on private grief. You go in and say, "James Nicholson, crime reporter, I'd like to talk to you." In a lot of circumstances you have to put a foot in the door.

'I've done undercover jobs. I've investigated paedophiles and in that case you enjoy telling them who you are. "I'm a bloody reporter." AAAAhhhhhh!

'Covering crime is more sophisticated now. In the old days you would take the telephone mouthpiece away so that the other guys couldn't file. Or they would take your distributor cap off your car if you were in an isolated place. Let your tyres down. It was as daft as that.

'People ask for money from the press, it's now become a daily thing. They've become accustomed to it by watching television. I've been in a lot of buy-ups. I even had to handle a kidney transplant and was asked if I could handle the buy-up. Buy-ups are a hazard to a general background story. The Ripper – everyone was buying everyone else. It becomes a situation where you call back to your news editor and say, "Who's buying who?" The *Guardian* is in a situation where they don't buy anybody. I don't think they buy crisps. *Telegraph* are the same. Dailies sometimes can't compete with Sundays.

'The only way to do it is to do it from Day One. Go in and meet anyone you can, get as many quotes as you can and you find at the end of the days someone's come in and bought up your witness. Some newspapers give you a buy-up form before you go out. With a stamp on it. You know when you're going to have to buy someone on a horrendous killing, horrendous rape. You say, "Sign this. We'll give you £10,000."

'I used to take a figure and double it. I used to lie, I'm afraid. Say it's worth fifty, all the time you know in the end your paper's going to give them nothing. I suppose that's a little bit dishonest, but it's true. Got to meet fire with fire. Jobs are being lost because they haven't bought the right people. You're not supposed to pay the relatives of a killer, but if there's a way round it someone will find a way. They go through the roof now. The figures are astronomical. £50,000 is not uncommon. You can go to a quarter of a million. It should stand out like a pools win but it doesn't. Big offers were made in the Ripper and the Black Panther. I don't pay policemen. The people I know would be insulted if I offered.'

Then there are the Rocky Ryans. Rocky is a man whose leisure-time pursuit is getting newspapers to print bogus stories. His philosophy is always to try to give a paper the kind of story it wants to believe. That is always easier to sell than the kind of story that does not fit too easily into the paper's notion of the world. Hence he has sold the *Sun* a bogus story about the Yorkshire Ripper going to discos on an evening out from Broadmoor and he has sold the *Telegraph* a story about a businessman being behind the Seychelles coup. When he phones the *Guardian* it is often with a security tale – a spy held at the airport, that sort of thing. He has a wide range of accents and the stories usually have enough detail to make them believable. He also employs an almost infallible trick – he threatens to take the story to another paper.

'He's sold everybody. He tried to sell the Krays to me. I haven't been caught. I had one guy tried to sell me down the river about one of the Krays trying to kill himself when I was on the *Mail*. Six weeks later, when I had just joined the *Express*, he came in again. He didn't recognise me. I said, "Right, I'm going to have you arrested for giving false information." The last thing I knew he was running through the swing doors. He'd done a lot of damage. He's dropped one or two editors in it.' But what does Nicholson do about those snippets of information he comes across from contacts that would make good copy, but –?

'If I am in a dilemma about something someone tells me, that if I use it, it will get them into trouble, if I can get away with not using it I'm often dishonest enough not to. If I pick a story up I don't think I'm honour bound, depending on the circumstances, to rush to the news editor. A couple of times I have deliberately let guys off the hook. I felt, no, I had better not write this. If the publicity would be more killing that the offence has warranted. But if I'm sent on a story, then I cover it. I've had two incidents in which friends of mine were involved recently – one was OK and the other will never forgive me.'

In any case the big crimes are changing. 'Insider dealing. The people in the City who have been getting away with this for years have been committing bigger crimes than someone knocking off the Knightsbridge safe-deposit box. The white collar people who live in palatial mansions are now going to have to go to prisons. Estate agents who marked down a house and then sold it . . .'

He is sanguine about dishonesty elsewhere.

'You'll always have corruption in the police force. There's 26,000 men in the Met. It's lessened. It went through a period when I had more police contacts inside than out. I would no more associate with a corrupt policeman than a corrupt lawyer. There is evidence that information is being passed from a lawyer to a crook to enable them to stay ahead of the law. There's a list of them. I was told there were over thirty names.

'I've been offered money many times to keep stuff out. Twenty or thirty times I've been approached. My advice is that you shouldn't talk to me because my job is to make sure it goes in. A barrister, now famous, who had marital trouble, asked me if I could keep it out the paper: "What's the procedure?" I said, "You're the bloody barrister – if I were you I would live in an hotel miles away and establish residence there for a month." It worked. He wasn't traced. He's eternally grateful. The barrister who buys me a Guinness is the one who did it.

'I'm one of the few guys that have kept my marriage together. I have a wife who understands. She thinks I'm a cop. I had a party at my place the other night and there were several police there. She has learned to live with it. She could have married a bloody sailor.'

His escape route is cowboy films: 'If you're mixing with crooks all the time you don't want to watch shows with them in. Today at the Bailey for instance, you can see two vicious murders – a case of girl whose mouth has been superglued, nose superglued and then stabbed and strangled. There's no need to watch Channel Four, you can go to the court and see it live, see it in the raw. The public don't see it. I do. Hence I would rather watch old John Wayne riding round the range.' And he's off chatting to a man at the bar, for booze oils all the wheels of crime – the old Fleet Street pubs, the police haunts, and the dark, downstairs dives.

4

The Club Man

You go into dark places to do dark
things.

David Mamet, *House of Games*

Harry Hicks. The name itself seems to come from a 1950s B movie, possibly starring a younger, slimmer George Cole. When people talk about him
they use both names, it's never Harry or Hicksy. It's Harry Hicks. Or 'arry 'icks.
First glimpsed from the other side of the bar, Harry has a night-time face, formed
by years of cigarette smoke and cajoling heavier men not to take a liberty.
Whippet-thin, with a mouth that seems permanently on the edge of making a
slightly dodgy remark, dark glasses and snappy clothes with genuine labels that he
is not shy to show you, he can explain with a straight face at a party how to pour a
bottle of Moët et Chandon without the heat from the hand affecting the
temperature of the champagne, and in the next breath wonder why he brought
such a good vintage along when no one there will bloody appreciate it.

Harry Hicks is a card. He started at the bottom of the pack in Finsbury Park,
north London, shuffled his way up to the top of the pack, then down again, then
up again. He is a club man. He has sung in clubs, owned clubs, run clubs, been
run out of clubs, had clubs closed down on him, been raided in clubs. And he is a
fixer. He can get you tickets for Arsenal at home to Spurs, or *Cats* in the tourist
season. He could probably get you an invitation to a garden party at Buckingham
Palace if he thought you weren't joking when you asked for one.

Right now he's established in the immaculate front room of one of north
London's more fashionable streets, with his pit-bull terrier in the back yard, only
a few miles away, yet very far from where he started.

'My father used to have gamblers in the house and they would play dice, that's
where it all began. We weren't well off at all. I didn't go to school except
prize-giving days or Christmas parties or whatever. So during the day I used to go
out collecting old rags, selling fruit, being a barrow boy. The truancy people took
me to court, but my mum was always by my side and said I was such a good boy,
and nothing ever happened.'

This idyll did not last long. He smashed his uncle's brand new car into a sweet
shop and the uncle was unimpressed. He was sent to Stamford House, a juvenile
remand centre, and did not enjoy it. 'That was my first taste of being away and I've
mostly managed to keep out of these places since.'

But he was not out of his teens before he was in trouble again for stealing a lorry-load of tomatoes from Covent Garden. He was remanded in custody for two weeks in Wormwood Scrubs. Due to an administrative oversight he was kept inside for a further four and half months and when he appeared again his mother did her stuff once more and the judge agreed that he should not have been inside for so long and released him. And, although Harry has had around a dozen convictions for all sorts of things since – receiving, stealing, taking and driving away, no insurance and the like – he has since avoided Wormwood Scrubs and the rest of 'these places'.

It was the fifties when he was released and there was still National Service, which presented a fresh challenge for the developing Hicks' imagination.

'I had to go to Russell Square for a medical. So I got dressed up in an army coat with a string wrapped round it. I had a plastic tommy gun under my overcoat and I came out of one of the little cubicles they sent you into to change shouting, "Kill them Germans!" They didn't want me. No one wanted to do National Service.'

But if his country didn't need him Albert Dimes, a big underworld name with a successful bookmaking business, did. 'I used to run around the West End for Albert. He used to like me with him to keep people happy and lark around and get up and sing at the Astor Club and places like that. I was quite good, Sinatra stuff, rock 'n' roll. I'd always get up at any cabaret. One time one of them wanted me to sing "My Yiddisher Mama" but I wouldn't so he chinned me.'

He preferred this life to the slightly riskier route chosen by the men who spent big in the clubs. 'I could be in a club and in they would come. In those days there was a midday newspaper and they used to look at the back page. They'd robbed a bank that morning and they'd look in the stop press and they'd say "That was us".

'I was in their company but not on the robberies. Mainly because I didn't like the prison bit. I suffer from claustrophobia. Loads of times they asked me along. I went on a bank robbery just once. I was the driver. My foot was shaking so badly that I couldn't drive. They didn't rob the bank that time because there was a police car. And that was my one and only go.'

Albert Dimes and Jack Spot were the then rivals for control of West End clubland. 'If any people were coming over from America, Mafia people, Albert would take them to the clubs and ask me to go with them as court jester. I made them laugh. They were gentlemen. If you get with the right people, they don't argue with each other, it's when other types come in that it erupts. They would look at premises, restaurants, gambling clubs mostly, and ask Albert's advice. Albert would walk into the clubs and someone might put an envelope in his pocket, give him a few, and once Albert Dimes had been in a club no one caused trouble. People made like it was protection but it wasn't really.' And the clubs led Harry Hicks to a couple of blokes who had recently seen their future in such ventures.

'I became very friendly with the Kray twins. I would make them laugh. They would call for me and I would go out to the clubs. I used to go to the Society Club, it's now Tramp, regularly with Reggie Kray and his wife – she was alive at the time. From there it would be the Astor Club. You would get all the girls, hostesses, there, so if you wanted a girl to sit with you they would do whatever you wanted.

'There were also a lot of women who just like to be around heavy people. Why I don't know to this day. Women don't have to buy drinks. They walk in and they get lapped up. There's a bottle of champagne for them. They weren't prostitutes, they were good-time girls. They would be in the club, go for a meal and then whatever happened happened.'

Although he had decided he was too light for heavy work, this did not stop him getting banged about a bit.

'It was New Year's Eve and I had to wish someone Happy New Year. I went to the Astor Club, they weren't there, so I went to the Palm Springs Casino. I was dressed properly – I'd been to the Grosvenor Hotel earlier – dickie bow, quite presentable. I said "Happy New Year" to the man on the door. "Don't take the piss out of me," he says. Crash. He's hit me. I've finished up out on the street under a car, four of them kicking me. They broke my cheekbone. Went into hospital. I saw the club owner. I said I've had a right beating. I said I feel like killing the guy but I want money. He said you can do that, we're insured, but you've got to nick the guy, grievous bodily harm. I wouldn't nick anyone, but I made sure that the guy got hurt. I didn't do it myself but a couple of well-known faces said it was a diabolical liberty what happened. I know it sounds wicked. We knew what time the guy came out of the club and that he had a flat in Knightsbridge. He pulled up in his Mini, he had to walk about three steps to his flat. These two guys were walking along – I know it sounds cruel – one bumped into him and said, "Who are you pushing?" That was it. They got stuck into him and he got a right seeing to. I felt sorry for the guy afterwards.'

But Harry Hicks had to watch his own manners on occasions. The Krays 'looked after' the Colony Club, one of the West End nightspots that hovered between seediness and glamour. Harry was playing American dice one night, losing a lot of money with a system called 'out' betting, whereby the gambler bets against himself. The system, as Harry discovered, has a basic flaw, and within an hour or two he had emptied his own wallet and those of his gambling companions. Around two in the morning the croupier announced to the clientele that it was the last game of the night. Harry, hoping like all true gamblers to recoup with just one more throw, was livid. He jumped on the table and kicked the chips over. His absence was requested.

'The next day I went to another gambling club in Stoke Newington and I got a phone call from one of the twins that they wanted to see me. I didn't have a clue. I got round to the flat and they said, "You've been a naughty boy."'

It is reassuring to meet someone who has actually been told by the twins that he has been a naughty boy but Harry, like naughty boys everywhere, was forgiven. The twins told him, however, that they had heard he had been making a fool of himself in a club that he knew they were involved with and this was not on. He was barred.

'But I loved it. There were film stars there, George Raft, Telly Savalas, Elizabeth Taylor. And I wanted to get back because of the gambling.'

So the Krays put a proposition to him: he should find a smart gambler and convince a casino owner that he was a millionaire so that he could get credit, the credit would then be parlayed into profits. Harry and his friend were duly given £2,000, a fortune in those days. They tried another system whereby they betted against each other, which worked fine for a while.

'What we didn't realise was that if the dice comes up two ones, one of us loses and the other doesn't win anything. Panic stations. It happened twice and we were £400 down. Now we were playing with the Kray twins' money because they don't understand gambling at all. This guy that I'm with clicks his finger and wants the credit. It's all been arranged that he's going to get it. The manager goes up to get the money for him, £5,000, a tray full of chips, the only person who wasn't in on it was the cashier. As he goes up to get the credit, this little Jewish guy walks up and says, "You can't do that, that's mad George." He didn't get the credit.'

Which left Harry Hicks £400 short. He went next door to the Astor Club where Ronnie Kray was hanging out alone.

'I couldn't get through to Ronnie. He didn't understand anything about gambling. All he understood was – are we getting our own money back or getting into the credit?' Ronnie did understand other things, however, and a man was despatched to get his money back and clear up the misunderstanding. 'You read about how terrible the Krays were. I didn't see that side of it. It would be have a drink, have a laugh with them, whatever. I was in the Regency Club, which the twins used to look after for the Barrys, another family, who owned it. One night Jack "The Hat" walked in, I'll never forget, pulled out a gun and said, "Where's that fat poof?" (He was referring to Ronnie.) He fired three shots off in the club. They got to hear about it and that is when everything started going boss-eyed. A couple of people got killed.

'It got out of hand, people were saying the Krays were nothing and the twins felt they had to do something about it. Especially people saying that Ronnie was a fat poof. That was the worst insult you could come up with, worse even than calling someone a grass. They got arrested and that was the last I saw of them. I don't see them, don't get me wrong, I do quite a bit of prison visiting as it is but I left them out because I thought once I go it goes on for ever and if you're working you just can't do it.'

The clubs at the time often had American names – the Kentucky, Palm Springs – and modelled themselves on the real or imagined establishments of the protection era in the United States. One story has it that Owney Madden, the 'English Godfather', who worked in America at that time and owned the Cotton Club, once sent his assistant Yankee Schwartz to sort out a contractual wrangle over a band due to play at the club. The impressario concerned asked Yankee what he could do to assist. 'Be big,' replied Yankee, 'or be dead.' Clubs were just the place for villainous one-liners. The Kentucky was used in the film *Sparrows Can't Sing*, starring Barbara Windsor and directed by Joan Littlewood. Lord Snowdon and Roger Moore attended the première as did the Krays who threw a post-première party in the club.

There were other places – the Stork Club, Winstons, Churchills, the 21 Club. There was 'top class cabaret' and afterwards parties with Christine Keeler and Rachman. Harry was invited to them all. He would go to the boxing with the honoured guests from America: Cassius Clay versus Henry Cooper. 'After the fight one of the Yanks said to me, "Get up there in that ring." Up I went and got in the ring. That's what they loved me doing.'

On the occasions when Harry wasn't actually invited as such to events he found his own way of not so much crashing the gates as giving them a gentle nudge and finding out they were open all the time.

'I used to say to people wherever I went that I was Alec Guinness' son. That gave me a licence. I don't know if he has a son. I went to the South of France to see John Conteh – the former world champion – fight in Monte Carlo. The film festival was on. I got all dressed up and went in the Carlton Hotel. I walked in, you had to have a black disc rather than a ticket. The man says, "Yes, sir, can I help?" I said, "My name's Bryan Guinness, I'm Alec Guinness' son." Robert Shaw was there so I introduced myself to him and he said, "Oh, how's your father?" I said, "Dad's in the Bahamas . . ."

'At premieres what we would do is park up behind the Rolls Royce. You'd follow them and go to the party. One time we followed Robert Morley. He drove off, past Staines or somewhere like that, right out into the countryside and we were saying, "he's not going this far for a party surely." He pulled into his house. All the lights were out. That was it. He must have been the only one who wasn't going to the party!'

Frank Sinatra had a do at a hotel around the same time so Harry and his mates got hold of a fake press card and a camera. 'People would get up and dance and if anything was lying about, Dunhill lighters, that sort of thing, they would take a walk. Paintings off the wall, sometimes.'

Life on the inside track was simple and, if you knew the rules, less terrifying than it seemed from the outside track. 'People wanted to pay protection because they didn't want troublemakers, not because they were terrified. All it was really was throwing them a bone off to make sure everybody was happy. Everybody got a chance in those days. If you lost your money there were people there to give you what they called rising money so you would wake up the next day with money for your breakfast.'

But the police took a less benign view of London's clubland at the time. In his memoirs, Gilbert Kelland, the former head of Scotland Yard's CID, recalls the raids of the late fifties and early sixties. Some seem quaintly dated, the pursuit of clubs and gaming houses in Chelsea and Belgravia where chemin de fer were being played. 'One of the frequenters,' he writes of one gaming house, 'was quoted in a newspaper as saying "this is the end for me, boy. I never want to see a gaming party again."' Alas for Kelland and his colleagues, not everyone they arrested was so contrite.

Some of the other offences being investigated at that time give an indication of the way that morality was as important as criminality when it came to clubland. For instance, in Soho, amongst the Malteste-led gangs and the protection rackets, there was also the Establishment club which, as Kelland tells it, 'achieved some notoriety as the home of satirical entertainment after the appearance there of the American sick comedian and drug-addict Lenny Bruce.' Kelland goes on to record that Nicholas Luard, one of the club's owners, was quoted in the *Sunday Times* as saying that they had been tipped off that they might be prosecuted for obscenity if Bruce appeared again but that he was quite happy to take on the police over it. A few days later, as Kelland reports, 'a routine observation by Clubs Office staff inside the club disclosed licensing offences. It was raided just before midnight.' The club eventually closed. (Bruce never made it in anyway. Banned at Heathrow by Home Secretary Henry Brooke, he went back to America and died of a drugs overdose in his lavatory.)

Throughout this period Harry managed to get by without taking on a regular full-time post but he still had to pay some bills.

'At one time I was a creeper, someone who creeps into a bank while another person gets the attention of the teller while I would slip behind the counter. Changed days – it would be impossible to do now. I know it was wrong but what could I do? I wasn't a bricklayer or a plumber. I was a plumber's mate but I lasted for about three days. I didn't know what to do with a washer.'

But he did know how people in trouble with the law could be helped out. One wheeze was the This Man Saved My Life mitigation plea. An arrangement would be made for the accused man, if he was out on bail, to be beside the Thames – any stretch of water would do – late at night. A 'stranger' would fall into the water. The accused man would gallantly leap into the swirling brine and rescue the drowning man. Two days later, when he appeared in court, the rescue would be brought to the judge's attention and the grateful rescuee would give the 'I owe this man my life' evidence.

'Judges started to see through it though and the other thing was that, once, the hospital I got taken to when I was pulled out of the Thames thought I was a nutter and had tried to commit suicide so they wanted to put me in a straitjacket.'

He moved into running clubs and pubs.

'If you were a bit of a character and people knew you, someone would finance you and stick you up to run the club. You got half of the profits. I must have enjoyed being the host. People would rob a bank one day, gamble it away and then knock on your door and say, "Harry, can I borrow a couple of hundred quid?" You were taking that much money it didn't make any difference. I was giving money away, lending money. But it didn't make much difference to me because I was a compulsive gambler.'

His big mistake was opening a pub in the Angel, when he should have kept discreetly away from his home patch. 'We should have done it in Mayfair. Everyone would congregate at my pub and when it closed everyone would go to the A and R Club on Charing Cross Road, Ronnie Knight's club actually, have a drink and it would go on from there. They were known as heavy people, the people who went there. They wouldn't allow strangers in – they thought you were a police or a spy. They would be talking about what they were doing. Today it's a lot different. You can't tell anyone anything in confidence without something going wrong. Years ago you could tell people. The police have got their grasses now so these type of clubs where you could talk freely have packed up. A couple of top coppers used to come up and have a drink, whether there was anything in it, I don't know.'

But fate in the shape of a shoplifting charge – he was chatting to a well-known shoplifter in Jermyn Street, pockets full of money – was waiting round the corner and Harry was arrested and held for three days, not least because the police knew of his associates. He lost his licence and had to sell the pub. He took a trip on the *Oriana* to Australia, via the Bahamas, Fiji, Honolulu. 'The youngest passengers must have been eighty. There were seven deaths on the trip.' Harry did a bit of 'bobbing and weaving' and performed with the band, though the captain for some reason didn't take to him, especially after he held up the ship's departure at Acapulco. In Australia he made thousands 'selling pots and pans to Aborigines. They were bought in Taiwan but we told them they fell off the back of a lorry'.

On his return he moved to a gambling club in Hatton Garden, a modest place that catered, with tea and sandwiches and flexible hours, to the gamblers and jewellers of the area, who enjoyed dice, poker, kalouki and rummy. The staff were often relatives of people inside.

But its activities were not so modest as to avoid the attention of the police and Customs.

'I didn't know it was under observation. Early one afternoon, the Robbery Squad, Murder Squad, Customs and Excise all came in. The Robbery Squad had guns on them. They wanted to have a word. They said I knew the guy they were looking for was in the club. I said I didn't know what they were talking about. They believed me and left.'

But the Customs did not leave and he was charged with evading betting tax and taken to court.

'They wanted £35,000. Outrageous. It meant I was taking £350,000 in bets a week. The judge believed me and knocked it down from thirty-five grand to five grand. So the police shut that place down, and I ducked and dived for a couple of years.'

There was another club, Pal Joey's, at the Angel, with an enormous, generous bar and a piano. It was to have been called Harry's Bar, this one, but the name was changed at the last minute. Then there was Alfies, in Clerkenwell, which kept long hours but made short profits. There were other irons in the embers.

In his world, Harry Hicks has mixed with what Mel Brooks calls the 'great and the near-great', both criminal and straight – including a lot of footballers and football managers. 'I know all the Great Train Robbers personally. They're nice people. I suppose I've got to say that because I've got convictions myself but I think there's a lot of people in high places who know them. And I've gambled, gone to clubs, everything the professional criminal likes to do without having to do the bird.'

But there were problems with the gambling. 'I was at home one Sunday and I owed a guy £500. I looked out the window and I saw him – and he saw me. I was going to make out I wasn't in, to be honest, but once he saw me I had to let him in. He said, "I want to do you a favour." I thought – beautiful – one minute I owe him £500, the next he wants to do me a favour. But I don't know what the favour is. He says he's going to come round and pick me up and take me to Wembley. I know this guy is a lunatic gambler so we must be going to Wembley dogs. Monday morning out I go because I didn't have any money. By night-time I had £800 because I genuinely think I'm going to the dogs. He picks me up. I didn't say anything because I owe the man £500. Whatever he says goes. We pulled in the back of a church. I thought – what's happening here?'

It turned out to be a Gamblers Anonymous Meeting and Harry's friend had been attending for the last two years.

'If I hadn't owed him the money there's no way I would have gone in. There were eight guys there and one of them says, "My name's Jack, I'm a compulsive gambler." He said he had gone to Haringey dogs, lost all his wages and gone home with a fiver. I thought, What am I doing sitting here? A fiver! He wasn't in my league, people betting fivers! He said he'd put the fiver on the shelf and his wife had taken it to pay a couple of quid out to the dairy on the corner or something. When he woke up the fiver's not there. He got hold of the wife and he put like 200 stitches in her. She went to the top of the house and hanged herself. I thought, I'm not that bad. I felt sorry for the girl that died but not for him. I thought what a bastard to do that to someone for a fiver.'

But Harry carried on at Gamblers Anonymous for eighteen months. During that time, with all the money saved from not gambling, he opened up shops in Southgate and Putney.

'I had loads of money. Then my best friend died and I thought, What am I doing, I love gambling. And I did the lot in a couple of days – horses, dogs, thousands and thousands of pounds.'

He had also taken part in the hoist of a briefcase which was meant to contain £8,000. 'We went to this place, got a ladder. I looked down and there were two of the biggest briefcases I'd ever seen. Took the two, dropped them out the window. I got back and there was £88,000. I didn't know what to do. I put a tarpaulin out and buried it in the garden. The guy who stuck the business up came round. I could see from his face he wasn't expecting the extra £80,000. I went to Spain, Valencia, with the wife and two children. I was laying there on the sunbed in the most beautiful apartment you've ever seen. I started fidgeting. We were booked for a month, I was back after three days. I put £9,000 on a horse called Falcon II. Within a few months everything had gone. I'm uncontrollable.'

The old heavies who would come round and read out their notices from the stop press of the *Evening News* are gone, as far as Harry is concerned. 'The only money now for people with a criminal mind is fraud. The police were getting really heavy, people being fitted up. So they went off to Spain. People think they have fortunes there but they have nothing. Life there is upside down. You don't go out till twelve at night. Sleep all day and drink all night. Nothing else to do. They can't rob a bank in Spain – they wouldn't know what to say.'

The exile's life in Spain, running a club in Fuengirola that sells Whitbreads and pickled onions and runs videos of English league football, does not appeal.

'People can say what they like about what a lovely life but from what I've seen everyone's bored to tears and getting into things they don't really want to be into. The wives sit around and have their hair done. Some of them open up clubs. They all want to be back here, all of them. They miss the adrenalin.'

Back here Harry stays in his Islington home with two of his five children; he makes his living as a purveyor of tickets until, perhaps, another club beckons. He regrets that few now have bands playing things like 'My Funny Valentine'. 'People used to go to them to drink, now they go to get drunk. People just go and talk crap – me included, you don't realise you're doing it – about horses, dogs, gambling.'

There is no shortage of such clubs, even with the relaxation of the licensing laws. Places behind anonymous, spy-holed doors and down basement steps, membership only. Places where people order up rounds without asking the recipients if another drink is required, where people come in, look around, depart and return for no apparent reason. Dark places where it could be any time or season. And where strangers are suspected of being detectives.

5

The DC

Thieves respect
property; they merely
wish the property to
become their property
that they may more
perfectly respect it.

G. K. Chesterton, *The
Man Who Was Thursday*

Policemen always say they can recognise other police officers and criminals say
the same. The height is a clue and, says the Detective Constable, 'They say we've
got searching, shifty eyes; if you go into a pub you're always looking round.'

The DC has the height certainly and the self-assuredness that goes with years
in the job but he was not born into the profession nor was he someone who
headed for it as soon as he was old enough and tall enough. He studied
commercial and graphic design at Lincoln School of Art but did not like the idea of
spending all his time indoors. He had a spell in the building trade, doing painting
and decorating but felt it was a dead-end job and joined up in the fire service.

'I really enjoyed that because I was serving the public. But I wanted to do
something more than fighting fires. I wanted to use my brain. So I applied to the
police force.

'I failed the entrance exam because of my spelling! That really upset me so I
thought "I'll show 'em" and I had a crash course in pushing up my spelling. I
think the thing that made me join was the social-conscience kind of thing, it
certainly wasn't the money in those days. It wasn't in the family. My brother runs
a driving school, my sister is a seamstress, my father was a bus-driver, my
grandfather was a preacher – so there's no links with the police force at all.'

The job took him south and he now works in the suburbs, dealing with
everything from murder to petty theft. He is a big, thoughtful policeman rather
than a smart guy in a double-breasted suit. And his work has become his life.
'When you check out all your friends who are policemen and you look to see what
other friends you have, you find you haven't got any. All your friends are
connected one way or another with the police force.

'CID and uniformed officers love to hate each other. They work together but
they don't drink or mix together. Some other officers call uniformed officers
"wallies" or "woodentops", and you don't want to drink with them. But when
it comes to the crunch, you do work very close to each other and rely on each
other.'

There has been much talk in the media of a masonic influence in the police force. There is a large and active masonic lodge which consists of many senior men at Scotland Yard and which was set up after the former Commissioner Sir Kenneth Newman had specifically counselled officers against membership. What do the police think about it?

'The big joke is the masons. It's got so ridiculous now that you don't know who's a mason and who ain't. If you don't like someone you'll call them a mason. Anybody who gets promotion and you think they shouldn't you say, "Oh, he must be a mason."'

The DC lives on a quiet, private, modern estate in what is almost the countryside. It seems far away from the high-rolling crimes areas.

'The average policeman nowadays has moved up classes. Now the majority won't live in the inner cities, they've got their own house in the suburbs. They're now, what – lower middle class? Upper working class? Somewhere in the middle class. Because they're now property-owners they tend to be more conservative. The majority now I know would vote Conservative. I'd have difficulty finding one who would vote Labour or anything else. Ninety-five per cent of the ones I know are Conservative. Our wage increases have come from a Conservative government and at election times the average policeman will say, "Oh, you don't want Labour, they'll stop this increase every year."'

Contrast this with what Gilbert Kelland, former Assistant Commissioner at New Scotland Yard, had to say about the politics of the police who joined up after the war: 'Although as police officers we were strictly apolitical, I suspect that most of us could be counted among those ex-servicemen who, while admiring Winston Churchill's wartime leadership, had a strong desire for domestic change and were responsible for voting in the Attlee administration.'

As police officers have shifted class so too have some of the villains they hunt, who also seek out quieter, suburban homes.

'You do get villains who have come here when things have got a bit hot for them in London, they look for safe houses. When you talk to them they seem very frightened individuals. They seem to be looking over their shoulders and watching their backs all the while, not just for us but for their fellow villains. They're more frightened of their colleagues down in London than they are of the police. I suppose that's what gangland is all about. Rather than big hard men they seem to be very small frightened men, frightened of their own shadows.

'When the Krays thing happened we had a chap who came down here. He was connected to them and I think he was worried to death. He's lived up here ever since. He's a bit of a scrap dealer, which is a cover for all sorts of things. Rumour is rife as to what he does. He is what I would call a typical gangland man. He has a legitimate business to cover up all sorts of things he's into. Now it turns out that one of this man's houses is being used to manufacture these drugs. I don't associate drugs and drugs factories with gangland but it shows you how things have changed. Years ago it used to be protection. Nowadays it seems as though all these gangland people are moving into manufacturing and selling drugs because they realise there's a lot of money to be made.'

But those souls worried about the shadows against the french window are not the DC's bread and butter, who are now a somewhat different breed. 'I would say that there isn't an actual criminal class. The majority are from the unemployed. When the unemployed figures were at their highest there was an enormous amount of thieving and that's dropped off as the figures have gone down. I was talking to one or two villains and saying, "I haven't seen you recently," but they say they've got a job, earning good money. If you look at it that way there is a criminal class, the unemployed.

'You don't have too much feelings about villains one way or the other at the end of a day. You do have a sneaking regard for a good one. If he's a good burglar, he's thought it out and done it well, you do have a lot of respect for them. A good villain won't admit the job. He'll say, "No comment, no comment." You can still have a high regard for him because you think, if I was sitting there I'd be doing the same thing. You're a bloody fool to open your mouth. You can't have a lot of respect for a man who does that. You think he can't be very smart or he would have kept his trap shut.'

Yet the inevitability of some villains' embrace of things criminal remains a puzzle.

'I can quote one family with four brothers. They're all villains. And you look at them and you wonder why have all four brothers been villains? If statistics say out of all twenty-year-olds only one in 150 is a villain, how come you've got four in one family? If the first one went to prison you would think that would teach the others. But it seems that the second one wants to be as clever as his brother. So he goes to prison. And you think surely the third one will get the message but he doesn't. You think, "What on earth motivates them?"'

One thing that does motivate them, or at least influence them, he reckons, as we drink coffee in his spruce living-room with its encyclopaedias and family photos, is the media. He thinks that crime programmes have educated the villain into knowing what his rights are and how he should handle himself when arrested. 'Lots of them will come into the police station and quote to you their rights of silence because they've read about it or seen it on television.'

He says that catch-the-criminal programmes like *Crimestoppers* and *Crimewatch UK* provide handy tips for crooks. A recent programme had shown how foam could be used to muffle an alarm and his force had had to deal with a number of copycat cases the following month. 'Sometimes they show how to dress for and execute a successful armed robbery. It's a sort of Open University of Crime.'

One other theme on television has been that of the bent cop, the bad apple. 'There was a period where it got very nasty – fitting up. I have one or two colleagues who moved out from the Met and I think there were a lot of frightened and worried policemen, although they didn't get very far with Operation Countryman. Policemen who had been involved in seedier types of things – I'm not saying dishonest – seedier, whatever that implies, thought, "I'm honest but as long as I'm in the Met I'm going to be part of it." They came out here where they can be an honest policeman. The Met have now got their house a little more in order.'

How much of his job as a detective is genuine detection as such and how much is luck and chance?

'There are a tremendous number of occasions when you know someone has done a particular crime because of little whispers that you hear and you've got no real evidence against him at all. If you like, it's an inspired guess. So we go out and lock him up and see if we can find the evidence. With a murder you have more detectives involved so you can be a bit more careful and it can be a bit more of a qualified, inspired guess.'

The pressures of the job, he says, take their toll.

'The domestic side you can't divorce from the working side. I've been married twice and I'm now going through my second divorce. I've had numerous relationships with women and I put it down to the fact that I put my job first, the hours, the stress everything. Half my colleagues have been divorced, women problems. It's very difficult to look round the office and find a happily married man. The domestic strife in that film *Closing Ranks* was real life. Often in these television programmes the Detective Inspector goes home to this little housewife and you think – that's fantasy. For some reason, they always pick out DIs as being investigators. The old Agatha Christie thing. My DIs sit in the bloody office all day!'

When he does return home he will take the dog for a walk. He does a lot of walking, climbing in the Lake District and Snowdonia, far away from blags and lags.

'I have a lot of female friends who don't live in the area so I don't tend to see them when I'm working. So unwinding can be going over there for the weekend because I can be just an ordinary person and probably the only person who knows I'm a policeman is the woman I go to see. I tell her, "Don't tell anybody I'm a policeman." But it's difficult when people ask what you do for a living. If it's a light-hearted situation I'll probably lie and say I work for the gas board. But if it's someone you can't lie to, you say, "Oh, I work for the local authority," which covers a multitude of sins, or I say I'm a civil servant.

'If you go to some sort of party and someone lets it slip that you're a policeman there's sometimes a false atmosphere sets in. People come up to you and say silly things like, "I've got to be honest – I went out this morning and I didn't put my seat belt on. You won't report me will you?" And you think, "How pathetic!" They talk down to you.'

He relates these exchanges without much rancour, as though the irritation is more to do with the inevitability of people's responses than the actual responses themselves.

'From the neighbours there's a mixed reaction to my job. The old boy next door can't understand why I don't wear a uniform and a tall hat. Some of the younger ones think, "He must have a bit of a funny job if he doesn't wear a uniform and I don't think we want to talk to him."'

Like all policemen, he complains of the amount of paperwork, of time spent at the desk, of 'memos from other departments who think you've got nothing to do but sort out their memo. Unless it's really important it just goes in the litter bin.

'Just recently we've had what's it called – there's a fancy word for it – "crime screening" come in. What they tend to do nowadays is give detectives crimes they think can be detected and all the rubbish they give back to the uniformed officers who probably reported them in the first place. I look for a job that's got an interesting and unusual element to it. The mundane you've done so many times before your heart's not in it that much. If you get an unusual one, a blackmail, it can be an interesting experience.'

But the very essence of police work for the DC is changing. 'Years ago detectives used to be part of the beer-and-bang-'em-up-in-the-cells brigade. Now they're more into computers and psychology and less into drinking beer. So you find that they go in pubs less. And this business of talking to informers in the pub seems to have died a complete death. It doesn't happen any more. If you say to someone, "Oh, I was in the pub speaking to an informant," they laugh. Because they know it's not true. You meet the informants you do speak to in their home, a car, all sorts of places, but very rarely in a pub.'

But surely the arrival of the supergrass helped change the rules of engagement?

'We don't call them grasses, we call them witnesses, sounds better. It's strange what motivates these people. You can offer some of them money and they're insulted. With other people, you think they're doing it out of the goodness of their heart and they say, "How much will I get for this?" The dangerous one is when they do it for revenge. Probably your best grass is the one who is doing it because his conscience is troubling him.'

But here the recurring police complaint about the meanness of their authorities presents obstacles.

'Sometimes someone will help you clear up a serious crime and you ask for £100 for them. The police force argue the toss as though you're asking for half a million. When you consider what you've saved and cleared up, £100 is nothing.

'One particular woman was a fantastic informant, she was right in among the villains. I could never get enough money out of the police force to justify what she was giving me. In the end she had to move out of the area. I had a word with the local council and I said that if they didn't do something they'd find her body lying around one day. In the end they agreed to move her and do a swap with another council and I went back to social security and they agreed to £300 for moving expenses, just like that, while I was having a problem getting anything at all for her from my end.

'If you get a woman as an informant she'll often be much better than a man. Villains tend to talk in front of women and treat them as part of the furniture. But of course women listen and work things out. Very often they can pick up a lot of things that men don't give them credit for. But the best informant is one who's been part and parcel of a plan for a robbery.'

But if the beer culture is changing so are other police practices. 'The greatest change that's taken place in the police force is the presentation of evidence. Of course, you're talking about the verbals. Originally what you're talking about is officers going in cells, interviewing somebody and then some time afterwards recording the conversation that took place in that cell. In the old days everyone would argue that it was accurate but nobody was fooling anybody. It is impossible to be accurate.

'I can remember standing in the witness box many, many times saying "This is accurate" and being unable to say, "Well, it's just a general summary." Because once I say that it's a summary there's less strength in it as evidence. So you had to stand there and say, "Yes, this is accurate." It probably was, to the best of your perception, but you had to say it was precise. But it's more than the human mind could comprehend to take an interview lasting more than a half-hour and then record it word for word two hours later.'

The arrival of the Police and Criminal Evidence Act meant the taking of a contemporaneous note: 'Terrible – while you were interviewing you were writing down questions and answers. It was impossible because their minds were two or three questions in front of you. People were reading questions as you were writing them down and working out the answers before you'd finished writing. It was a ball-aching job because some of these notes went on for twenty pages. It all got very messy and then suddenly we got the tape recorder.'

The use of the tape-recorder produced surprising results. 'Before it came in everyone said it's not going to work because suspects aren't going to talk and policemen are going to be very guarded as to what they say because they don't want to appear oppressive. But if you look at it today, the villains do talk. They feel they've got to talk because they think it's wrong if you put a tape recorder on not to talk – they feel uncomfortable.

'I've been on courses on interrogation. They don't call it that because it still smacks of something from the Gestapo. They tend to call it "interview development".'

What they learn, amongst ways of persuading people gently to unburden themselves, is how not to appear 'oppressive', offering such subtle inducements that a defendant is bound to come up with something. 'The oldest one in the book is "You admit this offence and I'll give you bail", but that's one you could never say on a tape nowadays. You've got to very much be a talker, a persuader. You say to them that it's in their best interests to tell the truth. One of my bosses says you've got to sit there and say, "You done it," and they say, "No, I haven't." So you say, "You done it," and wrap it into different phrases so that every time you say it it sounds different. If you keep going on and on and on eventually he will say, "Yes, I did."

'I do tend to exaggerate occasionally and imply that things have been said that have not necessarily been said [by a co-defendant] which if it came out in court later on I would argue was my mispresentation. But deliberately lying is very counter-productive with a tape recorder.'

Outside the station, the DC faces a more violent world but he says that 'if you did a survey on police who are assaulted, you'd find that eighty per cent are relatively young policemen with very little experience. They tend to jump in feet first. When you have a bit of experience you tend to use diplomacy. You learn the show of force principle: you get enough colleagues there and you say, "If you want to be violent you can take us all on." Usually the bloke will say, "All right, I've had enough, I'll come quietly." If it's one to one and you say, "Look, if you don't put that iron bar down I'm going to come over and wrap it round your neck,' he will probably take you on.'

The DC has faced the sharp end on occasions. On one occasion a woman against whom he gave evidence decided to murder him.

'She was a bit unstable and she decided she wanted revenge. She walked into the police station and asked if she could see me. I thought she'd come up for some of her clothing because it had been taken for forensic evidence so I showed her into the interview room and she pulled this flaming great knife out and said, "Right, I'm going to stick this in your guts." I pulled the door back and I was one side she was another.' She was pulled off before she had the chance to inflict any damage and charged with attempted grievous bodily harm.

'I'm one of these people who believe that if you resort to violence in a cell you've failed. I look on colleagues the same way. If one says, "What he needs is a good smacking," I think well, you're a flaming idiot. If you get away with it, all well and good, but if it comes out, you've put your job on the line. If you talk to the bloke you'll get the same result or probably a better result as if you turned round and smacked him.

'But it's not a deliberate act, it's very often that the suspect has wound the policeman up and has probably physically threatened the policeman who has reacted and gone to grab the lapels on his jacket.'

What about police chases, zipping through streets with sirens blaring and lights flashing, knocking over the occasional pedestrian?

'There were a couple of gypsy boys who were taking cars, XR3Is, and it got to the stage where they were driving past Panda cars enticing them to chase and they always got away. One day one of my colleagues said, "We've got to do something about this, they're taking the piss out of us. We know it's them, let's just lock them up." So he arrested them and while they were in custody they just lost their bottle and one admitted to stealing eighty cars. Some of the police get a thrill out of it, blue light flashing, horn blaring, they get a high, you can feel that, but you're loath to criticise because they're the ones who'll catch the villains.'

These shades of right and wrong are not spotted by the press, he feels, who see things in black and white when it comes to crime. They spend too much time on the offender, too little on the victim. He reads *The Times*, interested in the law reports and the effect they have on his work; his colleagues take the *Sun*, the *Daily Telegraph*. 'In our canteen at work they did a survey of what everyone thought they should have. The *Daily Mail* was selected because it was the middle of the road paper. Policemen don't want to be seen to be readers of the *Sun* because it's too sort of, well, the sordid end of the market.'

His other reading matter is also to do with his work, methods of interrogation and interview. Or Science Fiction. On television he steers away from the '*Juliet Bravos* and *The Bill*. In a sense they're pathetic because it isn't like the job as I know it. It has to be a story with a happy end whereas in real life it's the reverse. The majority of crime goes undetected but in the programmes they always get the villain and you know damn well it's not like that.'

He listens to his music in the car, instrumental stuff, not classical. *Planet Suite*, *War of the Worlds*, *2001*, a lot of the modern electronic music.

But the music, the Sci Fi, the walks with the dog are just an interlude. The real stuff takes place in the field, in the interview room, in the court.

'Cases go best when everyone works as a team. This very often doesn't happen. It's an old joke that the barrister probably reads the case up on his way to court in the train, while the detective gets there and he's had a late night and he's forgotten about the case because it was six months ago and all he's got is in his pocket book. That is if the Crown Prosecution Service haven't decided to offer no evidence or lost the file.' If files are lost between the police and the CPS, love certainly isn't. The service is blamed for delays, 'which means that sometimes witnesses get fed up or disappear and the villain has a chance to persuade people to change their evidence, set up his wife in a business, get his wife pregnant – judges are much more reluctant to send someone to jail if their wife is pregnant.'

Although the prosecuting counsel and the detective are indeed a team, quite often they barely talk. 'But where the detective and barrister know each other and get their heads together they can come up with a very good case. Not necessarily talking about evidence, but talking about feelings. Once barristers were treated like gods. It wasn't the done thing to speak to them. Nowadays you find that they talk together on equal terms, as investigator and prosecutor. In a private room at the back of the court you talk very casually but in court you call him Sir and you do make him out to be a superior person. I think that's right. That barrister has got to be in charge.'

Police officers almost invariably, even in these secular times, swear on the bible before they give evidence. 'I'm not religious but I swear on the bible. It's difficult to explain that. If I did things correctly I should affirm. But if you affirm then your evidence doesn't seem to carry so much weight. But if you swear on the bible you're looked on as being a god-fearing and truthful man; if you affirm they think, "Hmm, what's wrong with him? Is he going to tell lies?" I'm more of an agnostic than an atheist, more of a don't know. I'm not completely without religion – I'll sit on the fence in case there is a god.'

Quite routinely, in a case where a defendant is alleged to have made admissions, the DC is accused of fabricating the evidence. 'You expect to be called a liar and a cheat by the defence barrister. It's a nerve-wracking experience giving evidence. Even after nearly twenty years you still have butterflies in your stomach when you stand up, but when you get there you're all right. You think, "Go on, get it over with, I've heard it all before."'

He has often been accused of verballing people. 'Then you get the Memory test. You get a barrister who says, "Officer, these verbals" – they don't call them verbals – "these questions and answers – are they accurate, can you remember them quite well?" "Yes. Yes." Then he says, "Now, officer what was the first question I asked you when you stood up?" And you think, "Bloody hell, that's done me. I can't remember that." You can either turn round and say, "Can't remember," and then they say, "Well, therefore your memory is not that accurate so how can you remember those verbals?" Or you have a stab at it and hope that his memory isn't too good and he can't remember it either.'

Many of the barristers making these accusations are, of course, the same ones with whom he has worked as a team on a prosecution, they may even have a civil chat beforehand. No grudges appear to be held. 'In court there's a bit of mind-reading going on and he's saying in his mind, "You know I have to ask you these questions," and I'm saying in my mind, "Yes, I'll do my best to answer them," but it doesn't destroy the relationship you have.' Sometimes the barrister will apologise afterwards for his cross-examination.

He is warier of the solicitor. 'There are some that have a reputation for being, I won't say bent, because I think there are very few of those around, but I will say very devious and underhand in their methods. If you get someone locked up in the cells and he says I want a particular solicitor and no other, that's told you that he has got some sort of relationship with that solicitor and he is one to watch. It could be that he is just a good honest solicitor and he wants him because he does a good job. The other reason could be that he's got some sort of hold over him and can trust him to get messages out of the cell block or whatever.'

Juries remain an enigma. 'I've been in cases where the defence barristers are very crafty. They don't want businessmen in suits, they don't want housewives. So everybody in a suit – objection. In one case I was in they finished up with twelve hippie looking people on the jury. I think they thought they'd got it sewn up. But their appearance had not nothing to do with it. They weren't on the side of the defendants at all, they were on the side of justice for want of a better world. A lot had come to court not sure how to dress and had come casually dressed. Then they'd looked around and seen other people with suits on, so next day came like that themselves. When the defence saw them the next day they looked a little aghast. But basically you are looking for the middle-class property-owning type of person. The younger person, inner-city type, they're not going to convict.'

Often when a sentence is passed the arresting officer is still in court and while the relatives and victims weep or applaud they remain impassive. What are they thinking?

'I don't think the judges get it right with sentencing. We had an incident when a father was upset with the crying of his three-year-old son so he shakes him, hitting his head against the chest of drawers and kills him. It's a very tragic story. The father kept saying, "I love that kid." You felt sorry for him in a sense. He's very cut up because he's killed his son. He got twenty-five. I thought that was wrong. He's not only got to live with the fact that he's killed his son but he's got twenty-five years in prison. You get vicious rapists who kill their victims – we had one who raped a young girl of eighteen, left her in a ditch, thought he'd killed her. He went back and she was still alive so he got his shotgun from his home and came back and killed her. He'll be out in ten years.

'But I had one judge who I bumped into walking across the courtyard before he passed sentence. And he said, "What am I going to do to this lot? What do you think?" I thought, "I don't want to know about this conversation," so I was a bit non-committal in the end. It brought home to me the problems that judges have.'

He sees the opening up of Europe and the ending of the boundaries as opening up horizons for the police too, with travelling to the continent on investigations becoming more common. The computer will become more important, passing its current almost experimental stage. He likes using it.

'If you get a suspect, you feed the name in and say, "Please, computer, can you tell me what crimes have you got that fit this?" Usually it coughs and splutters and comes out with nothing. It's not very accurate. But the wonderful thing about it is that we get things out of it that we never anticipated. We find a tremendous number of people's names and addresses get put into it – witnesses, suspects, complainants – so you've got a fantastic index of people's names and addresses. I was looking for a particular man and I checked all the usual places – telephone book, CRO – and I couldn't find him anywhere. I fed him into this computer and he turned up as having been a witness in a particular case.'

We go for lunch to a pub where he's known and I try to see if he really does behave like a recognisable policeman, casting an eye around. But he concentrates on the food, facing the wall. We talk about what is, for some people, the end result of his work – prison.

He visits prisons to see convicted men and those on remand and acknowledges that police officers 'do tend to look down on prison officers. There doesn't seem to me much job satisfaction for them. My view of a prison officer is a man who walks around with a big bunch of keys opening and shutting doors all day long and that seems a very boring job. But they do have a better relationship with prisoners than we do. Sometimes they can be too friendly with criminals. The police officer can look down on him because you think he's a bit of a soft touch, he's letting the prisoners walk all over him. But then you can't really blame them, because they have to deal with people who are going to be there for ten or twenty years – murderers.'

6

The Gang Leader

Ronnie, love, you were born to hang.

Ron and Reg Kray's Aunt Rose, quoted
in *Our Story* by Reg and Ron Kray

'We never hurt any members of the public,' said Ronnie Kray, pouring himself a
Barbican lager and stubbing out the umpteenth John Player Special into a
biscuit-tin top ashtray in the Broadmoor Hospital visiting room. 'It was always
our own kind. Never members of the public.'

The members of the Great British public have duly showed their gratitude for
being thus bypassed by maintaining an interest in the Kray twins that, twenty
years from Mr Justice Melford Stevenson's adieu to the murderers of Jack 'The
Hat' McVitie and George Cornell, has never really waned. There have been Kray
books and Kray T-shirts and Kray boxer shorts and Kray mugs, Kray impersona-
tors and even a couple of comedians – Hale and Pace – whose entire act was based
on the concept of the twins. There was a Kray musical, *England, England*, by Snoo
Wilson, an autobiography, written with Fred Dineage, and, finally, a film. That
famous black and white David Bailey photo of the twins remains an icon, a last
image of British gangland, as outdated now as Tommy guns and Craven A. An
advertisement for Bailey's Royal Photographic Society Exhibition in Bath in
1989 used a photo of the Kray twins and older brother Charlie, captioned archly,
the Old Bailey.

Rarely a week goes past without some mention of them somewhere in the press
– Ron getting married to Elaine, Reg getting fit, Reg donating a painting to
charity, Ron getting divorced from Elaine, Ronnie getting married again to Kate
Howard, Reg hoping for release. 'Ronnie Kray: I'm still gay and mad,' says a
News of the World front page. 'Krays' car washer decides to come clean,' says the
Daily Express. 'Butchered by the Krays,' announces the *People*, 'the paper that
dares to tell the truth.' Many of the stories are fantasy, some invented or
embellished by former inmates who can make some easy money on release by
telling tales. Some are true.

Reg Kray was moved to Maidstone from Gartree in 1988, Ron resides in Broadmoor, where they meet every three months, a visit attended by prison officers.
Ron is the host. And he still looks the part: pastel blue suit, pale blue and white
shirt and tie, monogrammed cuff-links, monogrammed handkerchief, gold brace-
let, diamond ring; cigarettes and Barbican lager being offered across the table.

The Colonel, as they used to call him, still has the military shoulders, the neatly-clipped nails, the smartly-combed hair, the same ambiguous lop-sided smile. If it wasn't for the fact that there's no alcohol in the drink and that the only other people in the room – apart from Peter Sutcliffe, the Yorkshire Ripper, and his mother-in-law – are in white coats or uniform, he could be back in one of his old haunts like the Grave Maurice or the Colony Club.

Ron Kray is not making a pitch for his own release, which would anyway be highly unlikely to go through now. If he did ever get out, he says, he would like to revisit Morocco: 'The boys. The boys and the music. I like Arabic music.'

He listens to classical music inside – *Madame Butterfly* is a favourite – makes the odd matchstick caravan for a charity auction, a garden gnome for friends, watches TV. Ron thinks his brother at least should be released. 'There's lots of people who've done much worse than us. There's people who've killed little children and got out.' Reggie could find his feet 'in business,' says Ron. He wouldn't go running around after all the people who gave evidence against him at the Old Bailey. 'He wouldn't bother them. He's got contempt for them.'

Periodically a newspaper or phone-in programme conducts a readers' or listeners' poll to find out whether the twins should indeed be released. The *Sun* and *Sunday Sport* asked readers whether the twins should be released before they had served the thirty years that Justice Melford Stevenson recommended; the readers voted to open the door. However, the *Sun* poll asked only whether Reg should be released as though it was now accepted that Ron is inside for ever, a recognition of his mental state – he was certified insane in 1956 – and possibly a tacit acceptance that if the Krays were a *folie à deux* then Ron was that *folie*. A total of 25,407 Sun readers replied, said the paper, by voting by more than thirteen to one in favour of Reg's release. As a nudging endpiece the paper added, for whoever wanted to believe it, 'Auditors last night disqualified sixty-three phone votes from Spain on the basis that callers might have a vested interest.'

The Krays have remained a peculiarly British phenomenon. It is not just their own chauvinism – in their autobiography Reg apparently (apparently, because the twins have since distanced themselves from some of the statements in the book) demonstrates his contempt for outsiders: 'A Maltese gang came in and demanded protection money. We went straight for them with knives and never saw them again. They've not got a lot of bottle, these continentals, especially when the knives come out' – it is also that they set the markers by which British professional crime is now judged.

Face was important. Cornell called Ronnie Kray a 'poof' and was killed. McVitie was also doomed, as Reg tells it, 'Not only was he scamming us but he was also boasting about it as well. At any other time in our lives, maybe we wouldn't have killed him, just hurt him. But this was a bad time for us, a pressure time, so I killed McVitie. It cost me dear.'

He has kept himself fit while inside, body-building, exercising, although he still smokes heavily. Our only meeting was connected with an art auction he was helping to organise to raise money for the Addenbrooke Children's Liver Transplant Fund for a young girl with a fatal liver disease. The paintings were hung at the Norfolk Street gallery in Cambridge, auctioned by a Liberal MP and raised more than £2,000 for the fund. Charity has always been a theme of the Krays' operations. When they were outside they were forever raising money for boys clubs, pressing fivers into hands.

Brother Charlie, on the subject of charity in his book *Me and My Brothers*, said 'All their lives the twins have had an overwhelming compassion for the underdog – the little man who can't protect himself from the bully, the old lady who is ill or down on her luck. Often I've been sitting in the visiting hall at Broadmoor when Ronnie has spotted an old lady he's never seen in his life. "Look at that old lady, Charlie," he'll say. "Bless her. Get her a box of chocolates, will you."'

In Parkhurst, Reggie Kray thanked the prison officers for the plate of Kit-Kats and the cups of tea. He would like to be out. 'I still accept my sentence and the length of it, but these rules (the stricter parole requirements that were brought in by the then Home Secretary Leon Brittan to make parole harder for prisoners convicted of violent crimes and drug offences) make a mockery of the use of skilled workers in the prison service, such as doctors and psychiatrists. Two wrongs don't make a right. This country should bring itself into line with other European countries who cater for parole. These countries have less of a crime problem than this country does.'

He writes frequent letters out: to his adopted son, Pete Gillet, to relatives, to people who have written to him; letters scrawled in Biro on lined prison paper in a familiar ragged hand, ending with 'God Bless, Reg'. He has written a book on slang, done some work on another demonstrating 'How to exercise in a confined space', for which he plans a Jane Fonda style video, and was trying to get a celebrity cook book together.

In 1988 he contributed an article to *Marxism Today*, a piece on the hanging of a teenage murderer from Peckham called Flossie Forsyth, who was executed in Wandsworth jail in 1959 for committing what became known as the Towpath Murder. Kray had met him there while serving an eighteen-month sentence and was anxious that the magazine that was currently promoting the notion of post-Fordism as a political concept should include a piece of post-Krayism, too. The theme of the piece was that hanging does not act as a deterrent.

He writes songs and prison poetry, as does brother Ron. Ron won't talk about what happens in Broadmoor in any detail, the rules forbid it and he is not about to start rocking the boat.

Their former henchmen have surfaced periodically either to put in a word for the twins' release or to spill some well-baked beans in a paperback.

One of the latter is 'Scotch' John Dickson, whose book on his time with the Krays was published after a discreet interlude in 1988. Dickson promoted his book but he allowed no photos or tape-recordings. Not that Dickson, an ex-marine from Leith, Edinburgh, thinks that the twins would reach out after him. He had been their driver, hired because the twins liked the cut of his Scottish jib, and turned away from his plans of a career in the prison service to work for the men who were destined to end up there.

He is now a ruddy-complexioned man with sandy hair and the cheery demeanour of a mid-table Scottish football club manager. He has a protective wife – for their first date, he took her to see *Bonnie and Clyde* – and a ladies' dress business in the south of England. To look at him in his regimental blazer, tucking into a croissant at a West End hotel, it would be hard to imagine him standing on the running board of the strange, dark vehicle that was the twins' firm. Dickson himself seems to have felt that he was playing a part in some movie.

In his book, *Murder without Conviction*, he recounts his first meeting with the twins in the pre-estate agent world of Stoke Newington: 'I felt as though I had walked right onto a film set with Al Capone and his gang.' He refers to Ron speaking 'in true Al Capone style', and he felt himself 'lucky enough to go to a few London pubs with George Raft . . . I got the feeling I was an extra on a film set making a gangster movie . . . the funeral was like one you would see in a Mafia film . . . the passers-by must have thought a film was being made.'

But the Krays were real. The blood wasn't ketchup. John Dickson could not leave his seat at the end of it. He pleaded guilty when they were all finally rounded up at the end of the party, gave evidence for the prosecution and was inside but briefly.

'They took the good, they didn't want to take the bad. Rats. Parasites. I'd rather rot in here than end up like them slags. I've still got my friends,' is Ronnie Kray's response to the Dickson memoirs.

Ronnie Kray is anxious not to be misunderstood. The people they killed were 'gangland people . . . people like us'. To which Dickson says, 'But they were still human beings.'

The people who broke ranks in the end are all rats and traitors to Ronnie Kray. The ones who didn't – Freddie Foreman, Ian Barrie, brother Charlie – were the minority.

Dickson made suggestions in the book about the disappearance and probable murder of Frank 'The Mad Axeman' Mitchell for whom Dickson had acted briefly as a minder while Mitchell was on the run from Dartmoor.

'He doesn't know anything about what happened,' says Ronnie dismissively. 'We're the only ones who know.' Ronnie's account of the murder of Cornell, as relayed through his autobiography, has him saying, 'I have never felt so good, so bloody alive, before or since. Twenty years on and I can still recall every second of the killing of George Cornell.'

John Pearson, whose book *The Profession of Violence* is the best known, indeed the standard work on the Krays, is not one of Ron Kray's favourite people either. But Pearson does suggest in the latest updated edition of the book that Reggie could be safely released: 'As a free man he would have not the faintest chance of staging a comeback as a criminal – even if he wished to, which is most unlikely . . . Reggie's menace is confined to history.'

Certainly, there would be little that Reggie could do now, his greatest danger being an overkill of chat shows or the chance of some new Face wanting to test his manhood against him in a bar.

At the end of the visit, Peter Sutcliffe is still entertaining his visitor. He is dressed in late seventies flashback: double-breasted suit with flared trousers and purple shirt. 'I thought it was going to be nice weather today, a bit warmer,' says Ron, as he finishes the last of the cans, stubs out another half-smoked cigarette and looks out at the grey brooding skies.

Back at Waterloo, after our visit, the younger Krays stare out from the cover of the Pearson and Dickson books in the bookstall. They're stacked beside the latest Mario Puzo.

Twenty years have passed since those pictures were taken. So will the older Reggie Kray be released before the passage of another ten? He stays inside because, whatever the members of the public might think, he and Ronnie are dark reminders of a time when two young East End boys could make a public profession of criminality and live a real life gangland movie. They may never have hurt a Member of the Public, but then members of the public don't sit on the bench and pass sentence.

Their old stamping grounds have altered beyond all recognition. The Stoke Newington house where Jack McVitie was stabbed to death is still pointed out by locals who smile at the reggae music and the far from sinister parties now taking place there. The Blind Beggar sells quiche to lunchtime office trade. Their home street of Vallance Road in Bethnal Green is Asian rag trade now, although there's a car auction and a scrap-yard lingering on from different days. The clubs are closed.

Both parents are dead. Mrs Kray's funeral was turned into a circus by tourists and press. Ron and Reg both came to pay their last respects, kitted out in pinstripe and handcuffed to the tallest officers the prison service could lay their hands on; they looked small and old which was doubtless the intention. The famous names that the twins valued so much have mostly died – Judy Garland, Diana Dors, George Raft, Freddie Mills – or dispersed. A few still write or occasionally visit but, as Reg puts it himself, they are 'dinosaurs' now. Not that show business has abandoned the Krays. The *Sun*'s 'Free Reggie' poll quoted Roger Daltrey, Barbara Windsor and Jools Holland as saying that parole was deserved.

The great irony of it all is that the twins were jailed for that length of time not just for the murders – others have indeed committed more sadistic killings and in far greater numbers and received smaller sentences – but because of their extremely overt lack of respect for the established order; for the police, who they thought were too thick or too bent to catch them; for the courts – 'If I wasn't here now I'd probably be having a drink with Judy Garland,' Ron told Melford

Stevenson during their final trial; for authority in general. For that lack of respect the two men had to be taught a lesson. Yet the crimes that took them to the Old Bailey, the killings of Cornell and McVitie, were committed for precisely the same reason. The two men had showed a lack of respect to the twins and so they had to be taught a lesson.

7

The Footsoldier

The announcements in reply to the
questions as to the number of times
that any of them had been in prison
were received with great applause . . .
Some chalked on their hats the sum of
the several times they had been in jail.

Henry Mayhew, *London Labour*

If a pickpocket slipped his hand into John Masterson's breast pocket and relieved him of his watch he would probably take one look at it and just as swiftly return it to its owner. Inscribed on the back of it are the words 'To John, from the Kray Brothers'.

Masterson is a regular visitor to Ron in Broadmoor, and to a small circle of friends still giving Her Majesty pleasure in the penal institutions of the land. He is personally familiar with sixteen of them and if prison is the university of crime, then John Masterson has qualified for a PhD with honour. The longest period he has spent outside prison since his teens – he is now in his mid-forties –'has been five years.

He is a thick-set man, wearing glasses with lenses like the bottoms of the pint glasses he drinks from in the Rye Hotel in Peckham, a dazzling white shirt and double-breasted suit.

His crimes have not been spectacular, mere money-making exploits. He has been a footsoldier rather than a colonel but he came to national prominence when he was the first prisoner sent to the new Control Units in the 1970s. It was an experiment to see if troublemakers could be tamed by a system whereby they were kept isolated for ninety days at a time and, if they misbehaved in that time, the clock was restarted and a further ninety days began. It was not a pretty form of punishment and he has since tried to take it to the European Court of Human Rights and has sued unsuccessfully for compensation.

He lives in south London now, and although more than half his life has been spent away from his home country, he still has not lost his strong west of Scotland accent.

Punishment was an early experience. 'It was a strict school, St Cuthbert's, the local Roman Catholic primary. You got the leather belt. You couldn't backchat or anything like that. But when I got to thirteen or fourteen I did start answering back.'

In an English class he was blamed for having torn a book that was torn already. The teacher, as Scottish teachers did in those days, required that he submit himself for a blow from the strap. 'I refused to take the strap for it. They were punishing me for something I didn't do. Automatic to me, even at that time, was that it wasn't right. So there was a big argument between me and the teacher. So the teacher decided to strap everyone in the row that I was in. They were all putting their hands out like sheep to get belted. I'm still not taking the belt. I hadn't done it and that was the end of it. I was told to go out into the corridor and he tried to bully me into letting him do it. I grabbed the belt off him and whacked him with it and charged right out the school.'

Retribution was inevitable. 'When my mother got to hear about it I got a belting in any case. I had to go back to the school and in front of the headmaster. I explained all the ins and outs to him, but he demanded I should still get it – but from him. He gave me the belt right in front of the whole school, they were all lined up waiting to go into their classrooms. He called me up and gave me six of the best, each hand. I was angry and humiliated but I did it more or less to keep the peace with my family. Anything you did that was rebellious was like an embarrassment to my family because they were right strict, religious, church-goers. But it went against the grain to accept a punishment for something I hadn't done.'

His mother, a God-fearing woman and regular church-attender, was from Hamilton. His father, a steelworker and a teetotaller, had come to Glasgow from Cork when he was two years old. 'He was one of those old-fashioned types of people who handed his wages unopened to my mother every week and got his pocket money. He was happy with his pipe and television. The priest was a regular visitor.'

Masterson was bright at his sums but his teachers were more aware of his attitude than his powers of subtraction. He hung around with a group of lads, doing the sort of things that groups of lads like to do. 'We would annoy the adults, knocking on doors and running away. One trick when it was getting dark was to get black thread out, tie it to the knocker, hide in the hedges and tap, tap, tap. It drove them loopy.' On one occasion he broke a window, and fearful of a paternal bashing, hid for two days in a disused colliery. His parents were glad to see him back. Brushes with the local police resulted in a slap on the ear rather than a juvenile court appearance.

The other pastimes were Saturday matinees – 'most of the time was spent annoying the ushers' – with a fare of *King Kong*, *Tarzan* and *Hopalong Cassidy*. There were black and white crime movies, too.

'I remember one film where the baddies have robbed the bank and there's the sheriff, the goodies supposedly. They would chase the baddies. It came back to me when I was in the Special Unit, I used to think, "Am I a baddie? I'm having a right rough time now so I must be a baddie." All the kids used to cheer the goodies when they were after the baddies, but I always used to want to see the sheriff get shot!'

There were no holidays by the sea but there were trips: to Portobello, near

Edinburgh – with its massive open-air baths, where unsubstantiated rumour had it that bad boys put half razor-blades in the groove of the chute – and into the countryside. On one of these jaunts an eleven-year-old Masterson stole a box of chocolates from a little country store. 'It was a Sunday, Mother's Day. My father took a day off work to come to court with me. The sheriff called me a bad boy and my father – to show how naïve he was – stood in the back of court and said, "He's no' a bad boy at all," and had a go at him. He thought they were just like ordinary people. I was fined ten bob. My dad gave me a good thrashing. I was about the only one getting in trouble at school; a lot of it was "Dare you to do this, dare you to do that", and I was the only one that would go the full road.'

At fifteen most left school and started work, on the building sites or in the mines. Masterson started at Blantyre Farm pit, catching the pit bus at a quarter to six in the morning. He spent about a year at the pit head. 'It was hard work but it was the only experience you had in life and it was enjoyable.' He stayed for four years, until he skidded off the road on which he seemed set.

'I was taking a girlfriend home and we had missed the last bus. It was about five miles from where I lived. I had never driven before but I saw a car and thought I'll have a go at this, I'm not walking this road. I messed about with the controls, got it going and away. I got about two miles with it and I smashed it into a big wall. They said I must have been doing about eighty mile an hour. I sustained a fractured skull, four fractures to my back and a fractured pelvis. They had to cut the car up to get me out of it. I was given the last rites by the priest. I was unconscious for thirty-six hours and I never recognised any of my family for a week.' He was in hospital for seven weeks before he discharged himself and returned down the pit. He was charged with taking and driving away, reckless driving and various licensing and insurance offences and was fined £80.

Apart from that, life was quite carefree. It was drape jackets, crepe soles, drainpipes, winklepickers, a three and ninepence tattoo of a skull and dagger from Prince Valery's in Glasgow, which his mum did not like. The girls worked in the factories on the industrial estate in Blantyre, assembling things for Philips. There was dancing on Saturday nights to Elvis and Buddy Holly and the odd gang fight between teams from Hamilton and Blantyre. A few stabbings and stitches. But more serious stuff was yet to come.

'When I was nineteen I got done for a robbery. I was having a wee drink and I emptied the till of a pub in Hamilton and took £40. I was sent for Borstal training at Polmont. The family were scandalised. I was the first Masterson to go to jail. I didn't conform and I was transferred to Jessiefield in Dumfries. At Polmont they wanted the floor to be scrubbed with a scrubbing brush until it came up white. One particular morning I got black boot polish and polished the floor, the opposite to what they wanted. I got three days' solitary for that. You had to be immaculate, your bed had to be immaculate. I was fed up with the regimentation, I just got the boot polish out and did the floor.'

More confrontations followed. 'We were sitting at the dinner table, and I said what's this jug of water – it was the soup I was referring to – doing on the table? They got angry and I slung all the food up in the air, so they put me in solitary.'

When he finally emerged, guilt about what he had done to his parents pointed him in a southerly direction. He got a job sorting out reject shoes in Leeds. 'I met a girl who was a Jewess. She was living in digs and we decided to move in together. I took her up to Scotland to see my family. Had the bans in. But my family obviously wanted me to get married to a Catholic. I was determined to get married to her and then I got to thinking about it and my family and called the whole thing off. I stayed back in Hamilton for about a year but I couldn't live with my conscience. So I took a bus down to London.'

It was the London of Kings Cross bed and breakfasts with their smells of over-cooked vegetables and overpowering air-fresheners. 'It was rough and ready, beggar's corner. All they wanted to do was booze. I saw I was getting nowhere so I went to Birmingham.'

He met up with the other itinerant Celts, getting comfort at night on the edge of a stool in the public bar. With one of them he carried out his first wages snatch.

'There were three people who went every week to collect the firm's wages. We just followed them. We had a car – funnily enough it was the Chief Constable of Nottinghamshire's – which had been nicked from Brands Hatch. We got into a position where we could catch them on their way back to the factory from the bank. I just walked towards the bloke who was carrying the wages, dead casual, and jumped at him with a flying head-butt and charged back to the car. There were a lot of people shouting but one of them thought it was me that was being robbed so he opened the door to the getaway car. He thought I was the victim! Away we went, to where we had the other getaway car. So we sped off, down a one-way road the wrong way. Split the money up; all told we got £4,000 from the snatch. I lived it up, spent it. I'd never lived it up in my life before.'

But he had a row with one of his erstwhile friends who was treating a woman badly, which Masterson thought was not on: 'I was going to kill him.' To get a vengeful Masterson out of the way, he informed on him. At Shropshire assizes he was sentenced to four years' imprisonment. Back inside, he started where he had left off.

'I was always protesting. I was on the roof on two occasions. I threw all the food over a prison officer on one occasion and smashed up the cells. One time I went into the C of E chapel and there was this big chair there called the Bishop's chair. I nicked it out of there and took it to my cell. I'd had that much punishment by then, sticks over the head, ending up in a straitjacket, that they tried a different approach. The governor came to my cell about two days after I'd taken the chair and he just said, "Masterson, can I have the chair back?" That was OK. I gave it back.'

And the japes continued, too. 'One time there was an Irish officer and he wasn't having us going into the toilets for a smoke. So I got this drum which was filled with black dye for the mailbags and set it up in the office right above where he sat and attached it to a rope through the rafters. When someone went off for a smoke he tried to stop them, then when he sat down I pulled the string and he copped the five gallons right over his head. He was screaming, "Dirty bastards!!!"'

In Birmingham prison he took two hostages for two days because he wanted to see the governor, he can't recall over what. He was sent to Dartmoor. He liked the football and the table-tennis. But there was more trouble and more solitary. The governor tried a different approach again.

'He tried to do something positive with me. So I worked in the barrow party putting rubbish in incinerators, which I enjoyed. After he saw I was responding to that I ended up with an outside job. There was a lot of protest from prison officers. I was doing well working in the dairy but there was a prison officer who was a bit nasty so I ended up having a pop at him. He switched his walkie-talkie on so what we were saying was going straight into the control. The security officers arrived on horses, with bloody dogs. We were just arguing about the way some job should be done. I explained it to the governor and he gave me a caution and I was put to work on a tractor.'

On release he returned to Scotland as the black sheep, worked on a building site but headed south once more on a New Year's Eve. Temptation awaited.

'I got involved with this Scottish bloke who was involved with some policemen in Chelsea. He was getting keys from the policemen, at £250 a time, to the property of people who'd gone on holiday and left their keys with them so they could check up that everything was all right. He would turn the place over, smash the door in to make it look like a real burglary and get away. I didn't want to get involved but anyway he talked me into it.'

The money was paid over and a meeting arranged with the police in Hackney. 'I got myself a gun, a Walther PK 38 automatic. I had another two guys with me and I said you'd better go in the other bar and have a drink. I'll see him on my own in the toilet. I asked him about the keys. And he said, "Nothing doing." So I asked for my money back. He said, "You'll have to put it down to experience." I said, "You'll fucking put this down to experience."

'He kind of broke up because I had the gun. I pulled the slide back off the top and the bullet was in the chamber. He started pleading with me and his mate came in the toilet so I put him in the pisshouse. I told him to get the money. I'm trusting at this stage that there's no way he can stick me in without sticking himself in. He wasn't a policeman at this stage, he was a villain. So I said, "I'll keep your mate here till you get back." I waited with the other Old Bill at the bar. I was having Scotch and coke and I said, "Get them in." I had the gun in the waist of my trousers and I said, "If he doesn't come back you're getting your head blown off."

'About an hour went by. I thought he was off to try and get the money. Shortly after the hour was up, each end of the pub opened and there were policemen there with revolvers pointing at us. I thought, "Fucking hell". The story he stuck up was that I was trying to rob him. I was charged with attempted armed robbery.'

He was jailed for six years, a relatively small sentence for the crime, and was sent to Wandsworth. They tried to persuade him to sew mailbags and more hell was kicked up. There were some gangland figures there – George Dickson of the Dickson family, Little Caesar (Philip Jacobs) was there too. Masterson ended up with a job of putting chains on the little Brut aftershave bottles. 'I said I've got bad eyes so I couldn't do close work because I had a complex about wearing glasses – which I did at that time. Vanity, is it, they call it? So I just sat in the row when the others were working.'

There were more hijinks: pretending to be asleep when the governor came round, throwing an oily rag at a prison officer while he was having a spot of genuine shut-eye. 'It was just the same as being kids, my sense of humour hadn't altered that much.'

Then, in 1972, came the sit-down prison strikes over conditions and privileges inside. Masterson played a major part. During one of them, prisoners were moved to a different part of the jail. 'The only unfortunate thing that happened was the first day they had the film show the prisoners from F wing had to come through and a prisoner got his throat cut. This was a guy who had turned Queen's Evidence. Someone had told the bloke he gave evidence against to break a mirror and whack him as he's walking by. So as the grass is walking past the bloke says, "Hey you, I want to talk to you." The struggle started. Jack the Rat Duvall, who grassed up Frankie Fraser, was there. I whacked the guy on the jaw, and the bloke has cut his throat. By this time a prison officer has pulled him off. He's bang to rights, isn't he? Charged him, attempted murder. There was a lot of names got together to say that he wasn't there. We said that there was a crowd of us round the hot-plate and a fight broke out and the bloke has been pushed on top of him. That was the story. The governor tried to talk me out of going up. There were others – by this time we're in Parkhurst – who were meant to go and give evidence but they didn't want to go up to Wandsworth for the two weeks it was necessary to help this guy out. And they were supposed to be villains, trusted villains. Of thirty names that said they would give evidence on his behalf only five turned up.'

Masterson gave his evidence and said he was unaware of who had carried out the attack. The man was acquitted and delighted.

A brief sojourn in Swansea gave him a chance to set fire to some cells there and he ended up in the 'strong box'. On to Parkhurst where he went up on the hospital roof, throwing the slates off. He met the Krays, having been given a kind of introduction by their associate Freddie Foreman, whom Masterson had met while having a nose operation in Wandsworth.

He spent much of his time in Parkhurst in the punishment block and took to reading Wilbur Smith. One way out of solitary was to agree to go to the psychiatric wing.

'I thought what option did I have? I'll give it a try. One particular case in there had been convicted of baking a baby in an oven. I thought I couldn't live in the same cell block as people like that. It does prey on your mind. I'm not saying I'm normal but fairly normal and fairly sane. I thought, "I'll do something about these evil, dirty monsters." One was this baby killer and the other was a sex case. There was a little kitchen on C wing and they would go and make themselves something to eat at six o'clock. I switched the cooker off at the mains, got a soaking wet rag, put it into the fuse box, screwed it back up and wet the floor. So when they think the cooker's not working they would try and fix it and – PHEW! – that's it. They get cooked. The whole power for the whole cell block goes into that thing. I went back to my cell to wait for the bang and the scream. But another prisoner had seen what I was up to and he told a prison officer. I was put back to solitary and was happier to be there.'

Masterson's notoriety ensured him a place in the prison hierarchy. 'I was never a number inside and there are about thirty other prisoners like that in the system at any one time. Did I enjoy the notoriety? I certainly felt different from the rest because I was a bit of a star.'

'There's a class system in prison, same as there is out here. At the top you had the train robbers, Reggie and Ronnie Kray, armed robbers, bank robbers. They're not just looked up to by other prisoners, but by the staff as well. Bruce Reynolds, Charlie Wilson, the train robbers would tell their stories and everyone would listen. Bruce Reynolds told about how he went to Las Vegas when he was on the run. We were watching a film on television one night and Las Vegas was on and he said, "Oh, I remember being there, John, when I was on the trot." They were always quite polite and gentlemanly.

'Charlie Richardson was another. Despite the offence Charlie Richardson was convicted of – grievous bodily harm, for which he received twenty-five years – you couldn't help liking the man. He was a nice bloke. I saw him in Parkhurst and he looked after me because I had given an interview about his friend Frankie Fraser in the newspaper. His first concern was whether I was all right for a smoke, and for food and toiletries, but he was angry about the way the system had treated him.

'In the old days the safe blowers were important. Zef Boswell, he must be dead now. He used to tell wonderful tales. He was affronted when the young safe blowers used Durex for putting the gelignite into the locks. He was right establishment.

'Prison officers have the same attitude to rapists, child molesters as prisoners have. One time at Strangeways a prison officer offered to open up a sex-offender's cell for slopping out at the same time as the other men so that they could do him. They would tip the other prisoners off if someone was a rapist so that the other prisoners could do him. Boiling water in the bath, that sort of thing.'

The advantage of being at the top of the tree was the choice of jobs – in the stores, handling the food, or doing the laundry: 'You could get your clothes pressed every day; they were the smartest people in prison and that mattered to them.

'Your main gangsters, your bank robbers were from London. Like any other job you would come to the capital. When it came to real villains, nine out of ten times they were Cockneys. Ronnie and Reggie had a lot of respect for Scotsmen – they knew Jimmy Boyle – because they were reckoned to be hard men.'

There were occasional excitements inside, like attempted and even successful escapes. In one they went through the whole Colditz routine of scattering earth from the tunnel being built on to the exercise yard in Parkhurst. To no avail. In Brixton, the attempt was successful.

'I remember we were listening to "Top of the Pops" and the Scots Dragoon Guards were playing "Amazing Grace". The screw said, "That's a nice tune," and two of them tied him up and left him in the cell. Then they went into the kitchen, and the officer said, "Hey, you're a bit early for supper." They put him in the meat safe and then they went over the top. They got hold of a car outside, some couple had just come back from holiday, and they got off and away. Morale was high as a kite after that. The screws were not too boisterous, to put it mildly.'

But being in trouble inside meant additional time to be served. Masterson went on to Hull prison and further roof-top activity. Winchester and Strangeways followed before he was despatched to the experimental Control Units at Wakefield prison.

'I was met there by about ten officers – they were even rude to the officers from Strangeways. It was the first day of the Control Units there. We went through a gate, then through a wire like a hen run, in through a wooden door, across a little ramp, then came to an iron gate, spoke into the intercom, bom-bom, there was a fellow sitting behind this bullet-proof glass. There was an "in" chute and an "out" chute and the keys that the officers had on them had to be put in the "in" chute and only then did they get a key to the Unit. I looked at the cards outside the cells to see if there were any prisoners in there and there were none. They took me down and they all stood around me in a circle, arms across their chests.

'I had to strip off naked in front of them. I got changed, had a shower, they're all watching me all the time. The bed was bolted to the floor, the cell was all the same colour and you couldn't see out of it. There was a rule card on the bed and I picked it up and I could see from the flap on the spyhole that they were having a look to see what I was doing. The card explained: "You are now in the Control Unit and this is the regime. Right?"

'I felt lonely and alone in there. And that's how I felt when I came out. Except these last few years when I feel I have come forward.'

But while he has avoided the long sentences and seen the Control Units taken out of service, he has not managed to avoid trouble. Not long after he came out he was living in lodgings in Belgravia and met up once more with a couple of his Celtic counterparts, a Scotsman and an Irishman. It sounded like a bad joke and it was.

'There was a little bar in reception and one of them was all schizophrenic and hyper and he went behind the bar and took a bottle and some fags. The manager's there but he doesn't say anything to him because it's clear he's dangerous. I'm just sitting there reading the write-ups in the paper and he invites me up to listen to a Sidney Devine tape, "Crying Times". I said, "Look, I'm just going to watch the telly then I'm off." Later they come in with a stranger, who they're obviously going to roll. So I said, "Don't involve me, I'm just away." I said, "That's just low that is, that guy's just the same as everyone else. That's bollocks and I want nothing to do with it." So I sat down to watch the telly. Twenty minutes go by and the Scots guy comes down and says, "John, Paddy's killed the bloke."

'First reaction – I go up and check it out. He is dead. I'm off. They'd cut part of his face away with a bottle.'

Two days later he was picked up by the Murder Squad in Victoria. Paddy got six years for manslaughter.

Richard Ingrams, the former *Private Eye* journalist, always said that his greatest fear of going to prison was the thought that he would then be visited by Lord Longford, a man who specialises in visiting the unloved of the prison system and someone whom many prisoners contact in the hope of a bit of assistance or advice. Masterson came across him when he had been taken up by the Citizens Commission for Human Rights, a Scientology-run organisation campaigning on various penal issues.

'They were interested in me because of the time I'd spent in the Control Unit and so I was taken along to meet Lord Longford. He said, "Feel free to drop in anytime." The secretary, Gwen, said not to take him literally – but I did.' He chuckles. For since the first meeting he has become a regular visitor of Longford's, dropping in at the House of Lords for a cup of tea and coming away with the odd bottle of something to put in his drinks cabinet from the House shop. Longford introduced him to some of the other Lords: Kagan, Whitelaw, Kilbracken, Boothby.

'"Lord Boothby," I said, "I saw your old friend Ronnie Kray" – and he gave me a funny look. When I said I was an ex-prisoner to Harold Wilson I could see his eyes go like pools. Whitelaw was very genial, but when I said I was a friend of Lord Longford his eyes went – he must have realised I was a criminal – I don't think he thought I was a backwoodsman!

'I go to the House of Lords on a regular basis and I see Reggie and Ronnie and Charlie Richardson on a regular basis and I don't see much difference between them all. They're very polite and civil at the bar in the House of Lords and so are Reggie and Ronnie. I've spoken to a lot of the peers in the House of Lords and their manners and civility don't come higher than them three boys.'

As a penal *cause célèbre* Masterson was also courted by the Workers Revolutionary Party and their paper, *Newsline*, in the days before the terminal splits of the early eighties. He was introduced to the senior party members, Gerry Healey, Vanessa Redgrave, Mike Banda. 'They wanted me to be an honorary member.

But I didn't know the full ins and outs of it. I liked them as people and they were good to me. There wasn't much talk of politics inside. There was just a feeling that money was freedom. Most criminals of any intelligence knew that. And if it comes on top, they're inside, so they can't see the wife or go to the pub, but apart from that they're not worse off than they would be outside without any money. Some are even happier inside. It's a big world out here and there are some who find it just too much of a challenge. Personally, I never had a romantic notion of crime, it was just to keep me going.'

The Scientologists continued to court him too and he lived briefly at their headquarters in East Grinstead. 'They had parties every week, but not parties the normal man on the street would see as a party. Got to be worth half a million pounds their bloody house. I was to be an adviser to the Citizens Commission of Human Rights. Nice enough people but they did appear to me to be bug-eyed.'

His various involvements in matters penal has kept him out of most trouble. He has met Pat, a quiet and good-looking woman who keeps a tolerant eye on him. He tries to keep off the drink, going on anti-abuse courses periodically and feeling the better for it. He still cannot resist a difference of opinion with authority.

'The last problem was an argument with a cab driver who picked me up at the Hyde Park Hotel and I was charged with refusing to pay the fare. They locked me up in the cell and wouldn't give me my cigarettes. For someone who's addicted to cigarettes, well . . . I think there is an article in the Geneva Convention. It's everyone's right to smoke. Here I am, these policemen locking me up on the word of a cab driver, taking my cigarettes off me. So obviously I went crazy about it. Started attacking the cell, I sheered the bolt on the door. They moved me to another cell, gave me my cigarettes and said, "For Christ's sake have a smoke and go to sleep."' He was given two years probation.

He returns north on occasion as the prodigal son. One married brother now works in Ravenscraig steelworks, a sister is married to a scrap-metal dealer and has three children, the other sister works at a bookbinders.

'I saw a few of my old friends the last time I was up in Scotland. They look like the adults I used to annoy when I was a kid. So I suppose there's a lot of thirteen-year-olds annoying them in the same way. They work in the steelworks, one does private work, roofing, one's a building contractor. A couple have a fish and chip shop.'

8

The Drugs Squad Man

When you play, you pay.

Luis 'Kojak' Garcia, drug dealer turned police
informer, quoted in *The Cocaine Wars* by Paul
Eddy, Sara Walden and Hugo Sabogal

Graham Saltmarsh's parents ran a fish and chip shop and he was born and bred
on the Old Kent Road. One of his classmates from that time is doing life and
several others are well-known armed robbers.

'I really enjoy my job. I enjoy coming to work. The fact of the matter is that
actually hunting down drug traffickers – and I would put terrorists in the same
category – is very satisfying and very enjoyable because it's very hard. You're
unravelling puzzles. It's actually very stimulating. It's a great shame that a lot of
people have to suffer so that I can come to work and have fun. I don't mean that
cynically. I actually enjoy coming to work and solving a problem.

'I spoke to an American guy in the police force there and they've got
helicopters, all this kind of equipment and they still can't curb their drug
problem. They still haven't sussed out that it's fun.'

This is Detective Sergeant Graham Saltmarsh, Drugs Squad high-flier, the
man who suggested and helped organise the raid on the Afro-Caribbean Club in
Brixton from a train on the track above the street, a main proponent of the scheme
(for which he won the Churchill Fellowship) that would move drugs proceeds
from the convicted dealer to crime-prevention schemes. A former used-car
salesman, he has realised his long-held ambition to become a detective sergeant.
He is a clean-cut, self-assured man sitting in his chief's office in Scotland Yard,
expounding on his quarry.

'We're dealing with the tip of the pyramid – the international traffickers and at
the base is your street dealer. You can't stereotype them – a guy living in a squat
knocking out £50 deal bags of heroin – but the same character who's committing
exactly the same offence could be your yuppie in red braces in the dealing room of
a merchant bank, dealing out £50 bags of cocaine. He's got a BMW outside and
lives in Waltham Forest, but in terms of the view we take of them, they're the same
character.

'At our level, dealers are multi-commodity dealers. At street level they'll know
who's supplying heroin, who's supplying amphetamines. But some of them will
trade with registered addicts, so many litres of methadone for so many ounces of
heroin. It's such a complex industry that I would have to invite you to come for six
months to see how complex it is.

'There is such a crossover now between legitimate business and drug trafficking. We're dealing with politicians, Noriega, top industrialists – people who at one stage are viewed as completely legitimate and you suddenly see are actually dope traffickers. There are many well-known people, politicians and others, where drugs either touches their lives or they're physically involved in it.'

Saltmarsh's theory, which he has expounded in the pages of the magazine *Police Review*, suggests that there is in existence what amounts to a multinational corporation in the shape of Cocaine and Co., with all the trappings and style of a highly successful multinational: he identifies the directors as Peru, Bolivia, Panama and Mexico and the chairman of the board as Colombia with the company headquarters in Medellin, Colombia.

'The company motto is "*plomo o plata*" – the lead or the silver – take the bribe or die,' he says. And he points to all the rules of successful international business that Cocaine and Co. follow – consistent high quality, forward-thinking, creation of new markets (with Europe currently targetted for expansion), a committed workforce and a social conscience. 'Cocaine and Co. build housing for the poor, provide free hospital care, build schools, and bring drinking water and electricity to rural villages. One leading cartel member even built a zoo.

'And you will see people who once upon a time were smuggling gold bullion to get round VAT, with the logistics all set up, with their boats, their aircraft, now find it just as easy to smuggle cocaine.

'Traditionally it was obviously far more profitable. £2,000-worth of heroin in Lahore becomes £55,000-worth wholesale by the time you get it back here. And when you can hire dummies to bring it over as mules, time after time, it's far more safe than jumping over post office counters – and these days you get shot for doing that.

'That's the most important aspect of it because the one thing you can't do as an armed robber is pay someone to rob a bank for you. If they're prepared to do that, they'll keep the money for themselves. But what you can do now with drugs is pay idiots to do the hard graft and you sit back and take the money.

'There's no alarms, no policemen to worry about, no witnesses, certainly no complaint. The advantages for the intelligent armed robber are there for all to see. That is not to say that they will not occasionally commit an armed robbery to finance a drugs deal. You will now see some very established criminal networks here. They initially started off with cannabis, thinking that's semi-clean, we'll bring it in. But with cannabis, which brings in huge profits alone, there's a logistic problem with the sheer bulk of it, whereas with cocaine and heroin that diminishes somewhat – smaller amounts are worth the same kind of money. So this plea from the south London villain, "Oh, I'd never touch hard drugs, governor," is now crap. They'd gladly touch everything.

'Legitimate business is now intricately entangled with illegitimate business and crime. The edges are really so blurred now. You've got these guys setting up their own airlines, transportation companies, things one only saw in films ten years ago we are regularly breaking up here. A whole legitimate string of restaurants which is a front for laundering money. A TIR freight haulage company – doing very good legitimate business and at the same time smuggling dope on money that they have borrowed from major clearing banks. It's complex crime without a victim banging at the door of the police station saying, "Look what these guys have done to me."

'Without wanting to say how wonderful we are, I honestly think that, apart from terrorist crime – and the two are very connected – it's the most difficult form of crime to investigate. There are no victims there screaming, "We've just had our bank robbed," because the victims are the junkies further down the pyramid. That's why the Drugs Traffickers Offences Act has become so useful to us because we can approach drug traffic enquiries from the money end of things.'

'My specific job is to trace the assets of major drug traffickers. That means that I have to look at some of our proposed targets and from a money angle see what they're doing, see how they're operating and give the other side of the Drugs Squad information which helps them with their operations. The second part of my duties involves handling the declarations that come into us through the National Drugs Intelligence Unit, where the banks may be concerned that someone may be involved in drug trafficking. Thirdly – though not quite so much – is dealing with people who have been arrested by the Drugs Squad where it's quite clear that they've got assets concealed anywhere in the world. And fourthly, I investigate bank officials and other people who have actually contravened the Drug Trafficking Act. We have been quite pioneering in that we were the first squad in the country to take out a bank official.'

So what is an average day?

'I'm obviously involved in the administration in the office, preparing stuff for court. It does mean I travel a lot, both around the UK and abroad. In addition to that both my partner and I lecture at the detective training school. We're frequently invited by banks and other financial institutions to brief them on the provisions of the Drug Trafficking Act and other legislation, such as PACE, the Police and Criminal Evidence Act. I also teach at the Staff College, Bramshill.

'I work basic office hours of nine to five, five days a week, but everything else is tagged on around that. That's merely an administrative level of hours simply because it's easier than calculating overtime. There are frequently times when we are out at night, when we do observation, looking at people's property, how they're living, following up information that banks give us. We do travel to find assets abroad; in this year alone at least four times.

'We don't arrest as many people or go to court as much as guys on the regular operational teams. Much of the work we do is really information gathering. That's not to say that we don't arrest people but they do a great deal of that. A great amount of our work is often sweeping up, after we've got the bad guys in custody, just to see where their assets are, and at the end of their trial we can say John Smith has got XYZ.

'I was in Brixton for many years and was one of the officers in the case that raided the Afro-Caribbean Club using a train. That was the first time we took a look at the Yardies. They are not in my view as organised as they were in other parts of the world, certainly not like the Jamaican gangs and posses in the States. There is a danger that they will become more organised and this force has grasped that particular nettle – not before time – and there are organised teams looking at black organised crime. They are solely drug traffickers in the States but over here, certainly in some areas of London, I hate the term but I'll use it for the sake of expediency, black organised crime is heavily into prostitution, illegal drinking clubs and drugs.'

This is international business.

'We have drug liaison officers in several countries. We've got very close relations with the Royal Hong Kong Police. In fact we had an officer attached to us for a month from Hong Kong. We don't specifically target Triads but if we have information that Triads are involved in Chinese white heroin which we get from time to time we deal with that as we go along. They are monitored but they're not monitored specifically by us.

'So far, in this country, the Triads don't seem to have too much of a hold. But you've got to be very careful not to generalise that every time you've got a black criminal, it's a "Yardie", every time we've got an Italian American he's a "Mafia". We've got to be careful about that. These terms – Yardies, Triads, Mafia – are very journalistically convenient. I'm not being rude, but they are particularly convenient. In reality, the edges are not so clearly defined. You've got criminals in one country, dealing with criminals in another country – you don't need the Mafia involved. They produce the drugs or supply the drugs but they supply them to their English criminal counterparts. At this side there's no Mafia involvement, it's all dealt with by traditional criminals. There's no need for these flowery terms because we've got the criminals here who are quite capable of dealing with it themselves.

'The proliferation of cocaine in this country rapidly changed the market place. Cocaine being synonymous with Lamborghinis and swimming pools, brought in a whole new market; instead of flower-power hippies and dirty-looking people using heroin you suddenly had cocaine which at one stage was described as a recreational drug, acceptable. Even now it still is amongst the group that use it. They started using other drugs and it changed the whole perception of drug taking. Being a druggie ten years ago was socially unacceptable but now you're nobody – I read it in one of the papers – you're nobody unless you've been dried out for cocaine or alcoholism in the Betty Ford Clinic. Everybody comes out and admits it. I honestly think that that's spilled over into the perception of drugs, certainly cocaine's on the up and up.

'Everyone's got a filofax, everyone takes cocaine. It's become synonymous with a certain aspect of life. America is absolutely flooded with the stuff. It's bouncing into us through Spain and on to Europe as a loss leader.

'You've now got traditional British criminals going to places like Spain – let's say – to buy cocaine and when they're there being offered cannabis, ecstasy, even LSD and saying, "Right we'll take whatever you've got." They are commodity dealers, there is no distinction in them at all.

'There isn't such a thing as gangland now. There are blurred edges. Just as you work for the *Guardian* now you may well go and work for the *Telegraph* next week, just as I work for the Metropolitan police I may transfer to Strathclyde tomorrow. There are organised elements, cells, they're certainly organised but this vision of a Mr Big lording it over south London or north London – I personally never had any knowledge of that. But elements from one team do work with members of another team on specific jobs according to their specialities. They're also linked by some of the lawyers they use. And they're linked by some of the banks and financial institutions that launder their money. They become linked on the next level up, the legitimate level.'

There are various images of drug squad officers which float through the public imagination. One of the main ones came through Operation Julie, the massive acid bust of the late 1970s when a group who were producing LSD and selling it were tracked by undercover officers disguised as hippies.

'A drug squad officer is still portrayed on television as some flower-power hippie with a beard and long hair. I could take you round this floor and the fourteenth floor now and I guarantee over half the guys are wearing suits and ties, simply because in our undercover work you're dealing with legitimate businessmen.

'You look at some of the armed robbers that are now drug traffickers – they're smarter than me, they're sitting in the cocktail bar at the Inn on the Park right now. They're not living in a caravan on a gypsy site on the outskirts of London. You're talking about commodity dealers. There is this old image of the hippie drug squad officer going back to Operation Julie – forget it.

'On television there's nothing that comes anywhere near showing the pressures and stresses and strains involved in the job. It's difficult to get your foot in the door and it all seems so easy on TV. It's just the very smallest things that make us move and investigate something.

'A really good undercover officer is worth his weight in gold and they are not common. Just a silly example, which you couldn't portray on television, we had an antiques dealer who was a heroin dealer. We knew damn well and we needed to find his bank accounts. We tried every way, even putting him on surveillance. I ended up buying a horrible antique vase off him with my own cheque just to see where the cheque got presented. So many routine things you have to do that they can't portray on television.

'The only one that actually gives any atmosphere of police work – and it's not even British – is *Hill Street Blues*, because it portrays the pressure. I'm not for a moment suggesting that the Central Drugs Squad is an open house like that. We're a little bit secret in that not just anyone can walk in here, but that is closer to the reality of a modern-day busy police station because that is the pressure.'

Graham Saltmarsh talks with great self-confidence; you could see how someone might happily confide in him. I asked about informants.

'We have all kinds. We now have participating informants in the shape of bank managers, insurance fund managers. We have a whole new breed of professional informants who are doing it not for reward and many of them are glad to do that. Informants are important but we create many of our own informants by initial investigation. They are crucial to us. Even the criminal one, he's crucial to what's going on. If we can get him on our side even for money . . . that's really all I'm prepared to say on the subject.'

I once met a former drugs squad officer when visiting a prisoner at Ford open prison. He had come from the midlands into the drugs squad in London in the seventies and found from his first operation, he said, that he was expected to take a piece of the seized drug or the seized money. He went along with it and was eventually caught when a straight squad realised that a piece of seized hashish still had traces of fingerprint powder on it and had obviously been recycled. He was not bitter, merely reflective and a bit broken. So are there temptations?

'The format of the squad is unique in as much as we're dealing with the highest level criminals but we're actually a 50/50 uniform/CID split from Chief Inspector down to constable. That helps in terms of the possibility of any corruption. You don't have the old traditional CID clique whereby you might be in a position of vulnerability. The other way to overcome it is by sheer hard work in supervision. Nothing goes on in the squad that we, the middle management, don't know about. We have regular Monday meetings, we know exactly what's going on. It would be very difficult for an officer from a low rank to get involved in corruption because he's so closely supervised that it would be – I won't say impossible, because that would be tempting fate – it would be very, very difficult.

'The other thing that serves in our interest is the change in drug traffickers. You're not dealing with sole traders any more who maybe in the old days could buy somebody off, not necessarily a policeman, to leave them alone. But because we've reached an era where we are dealing with multinational businessmen with a whole infrastructure of logistics and organisation, they are not particularly interested in one policeman who can't do them any real damage anyway.

'There is no one-to-one on the drug squad. You're not the drug dealer any more working from a tenement in St Pancras and I'm not a TV drugs squad sergeant saying, "Give me £100 or I'm going to arrest you next week." It ain't like that any more. You're dealing with multinational organisations where you need a whole team effort to deal with them and take them out so in many respects it's served our own interest. I'm more worried about corruption in some of the banks and financial institutions than in the police force.'

What about going to court?

'We lose very few cases. Most good detectives can probably count on the fingers of one hand the cases they have actually lost. That's not to say that we don't get a lot of time wasted in court. The Police and Criminal Evidence Act, a great hobby horse of mine, was a piece of legislation created by lawyers for lawyers. We're getting bogged down all the time with administrative processes. That's one of the main problems of the adversarial system in our courts as compared to the rest of Europe who have an inquisitorial system. Because of this trials take a long time. We still win them. With most of the bad guys, and we're talking about organised crime here, we lose very few because we go with the right kind of evidence and the case is rock solid. So the only way we can be attacked is because of the administration, the way the prisoner has been housed. How many meals he's had, how many visits he's had. I'm not bitter and twisted about drug dealers being acquitted because I don't think many of ours are, but it bogs us down for weeks on end in court and stops us from being effective. That's a symptom of the adversarial system.

'They say we've got too many prisoners on remand and banged up in police stations awaiting trial. Why? Because trials take three to four weeks here on average, whereas they're disposed of in eight to ten days in France and Germany. They have an inquisitorial system and it isn't who's got the best lawyer and who can score the best points, and look you've made a mistake on the custody sheet.

'I guarantee the prison population would go straight down because cases would be disposed of quicker. I've sat in on a trial in France and we have a lot to learn from the Napoleonic system. The American system is almost a concentrated form of our own and look what a state that's in – you enter the premises without a warrant, the murder weapon you found is now inadmissible. We've not quite got there yet but PACE is the first step. Solicitors and barristers are shopkeepers. They're there earning a living.

'We have the luxury in that once we get to court, if the evidence is there, Joe Public is very much opposed to drugs. Even some of the youngsters know what's going on. So we not only enjoy juries that are sympathetic but when you need help from a member of the public, you may need their roof for an afternoon to watch a drug deal go down in the street, you get it. I am likely to get some old stall holder in the East End say, "No problem at all, use my roof." But if I told him I wanted to watch someone hand over a bit of nicked gear he'd probably tell me to go away and never come back. You can see we do enjoy some public support from some quarters that otherwise wouldn't give us the time of day. Some of the press coverage we get is extremely good and extremely constructive. I remember Neil Derbyshire when he was on the *Standard* three years ago did an article about Yardies and black crime and it being pooh-poohed. But three years later we have a team rightly targeting the Yardies.

'What's in the *Sun* or the *Mirror*, quite frankly, is more worrying than what appears in the *Independent* or the *Guardian* because so many people read them. It's easy for some of the public to dismiss the *Sun* as irrelevant – it bloody well isn't irrelevant. When papers like that do things they can cause a lot of good or real damage.'

We were talking at the time of the Great Acid House Scare – when acid house music and parties were featuring regularly in the papers as the new threat to the nation's youth.

'One of the things that happens, a spin-off from that fuss about Acid House is that there is a demand to get results. Look at this. This becomes political pressure and is one of the pressures on the police service. Get results, get results. We can't have this going on. Football hooliganism is an excellent example of that. Great deal of media portrayal of hooliganism – sure, it's bad – great deal of pressure on the authorities to do something and when you foul up because you've got that pressure on you that very same media has a field day. They're in a no-lose situation, that's the luxury that newspapers have. They have a field day with us. If we screw up we lose. The media never lose.'

So what about the media's concentration on crack?

'I would say America had, rather than has a crack problem. It was very serious but they've now weathered it. It peaked in the late summer of '86 there. I may be proved wrong but I don't believe we will have a crack problem in the way they had in America. The social make-up here is entirely different. Crack in America has in the main been used by a terribly disadvantaged black population, the kind of disadvantage that we don't have here. In addition, crack has been spoken of often to the detriment of heroin, which is often the drug of preference among blacks in America, and that is also a pointer to us because the black population here has always regarded heroin as a dirty drug, which I have no problem about, but they have not had the same scruples about dealing with cannabis, of course, or cocaine. But I've rarely dealt with black heroin dealers and indeed users and that's a pointer to me.

'We don't have the infrastructure of black organised crime that exists in America. I think there's a blurring between crack abuse and crack crime. They are two distinct things and people who have gone over there on so-called fact-finding tours have come back here and blurred the two together. Yes, there is crack abuse but crack crime has certainly increased as organised criminals chase what's become a decreasing number of users. The crack crime in Washington and New York was essentially a turf war and that turf war would have existed whatever the commodity – it could have been water melons if they'd been illegal. The portrait has been of crack users killing each other but the bulk of the killing has been between crack dealers vying for a shrinking market. They're already adopting methamphetamine, MDMA [ecstasy] and "ice" [crystallized methamphetamine] as the next drug of preference and I foresee that that will be the real problem that comes here. A personal opinion, and I stand to be shown entirely wrong. We mustn't be seen to be crying wolf over crack cocaine because when it doesn't occur and when we do have a serious methamphetamine problem people will say, "Well, you said this about crack and it didn't happen so why should we listen to you now?"'

In the late sixties and early seventies there was periodic talk of the legislation of marijuana or at least its decriminalisation. It coincided with changes in the law in some states of America, where possession of less than an ounce no longer merited arrest, and similar attitudes in Holland and Spain. There was even an active Legalise Cannabis Campaign, smiled on privately, if not publicly, by some politicians, which would hold smoke-ins in Hyde Park. The theory is that much of crime related to drugs is caused by its very illegality and the decriminalisation of the soft end of the market would remove the people who were only interested in soft drugs from the frame and free the police to concentrate on heroin. The extension is that much drug crime – shootings, robberies, kidnappings – would fade away with legalisation just as much of the Al Caponery around bootlegging faded away when prohibition ended. Graham Saltmarsh does not go along with this argument.

'We're stumping around doing all this with drugs and yet there's so much alcohol-related crime. We've already legalised one drug, if you like, and look what damage that's done . . . the media have had a field day with lager louts, drunk driving – rightly so. Yet with the same breath, that same media talks about legalising drugs. They're not advocating it but they're giving the guy airspace . . . I don't mind that. How many people in their right minds can even consider it? It's a non-starter anyway, it's not worth getting hot under the collar about.

'I believe in custodial sentences for users of any class of drug, even if it's for a matter of weeks – it takes them out of circulation, it brings them a bit of social disgrace at work and at home and it may well be constructive. I don't believe in fining drug users – it's like fining prostitutes: if a drug user can find the money to buy drugs he can find the money to pay the fine at a local magistrates' court. Self defeating. For drug dealers I believe in maximum sentences. I don't believe in the death penalty for anybody, that's a personal view – if I'm dealing with a drug trafficker in central London and he's arrested in the hotel and he's got five kilos of cocaine in a suitcase and he knows he's going to get life imprisonment for it he'll have no compunction in killing me to get away because he'll get just the same.'

When he's not working he reads. 'A lot of books on the police. I'm doing a degree course at Exeter University, an MA in police and criminal justice studies which takes up most of my real spare time. I've no children. My wife is a head teacher in south London.

'I switch off with holidays, weekends away. I ride, walk, that's it really. I don't read fiction but I'm passionately interested in politics and the way power is exercised. I found Michael Shea's book *Influence* fascinating. Good social life. Friends outside the job. I've got lots of good friends in the job but during my weekends I prefer to associate with friends that I have made in the village where I live and get totally away from the job. I have no problem with that.' The cassettes in the glove compartment in his car range from Paganini to Status Quo.

He does have strong views on what happens with the money he helps seize.

'I believe the bulk of money seized from major crime should be ploughed back into the community. I've devised a plan which I hope is going to be accepted and there are banks and other organisations here interested. It works like this: I'm the policeman, you're the banker and I say I have £10 million which I've seized from major criminals and I'm going to deposit it with you. All I want from you – let's take a figure out of the air – is two per cent interest on it. But, I want you to make risk lending to people like Shelter, that you wouldn't normally make. For instance, a charity might want urgently, say, £1 million for a rehab programme or for AIDS say, the Terence Higgins Trust. They know that over a period of two years they will collect it through subscriptions so I would say to the Nat West Bank – lend them the money now but only at five per cent interest, give them access to money they wouldn't otherwise have. That's really a great British compromise because we're not giving the money away and, for my senior officers who quite persuasively argue that it should be for law enforcement, it's available for the police service in an emergency. The beauty of the scheme is that there are no great administrative costs because we just deposit with the bank. I got a great deal of interest in the States for the idea.

'Effectively we've been privatised because we are collecting money for the Treasury. I would have no qualms in some of the DTOA money being used for crime-prevention schemes like the Middlesex Polytechnic one for improved street lighting. That's natural justice. We've frozen ten million quid this year and it's only a quarter of a million to light an alleyway. That stinks. Because that is money that is dirty money, homeless money. It doesn't feature anywhere but it's given a home back in the Treasury. Why can't we use it for schemes like that?

'It is very galling. I see it possibly more than anybody else. These are people sometimes we don't arrest because we haven't enough evidence to take them out and yet I can see the kinds of budgets they're on. Tens of millions of pounds.

'There was an economist just recently who said that the world has a balance of trade deficit of $200 billion. That money has vanished out of the system. I've got a fair clue where a lot of it is. This money is rolling around the world like a pinball machine.

'It's suited many nations – Switzerland was one and Panama another – to deal with that money. This hot money bounces from place to place to place. It has to be increasingly dressed up to disguise it from us. When the Swiss had the strictest banking secrecy laws the Social Democratic Party said right, a lot of criminals, terrorists, Mafia, are using Swiss bank accounts to hide their money, we're going to have a more open policy. The bankers said "There's no need, all the money is quite legitimate", but when they passed the law the bankers said, "Well, hang on, everyone will pull their money out and put it in Panama and the Cayman Islands," and it was said immediately to them, "Well, you said there was nothing wrong with it . . ."

'Our morality has become blurred in hiding money. Dirty money is hot money but hot money is not necessarily dirty. The leader of the NUM will find himself in the same queue at the bank as a major cocaine dealer because they both want to hide their money. The union leader doesn't want his money sequestrated by the government and the cocaine dealer doesn't want his money seized by me. They're in the same bank and the same queue.

'International fringe banks, some based in the City, have been doing it happily for years. Because of tightness of credit, a lot of money which is hot is not necessarily dirty. But the same banks and financial institutions provide the service of hiding it, be it for the chairman of a big factory or a heroin dealer, those services are in place. This blurring of morality in dealing with banks makes life doubly difficult for us.'

He also ponders on the morality of the American government's crackdown on drugs, with one arm of the administration waging war on narcotics, while another works complicitly with Latin-American drug dealers to 'stop the Bolshevik hordes'.

'In this era of detente, with things changing so much in the Soviet Union and Eastern Europe, some people are looking for a new folk-devil on which many of the ills of society can be dumped and with which they can worry the electorate,' says Saltmarsh. 'It's true that many of these ills can legitimately be put at the doors of major traffickers and the Noriegas of this world, but there is a tendency to go over the top, although some would argue that you cannot overemphasise the problem.'

He elaborates on his theme: 'It would be disturbing if at some time in the future some politicians or some very senior police officers were accused of having hijacked the issues of drug misuse for political reasons or to explain away other failings. Because policing alone will never bring the problem under control. At best we can keep the lid on it.'

Saltmarsh sees the future of organised crime as increasingly international. 'It's the same with the police. If we have information about some of our people going out to Germany we will make contact with our German counterpart and say, "Look, can you do something for us?" If the German criminals want something done over here or want stuff shifted over they will make contact with known villains over here. It's as simple as that. It's just a big happy trading family.

'The only difference is they have more money. They don't have to worry about the overtime bill or getting an extra car for the surveillance team.

'So I travel a lot, north America, Europe. I have a very good relationship with the Paris central drugs squad because I've done a couple of jobs with them. I don't speak French. To my eternal shame I went over to France and even the bad guy spoke English.'

9

The Dealer

The only reason that cocaine
is such a rage today is that
people are too dumb and lazy
to get themselves together to
roll a joint.

Jack Nicholson

Stuck in a traffic jam on the Marylebone Road on the way to the meeting I note a grubby cream-coloured van in front of me with a sticker on its rear window that says 'I'm a dealer and I've got a great deal to offer'.

Will later explains that sometimes, when carrying out his deliveries, he used to wear a brown dustcoat over his normal clothes, partly to look like a delivery man engaged on lawful business and partly so that if he suddenly had to make a dash for it he could dump the coat and thus change his appearance.

Unlike 'pusher', which conjures up the notion of men in dark glasses and shiny suits hanging around outside the gates of comprehensive schools going Pssst, 'dealer' has a slightly ambiguous ring to it. Will is definitely a dealer, not a pusher. In fact, he is now not even a dealer but an ex-dealer, one of that quiet breed who have survived the attention of the law long enough and successfully enough to fade politely out of the trade, retiring from a business that does not throw any retirement parties and provides no pension scheme. A handsome, open, broadly-built man with a wife and young family and a flat full of things you want to ask questions about, he might be an architect or a theatre director, a northern working-class background hidden behind an almost unplace-able accent, anything really but a commodity dealer. During his years in the trade he has been a party to cannabis deals worth literally millions of pounds.

'There's lot of different types of dealers. There are those you might go to and buy an ounce of hash from. They tend to have been doing it a long time and they buy one or two pounds. They might be forced to buy more, say five or ten, by their wholesaler. They're nearly always hippies in their forties. Financially, they're doing OK, no great shakes but they're doing fine. Quite often single mothers are dealers. It fits really, they're at home the whole time, always there if anyone calls in.

'Above them is a wholesaler who's taking it in ten, maybe even twenty, sometimes fifty pounds. He will be slightly protected, he won't see everyone and he'll be fairly careful about what he does. He's bound to have a warehouse man working for him, often a guy who lives in a cottage out of town with an outbuilding. That guy takes the whole heap, breaks it up into tens or fives or whatever and then he'll do his deliveries for him.

'Above him you're talking about wholesalers who deal directly with importers. There are some, not many, who would lay a hundred kilos on you.

'When I was wholesaling I used to think I was quite good. I suppose if I really put my mind to it, got up in the morning and got going, I could sell a ton in six weeks and get the money for it in eight or ten weeks.'

But the market – which is tiny in the United Kingdom compared, even per capita, with the United States – could be queered just by someone else bringing in another product. 'Someone arrives from Jamaica with something slightly better or cheaper and it'll knock you sideways. I would say a ton every six weeks is about it.'

So vast sums of money are floating around, quantities of drugs that, once retailed, are worth the price of a nice little place in Surrey; how do the dealers trust each other?

'The great thing about all these people, which was lovely, was the fact that they weren't drawn from traditional criminal classes. Everyone got what they got on credit so there was a big thing about loyalty and trust. There was a great pride in being honourable. Someone lays half a million on you and expects you to do the same next month.'

The people Will worked with were well educated, had been to university and smoked hash. 'There was a massive amount of kudos about it. When I was a kid I remember that the guy that sold you half an ounce was a bit higher up the hierarchy. The way I got into it was that a friend of mine was fairly big and I simply made it known that I was available. They are bright people: a twenty-one-year-old who had got it together enough to organise some farmers and troops in Afghanistan, get the stuff on an aeroplane and into Shannon. Get it out of Shannon and into a country house in Ireland, have it packed in cars and driven over here. They are all slightly megalomaniac.

'I don't come from that class. We were very poor – not criminal class, because if my family ever thought there was anything illegal going on they would be really upset. I didn't know anybody poorer, but they worked. I was very rebellious and I was in the forces when I left school. I hated it and I thought that laws I didn't agree with didn't have to be obeyed.

'So I loved the idea – childishly – of having so much money I could treat it with amazing disrespect, where I could be in the position where it really didn't bother me. I always found the negotiations about the price and the argy-bargy a bit distasteful. Which is stupid, as I know now, because of the terribly reality of paying off a mortgage! I liked being able to go where I wanted and when. But it's not quite like that – you would sometimes have to hang around and wait for as long as three months.'

The loyalty and trustworthiness of the people involved in the business is a theme he returns to.

'There were very few rip-offs although it was well worth your while. You could bugger off and start a new life on what you were holding but it very rarely happened. Until the East End firms started – they don't like all this credit. So what they have done is increase the risk by making you go three or four times, bringing money each time to pick up things you would only have gone once for.

'And there was great loyalty if someone was locked up. I do know someone who is looking after two families of two people who are doing clink – it costs him £20,000 a year. It's difficult because he's retired and he doesn't do it any more. We certainly always expected people to behave in an honourable way and in return if they got into trouble they could rely on us for help.'

The 'fat cats', says Will, were usually foreign, generally coming from the drugs' country of origin, where they have the necessary governmental, military and police connections to send the cargo on its air-freighted way. They have a home in England and their children at English public school. 'They have weird things – this Lebanese had a sheep farm and a horse farm. Those guys are very, very rich. They don't spend their money on the same things as the rest of us, they don't go on posh holidays or booze it too much. They're not even generous.'

So what route do the drugs take?

'One situation would be, say, from Karachi where it's been brought by lorry by people who are protected and know no one's going to pick them up on their way to the delivery. In the old days it came from Afghanistan, of course. Then it would go into containers on to aeroplanes, or sometimes to India or to Dubai by boat. That's because almost anything from Karachi coming into an airport would be opened so it's much better if it looks as though it comes from somewhere else – I once picked up an air-freight shipment from a west African diplomat in Golders Green; he got it through the diplomatic service via Japan, although it originated in Pakistan.

'The other situation, the Lebanese one, was completely military. Someone would turn up in a boat and a military convoy would be laid on and loaded up in some very strange little port in the south of Lebanon that's probably not there any more.'

Once arrived in this country, the drugs go to the major British dealer who has already agreed a price while the freight is in the air. 'It's a slight nonsense really because they all go in percentages and at the end of the day hardly anyone knows a percentage of what.

'Below that big foreign dealer is the one in Britain who can send it anywhere he gets a "gate", an in, a facility in an airport. They are available in every country more or less.'

The actual packing of the drug is carried out in an almost clinical situation, with special clothing. It is usually sealed in tins and the tins are then washed thoroughly in a machine. People handling it get 'scrubbed up' so there's no smell on them at all which could be detected at a later stage. Further precautions against the aroma are taken through the use of camphor or mothballs. If the cargo is going by boat it is crated and wrapped in as much polythene as seems necessary to keep it dry.

'Nowadays it comes through straight freight and it's computerised – so the computers are messed with. It's all quite high fallutin. It's just a normal freight cargo which will "disappear" and all evidence on the computer will disappear, too. Very often those guys involved – the whole facility at the airport – will demand half the money. They've got to be very good. They've got to be the kind of guys who after doing one job don't go off and buy BMWs and take three months holidays and find they haven't got a job when they come back.'

So how much money was to be made?

'You might be taking £30 a pound wholesale and you're moving a hundred pounds a day then you're talking a lot of money.

'Usually these things are kept absolutely secret until they've been here for a while and they've been asleep for a little bit. So it will be moved and put to sleep and moved and put to sleep again. Then it will be broken up very quickly and then people start talking about money. You would say how much it was and they would then go away and see if they could get that sort of money and come back having found out. You could always trust them. They would say, "I can't get that kind of money for it because my main guy is getting troubled by some guy who's got some Colombian weed and he won't be able to sell it." Then there's a bit of argy bargy and it all gets settled.'

In the first boom period of recreational drugs, when tobacco companies were patenting names like Acapulco Gold and Lebanese Red in anticipation of the eventual legalisation of cannabis, prices and details of drugs were readily available on the underground press throughout Europe and North America: *High Times* magazine, founded in 1974, even published Trans High Market Quotations detailing how much everything from Guadalajara Green to Thai sticks, from peyote to Moroccan kif should cost by pound and ounce; it was all printed in the same exhaustive way as the daily stock market quotations and was used by dealers as a way of reassuring their customers that they were getting a fair deal. In the United Kingdom, drugs magazines as such had a short-lived existence, but papers like *IT* and *Frendz* did print current prices as well as health warnings if 'bad acid' or heavily cut drugs were being sold. Those days are over now and there is very little published information of running prices and quality. So who judges the quality? And what it should be selling for?

'The guys at the top don't bother too much about quality. They have a great saying – "Oh, it's good commercial" – which means that it's nothing special, which means that it's piss-poor. It's always an annoyance to everyone else that people have to go through all the risk anyway so why not bring something really nice in?

'Some of them can tell by looking at the dope what quality it is. One guy I know can hold it in his hand rather like a Frenchman assessing a cork on a bottle of wine. He'll hold it in his hand and make it warm and run a bit through his palms.

He sat in Kandohar, in Afghanistan, for a few years, hand-pressing the stuff so he knows what he's talking about. He does a weird thing too: he eats a tiny bit and after five minutes he looks at his hands; he says it heightens your perceptions and if the stuff is good quality the lines on your hand become terribly clear and you can actually see your fingerprints quite clearly.

'The "street value" you see quoted in papers is always miles off, a massive overestimate. I suppose it's half ignorance and half deliberate. Someone will say they paid £20 for a piece that big," he indicates a small amount with finger and thumb, 'so when they put it all together they think this is going to look like a room full.'

What kind of hours does a dealer work?

'It can be very hard work. There was a time when I would start work at 5 a.m. to beat the traffic. I would like to be back in town having been to the warehouse and got what I wanted by 8 a.m. If I was quick I could maybe do another one or two runs at night.'

The 'good' dealer is judged by his or her connections, how much they can sell, how fast and how safely. A 'bad' dealer talks on their own telephone, or is always late for meetings, or turns up in their own car. There is a constant possibility that a tail has been placed on a dealer, so to arrive in a traceable car is regarded as foolish. 'If I get into my car they know immediately who I am and where I live so they stick a tap on my phone. Another thing is that you wouldn't dream of having a conversation in the same room as a telephone because they can hear everything in the room through the phone without a phone call taking place.'

So people talk in code. Will laughs at the transparent nature of some of the old coded calls. 'People would say, "I've got ten kilos of shirts." The other firm would know about that. They must pick up about eighty-five per cent from telephone conversations. I'm sure they must find it laughable how people carry on.'

Throughout the conversation, Will often refers to 'the other firm'. When it first cropped up, I assumed he was talking about another team of dealers before it dawned that the Other Firm are the drugs squad and Customs and Excise.

'One friend got picked up because he made a silly telephone call. The following day he had gone out and made a sensible telephone call so they had come steaming in and picked him up prematurely. I had said to him, "Do you know that they have these machines which can hear everything in the room through the phone, it's been in operation since the Wilson government." It's in *Spycatcher*, isn't it? He didn't believe me.'

People sense by instinct if they're being followed: 'It's very difficult abroad because you're in somewhere fresh and all their guys may look like hippies or something. They don't all look like debt collectors and drive the same kind of cars as they do here.'

The best known infiltration of a drug dealing and manufacturing group was carried out in Operation Julie, a massive operation involving 800 officers that led to arrests in 1977 and sentences totalling more than 100 years for a team involved in the production and distribution of LSD.

Leaf Fielding, the 'tabletter' – converting crystalline LSD into microdots – and head of its distribution network, used packets of tea and dog biscuits for concealing his wares.

Writing in *City Limits* magazine after his release in 1985 Fielding describes the effects of the success of the scheme, nicknamed, by him, 'Lucy' after the Beatles' song: 'The carefree times were over, days spent contemplating creation and cruising the cosmos became days spent looking over my shoulder and counting my money. In this stressful context acid had lost its numinous aspect of inexplicable joy – it was becoming a commodity which signified riches, deception and paranoia, which increasingly wore me down. It is a lonely life when you can't tell your friend what you are doing.' However, they did not lose their sense of humour: when the laboratory was finally surrounded by dozens of police who started battering the front door down with a barrage of sledgehammer blows, one of the crew unlocked the front door, opened it, stood back to dodge the swinging hammer and said, 'I suppose you've come about the television licence.'

Will reckoned the Operation Julie officers were good. 'I think they were a bit upset about it in the end. I don't think it was anything they relished. The guys weren't bad guys, they weren't doing anything morally wrong.' Indeed, after the arrests Fielding became friendly with one of the officers, who had – inadvertently according to the evidence – ingested some acid and had a strange experience in a pub along with fellow officers in the same situation. One thought his pint of lager so large that he felt unable to lift it, others burst into uncontrollable mirth when they went back to where they were staying and watched *Jesus of Nazareth* on the television. By the time Fielding had emerged from jail the drugs scene had altered dramatically – 'Today's drug is very different; heroin is used to blot out the unpalatable present and the uncertain future' – and different dealers had arrived on the scene.

Will has watched their arrival. 'Before, there was virtually no cross-over between cannabis and other drugs. There might be at the bottom of the retail market – in some blocks of council flats in Tottenham you might find kids who are knocking out crack and hash and speed and whatever. There was a time when it was thought OK to deal in cocaine, but when all the new information came out the people I knew stopped doing that.

'But the new people, that lot,' he squashes his nose to depict a heavy, 'go for anything. I don't think they give a flying shit what they're dealing in – people, even. There is a hard core who don't like having anything to do with drugs. That was part of the reason they didn't go into it in the beginning anyway. They thought it was going to kill their children.

'Some people shouldn't be in the business at all but they needed the dosh for a one-off thing and then got very frightened, but by that time everything had gone so far they couldn't jump clear.

'I remember one guy was in a terrible state – I had a van full of cardboard boxes of the stuff and nowhere to put it and I didn't want to make a big deal out of warehousing it. I had this very old friend who was on his arse and could do with a bob or two and he was going to get quite a lot of money for keeping it for me. I said, "You mustn't now get in touch with me, I'll get in touch with you." I went down there with it and the next morning he was on the phone in tears saying, "You're going to have to get this away from here." His wife had been awake all night and walked out at daylight saying she wouldn't come back until it had all gone.'

The heavier sentences have also deterred the amateurs and left the professionals in the field. 'Most people know it would be considered a very, very serious offence, especially nowadays. It's become a worldwide thing because politicians, when they visit another country in order to get some sort of arms deal or arms reduction going, will say, "Well, we haven't got very far with that but we've signed a few things on human rights and drugs."'

The dealing world divides, in the United Kingdom, fairly strictly on racial lines. 'I never knew any West Indians doing it because they were considered too high risk. First of all they wouldn't have been trusted because they are renowned for ripping off and buggering off with very small amounts and secondly those poor buggers can't really walk down the street without being stopped and searched and they can't walk through airports without attracting attention. And ditto Pakistanis.'

It has remained a predominantly male job, at the higher level, with a few exceptions. 'There were two girls involved at one stage. One went off to Thailand, came back via Brussels with a suitcase full of Thai sticks, did very well out of it and decided to take her best mate with her next time and bring a bit more back. They did the whole thing themselves – they shouldn't have done but they did. And they got caught. Normally they would have given it to someone like me who has got channels that are open and can send it off all over the place. But they didn't trust anyone and they started selling in ounces which takes too long. Also when they were packing in Bangkok they found they'd got too much so they put the rest in a package and sent it. It arrived six weeks later – it was addressed to a house over the road so the Other Firm just watched the house. They are very skilful at questioning and the girls told them how much they'd brought in. They got a year for that.'

The false address delivery is a favourite ruse: 'Say I live at 199 Everling Road, I might go to 199 Everling Gardens and say "I know I have some mail coming which has been sent to the wrong address by mistake," and you can just turn up there every morning for a week until it shows up.'

But the professional full-time dealer pays a social price. 'One chap I knew was very, very good at his job but because of that his life was no great shakes because he knew practically no one socially, spent all his life walking round London, going to obscure telephone booths and receiving calls from all over the world, always looking slightly down-at-heel. He used to say there are a lot of sacrifices you have to make if you want long term security. I used to think he was far too greedy to stop but he has stopped.

'In terms of how we presented ourselves, there was a desire not to look like a dealer but there were the punk guys who quite liked the idea of looking like rich men. There were a couple of guys who were slightly Boy's Ownish about it, into heroics, and you'd hear a lot of talk about a very small thing, blown up and dramatised. I was there at the time and knew it was boring as shit apart from the fact that we very nearly got popped because someone made a mistake.

'Then there was the Gold Rolex mob. You could go to certain islands in the Caribbean and they all have gold Rolexes and all know each other. And in Ibiza, when I was there, I thought if you really want to know what's going on you only have to come out here, hang about, get taken to a few houses. There were a hell of a lot of them there, Dutch guys and German guys, big wholesalers, sending steamers into Rotterdam and exporting to the whole of Europe, moving twenty to thirty tons in six weeks.

'London is very difficult to get stuff into but there is a bit more money to be made because the prices are higher. But the Other Firms are much better and much more on their toes than anywhere else. Elsewhere, in America and Holland, marijuana and hashish are not that much of a serious offence. I remember a guy telling me his mate had been caught with 100 kilos and that's quite a lot and he was terribly worried that he might get a year. It's like smacking his bloody legs, isn't it? A year! He'll be able to choose when he wants to do it, see his wife at weekends inside. They can be quite dangerous to work with because of that. Their drugs squad doesn't have the same sort of budget as ours and they're not mad keen. So the dealers tend to work in a more relaxed way and use their phones, so you have to watch them. They kind of forget how we have to behave here.'

It is this carelessness rather than the possibility of being betrayed that is the main cause for arrests, 'although I did learn that someone I know offered to do a deal with the police and met them twice'.

Some dealers talk of the adrenalin that comes from pulling off a major big-money deal but fear is another by-product.

'I've been frightened a few times. It's not very nice to look round and see you're being followed and there's nothing you can do to get rid of these people. You can do strange things, jumping on and off tubes, and all of a sudden they're there. It usually bloody happens when you're right in the middle of something which you can't stop.

'I can spot policemen a mile away and in fact it got me out of trouble when I was in Barcelona once. I thought, what's going on, I haven't been doing anything for a long time and yet there are people looking at me. In fact we were being followed around by criminals, who were waiting for us to go down a side street and rob us, and they were dressed in the same kind of smart mediocrity that an awful lot of policemen choose so they can blend in.'

So some people create a new persona for themselves. 'I never travelled under a false name. There are two schools of thought: if you go under your own name and something happens and you get locked up, what you're looking for is some bail in order to bugger off. If you are into false paperwork there is no question of bail being granted. The other school believes that it is worth it. Some people have a lot of IDs: one for work, one for travel, one for home. There are people who sell IDs in packages – they'll take a driving test, go to Ireland and get a passport for you, open bank accounts, get credit cards. But most people know that the safest way to do it is to create your own identity – find someone who died at a young age a long time ago or is in a mental hospital and has never applied for a passport. Then you go off and open your bank account in that name.'

To hide the proceeds, some dealers set up small businesses but there can be problems.

'One friend had a small business like that and when he was arrested all they found was a key to a safe-deposit box and £35,000 in it. He was inside for six months awaiting trial. During this time his girlfriend packed in her job and she ran his business for him. She worked all the hours that God sent and made it terribly successful, quite genuinely, and she produced the audit and showed it was all possible. So he was found not guilty.'

But if loyal girlfriends and wives are in the know, how many others are aware of a dealer's life?

'It's a bit of a drag if they know although it's not really that important as long as they don't know exactly when you're doing it. The favourite euphemisms are "I'm an antique dealer", or "I deal in Persian rugs, import and export".

'There is virtually no home-grown stuff here. Occasionally someone would come up from Cornwall with a carrier bag but the weather's not good enough. And the market is already set up. It's the same as any other kind of produce – the important thing is not the growing but the marketing and the distribution. I was talking to someone about producing garlic over here and he had some experience of asparagus production and he said, "If you can't get it into Marks and Spencers and Sainsbury's forget it." The same sort of thing applies to the drug market.'

What Sainsbury's don't have to worry about, however, is suddenly abandoning their stock because the Other Firm are on the scent.

'On two occasions hauls have been dumped. One time was a highly organised job in Scotland. There was a gang of guys from Brooklyn who had been together a long time who were flown in for it. I know that two of the guys who arranged for that Brooklyn mob to come over were CIA. That's for sure. They were incredible. Try and put twelve guys together here who will keep their traps shut and go anywhere in the world on the passport that you give them, do the job, disintegrate and turn up for their money three months later. They were built like brick shit-houses, they ate nuts and drank mineral water, did press-ups all day. They would arrive in London, go up to Scotland to some stately home where they would eat more nuts and do more press-ups. The boat would arrive and they would paddle these canoes, they really do shift, and in no time at all sixteen tons would be off the ship and back into the lorries. The lorries would be pushed along without the engine on in the places they didn't want any noise. It was financed by the mob in the States and they thought it was taking too long and they wanted to do a kind of audit. We had never met organised guys before. All of a sudden these guys arrive and they start wanting hookers! A bit of high life! We thought – what are they going on about? Hookers! We hadn't got a bloody clue, where do you go for hookers? They were bloody disappointed. They expected penthouses and they ended up in short term flats in Pimlico. Anyway on this occasion these guys were clocked as they came in at the airport. They were taken to the Dorchester and the phone was tapped. The person who picked them up in Glasgow saw he was being followed so he dropped them off and immediately buggered off back to his island, loaded his boat up and dumped it all in the sea. It ended up on the Mull of Kintyre.

'Then not long ago there was a large freighter steaming up the Atlantic which was met by a small boat which took six tons off him. The weather was really bad and he was driven up the Irish Sea and in the end he couldn't wait any longer so he took off – quite a brave thing really – went to France, through some canals and ended up in Holland. Everyone thought he had buggered off but they marketed it there. They had another eight tons which no one was coming for and they just threw that over the side.

'There's also a lot of money hidden and not found. People freak out and put their money and phoney IDs in the ground and can't find it again. Put it in a drainpipe and seal it up or in lots and lots of plastic bags. There must also be a hell of a lot of bank accounts in Switzerland that no one is going to pick up.'

But does no one claim that they have had to dump a haul and then just quietly re-sell it for their own profit?

'There was one occasion when a guy was supposed to meet up in a lay-by and do a switch – quite a large amount – between lorries. Their story was that they had been followed so they drove off and left it, then the story was that they were too frightened to stay with it so they parked it and were too frightened to go near it and when they went back it had disappeared. There was nothing in the papers about that but then it's quite well known that the police do sell it or pay informers with it. But the general feeling was that their story was a bit iffy. Still, I've never known a comeback, a punishment, on anything like that. The guy who did it was a major criminal, had been in the SAS, been a mercenary, an unpleasant guy, so I don't know why they got mixed up with him. It was a direct result of going to the clink and meeting people like that.

'We never went armed and it was a great shock when a Customs guy stopped a lorry in the City, opened the cab door and got shot. That was a great shock. We thought, "Who are these guys? What's happening? We'd all better look for another way of earning a living."

'Then it dawned on me – my wife was pregnant and I thought I can't carry on the life I live, it's not fair. The other thing was when people of my background have a lot of money they tend to socialise with it, so the more money the more socialising. So I ended up with a massive drink problem, purely through having an awful lot of money. Where I come from that's what guys with lots of money do – they buy the pub a drink. And when I was in a position to think clearly, when I had stopped drinking, the moral side of it came up. Not that I think there is anything wrong with anyone smoking or selling marijuana, or even making a lot of money out of it, it's no skin off my nose, but I did seriously think that if I did want to live in this country which, although it has its problems and has a long way to go, is not really as bad as a lot of other places, it's not fair to pick and choose which rules to obey. Otherwise the whole thing breaks down and places are run by horrible people as happens in Marseilles and New York where no one gives a flying shit about the rest of the world.'

The final decision to quit the 'import–export' business was made for Will by the Other Firm. 'When I came back to this country once after a trip all the others had been arrested. After that I couldn't go home so we had to abandon our flat and never go back. My wife went back in the middle of the night once and a lot of our things had been gone through, although I don't know whether anyone had been there or whether the landlord was just wondering what had happened to his rent.'

The others were not so lucky and most were jailed, where initially they have to remain in quarantine as far as their colleagues still on the outside are concerned. 'No one will go near anyone who's been arrested or touch them until the trial is all over.'

And prison sliced through the relationships of the dealers probably more thoroughly than those of the old-style criminal whose family were brought up to regard it as an occupational hazard.

'Clink always screws up families. People come out of prison very strange animals. They didn't see other people very much because they didn't want to share cells with young burglars. Everyone who got into that sort of trouble ended up splitting up with their wives and losing contact with their kids. Inside, they were treated differently. They were slightly looked up to. They could put a letter together and they were in a very moneyed business so they got some respect. But one of them, when he first came out, for a long time couldn't go through a door – he would go and stand at the door and wait for someone to open it for him. They become very fastidious about cleanliness.'

While the others were inside Will was despatched to deal with unfinished business in America.

'I was told to go to the States and explore an investment that some unspent money could be put to. I met the guy, the lieutenant, who was in the CIA. They live a very different life. They bounce you around in first class hotels and you think you're just about to crash out in your room and there's a knock on the door and the most beautiful woman you have ever seen in your life is there. This is your present for the night. I didn't know how to handle it. The first night I flew to Miami and I went to this hotel and there was a knock on my door. I was very tired and jetlagged and I was falling asleep and she said she would go out and get some food. I fell into a deep sleep and when I woke up there was "You Asshole" scrawled on the door in tomato ketchup. She'd been to a pizza place and all this Italian food was floating in the swimming pool. The next day there was a message that I had to go to California so I had to take off and then the same kind of thing happened.

'America has always frightened me a bit. I remember some of the people there had a ranch they could go to and they used to do daft things there – drive motorised sledges and put Rolls Royces into swimming pools because in town these guys had to act very serious to blend in.'

Now with nothing stronger than a cup of tea and a roll-up, Will contemplates the drug laws. 'Marijuana and hashish are not like the other drugs, they're not addictive, they might be habit forming if anything can become habit forming. It's not really the kind of thing that people take and then go to football matches and get out of their crust. They should decriminalise it because there would be so many less criminals and you wouldn't have guys going to those flats in Battersea and Tottenham coming into contact with white powders.'

However, there is little chance of that, he says, in the current climate. 'The press on drugs are completely inaccurate, you get much more sense in the police's own magazines. And no books have captured it – because the reality is not really worth bloody writing about: sitting in a hotel room for ten days waiting for a telephone call that doesn't come until the ninth.'

But Will got lucky and got out. Many of his contemporaries were to fall foul of the Other Team – or the other kind of grass.

10

The Grass

You couldn't make mistakes
when you trusted nobody.

Graham Greene, *Brighton Rock*

'I have been to bed with literally hundreds of women and I could call five hundred into this court to testify to that fact. I have also had dozens of jobs of a masculine nature. I cannot bear men touching me. My crimes, I know, have got progressively more serious, ending up with armed robbery. I would interpet that as an attempt – or at least a subconscious attempt – to regain my manhood.'

Tony Wild was giving evidence in the murder trial of Reg Dudley and Bob Maynard, sitting as cool as a lager commercial in Court One of the Old Bailey, sucking on a wine gum and deconstructing his sexual history for the benefit of Justice Swanwick.

He had arrived in court with a close escort of plain clothes policemen. He had already given evidence against former colleagues who were on armed robbery charges, assisting in putting them away for dozens of years, was offering to inform on Ulster Volunteer Force men he had met inside prison and was now about to play his part in the Torso Murder trial.

Tony Wild was a grass, a super one.

He was not like some supergrasses giving evidence in court; studiously avoiding catching the eye of their old compadres, hissing the evidence out through gritted teeth, a justification of it-was-them-or-me scrawled in furrows across the forehead. Wild gave evidence as if he were eating an ice cream: he lolled, he smiled, he joked, he beamed. He was in complete control.

'May I sit down, my lord,' he asked Justice Swanwick. 'I have a fissure on my anus.'

He was born in Sussex in 1946. His father died while he was a baby and his mother remarried. He did not get on with his stepfather and left home at the age of fifteen to become a boy soldier. He did not like the routine or the discipline and after six months high-tailed it to London.

He was a good looking boy and, he says, was approached by three homosexual men who, after pursuing him, raped him. He contracted syphilis and suffered the fissure that was to discomfort him for the next twenty years. But, as Wild saw it, the major effect of the rape was not physical; it was to make him prove his masculinity to himself. He became a farm worker and a labourer, seeking out the heaviest of building-site jobs. The next logical step, the most macho profession open, was clearly crime.

At sixteen he started his apprenticeship: theft, in Dover. A few months later he was caught shoplifting in Walsham. Then stealing cars in his home town of Littlehampton. The litany was familiar.

An office job led him to steal some of the money with which he had been entrusted. By 1967 he was shop-breaking. There were fines, spells on probation, then Borstal. A term in Grendon Underwood, which specialises in prisoners who suffer from disorders, followed. Outside he found work on a farm but not for long. Dishonest handling, criminal deception, shortening the barrel of a shotgun indicated that he was not about to become the leading light of the local Young Farmers Club.

Not that he was at that stage a cocky soul. He appeared 'suicidal' to the matron at Lewes prison. He told police who interviewed him that he was considering going on a hunger strike but had 'heard it was an unpleasant way to die'.

Outside once more he joined his brother-in-law's window-cleaning business and 'window-cleaner' was how he described himself when he was next pulled in. A more accurate description at this time would have been 'armed robber'.

He and his friends now robbed Securicor vans, stores, and cashiers with industrious regularity. In two months they carried out six raids and netted £65,000, hitting the London suburbs of Ruislip, Croydon, Redhill and Uxbridge. Then they hit London. Lining up terrified commuters against the wall at Kings Cross underground station, they made off with £6,000 from the ticket office.

The money didn't go far. He gambled at the Golden Nugget club off Piccadilly Circus. He liked to drink at the Inn on the Park and the Hilton Hotel. He loved gold chains and jewellery and treated himself to a £1,200 fur coat. One of his fellow-robbers remembered that he liked to hang out in a coffee bar in Hampstead and write what he called poetry – his friends knew he was talking cobblers because it didn't even rhyme. His last address before he was arrested was the Kensington Palace Hotel.

In February 1976, Wild and two accomplices held up a Securicor van outside Sainsbury's and robbed it of £7,274. They sped off in their Ford but were pursued by the Securicor men. Wild and his companions turned and fired at them, Wild letting off two barrels of a shotgun.

'I think my eyes must have been closed, for when I looked up I saw bullet holes appearing in the windscreen,' he said later. He escaped separately in his Volvo, which had been parked nearby, and he headed off for the Brighton road, sideswiped a roundabout and crashed into another. He jumped out. He ran across a field. His luck ran out. He was captured ten minutes later hiding under a bush.

When he was first caught he was not contrite, according to the police evidence which recorded him thus: 'Look I'm pissed off. That cunt of a security officer, chasing us with his van – he ought to have more thought for his wife and children. He must be some fucking idiot. He's just paid to deliver the money.'

Jebb Avenue in Lambeth, the ugly, noisy, fume-filled thoroughfare that leads to Brixton Prison was Anthony Wild's Damascus Road.

'When you're lying in bed in your cell and you're thinking about facing twenty years inside, you damn well wonder how you got there in the first place,' he told the Old Bailey court. 'I realised there was something in my mentality, something that made Anthony Wild different from these animals, from people who laughed at the killing of a man.'

And very soon there was something different about Anthony Wild. He had become a police informer. The deal was, as always, a shorter sentence. Five years for Wild compared with eighteen for Tony Cook, the gregarious fellow-robber who had been caught with him.

He was not going to be one of those pushy grasses though, not like the ones who ended up in the papers, having a good time in a police cell and taking advantage of the people who want to keep them sweet. 'I don't want a telly, police discount on clothes, carpet, or any facilities not accorded to me by normal remand regulation!' he said in a jovial postscript to the police as he outlined how he could help them.

But if the police were keeping an eye on Wild, so were other services in Brixton.

'This man has an intelligence in the upper average range which has apparently been unrequited in his choice of lifestyle,' wrote the principal medical officer at the prison. 'He tries to impress upon me his lifestyle was not a choice but that it was the product of the instability of his early environment and his feelings about his homosexual rape during his formative years . . . He has an impressionable, a notively labile and introverted personality, sensitive to adversity in his environment, and engendering periods of depression reactive only to adversity in his life. He over-compensates all these depressive feelings of inadequacy by drinking heavily on occasions and succumbing to suggestion by his criminal fraternity that he has got to know so well. He appears to be considerably over-indulgent in alcohol, cigarette smoking and sexual activity.'

But during what he had hoped would be his last spell inside in Brixton he was more concerned with keeping his diary and helping to put away criminals. Or so he told the court.

He started chatting to another inmate, a publican called Oliver Kenny, an old friend of Reg Dudley, who was also in Brixton awaiting trial for the murders of Micky Cornwall and Billy Moseley. Kenny was awaiting trial on an eleven-year-old offence of 'tom' – false jewellery.

At this stage the letters from Wild to the police appear to indicate that they weren't too interested in what he was passing them and indeed most of it was gossip, hearsay, or so vague as to be of little use in the witness box. So a couple of weeks after he had written up his last diary of his chats with 'Jolly Olly' he was striking a plaintive note in his letter to the police: 'Although I have passed on information that I believe would be useful to your inquiries, I have received from your office not even an acknowledgement of the receipt of my letters let alone a routine questioning as to the validity of their content. Perhaps you feel that I am trying to work a ticket or something.'

So he offered something a little tastier. He had now met Dudley. The police were anxious for evidence against Dudley. Things were moving.

Wild wrote to the man heading the murder investigation, Commander Wickstead: 'I hope you will appreciate that I have been very forthright in this letter and that in itself will indicate to you that I have other more serious matters to impart to you.' He had found that his memory was getting sharper. He wrote to the police again: 'By making statements to your officers I find that at night when I return to Brixton that I am able to recall events more vividly as I try to reconstruct the early days of my remand at Brixton.'

His statements to the police give a neat example of how an informer operates.

'I started a bit of name-dropping,' he records as he mentions a number of north London 'faces'. He notes his quarry's moods: 'He seems to be rather a chameleon – he changes his pattern of speech frequently according to the response of myself, also his ideas seem to change, i.e. he was mentioning some of the stunts the knocker boys use and when I showed disapproval he would say quickly that he didn't like it but when I said I like the knocker fraternity he'd quickly perk up and launch into a massive campaign of naming their finer qualities! . . . I then went on to say "I've generally found that villains – I don't mean pickpockets and burglars – but villains are very pleasant company, gentlemen a lot of them."'

But gentlemen do not grass. Or at least they tended not to when Wild first went 'talk and walk' in 1976. Wild came into the grassing business around four years after it had started and was there during its boom years.

Bertie Smalls, a very major bank robber, had been arrested in 1972. In exchange for evidence against his former colleagues he was granted written immunity by the Director of Public Prosecutions and Scotland Yard. As a result of his evidence twenty-seven London bank robbers went away for a total of 315 years.

The next major informer was Maurice O'Mahoney, a twenty-eight-year-old armed robber at the time of his arrest. He helped to have twenty of his former associates jailed, thanks to a terrific memory for dates and details that coincided with the police case against the men. He was jailed for five years instead of the twenty he would probably have got if he had not been so cooperative. He spent most of his time in the cells in Chiswick police station where he was given 'certain facilities' to make confinement more bearable. His score was impressive, if not as big as Smalls' – twenty were convicted out of a hundred against whom he had informed.

But O'Mahoney's success in the expanding business of supergrassing was soon overshadowed by Charlie Lowe. He admitted to eighty-seven burglaries and robberies. He started talking and dozens of his former colleagues were arrested. By 1978 informing had reached epic proportions. Suddenly the police had a highly effective way of sending down criminals who had evaded capture for years because no one could prove for certain that they had committed the crime; if the police brought into the witness box a man who said he had been there and so had the two defendants in the dock, most juries were inclined to convict.

Leroy Davies, James Trusty, Billy Williams, Edward Martin, Billy Young, Keith Warne, Ronald Simpson, George Williams, Christopher Wren, Micky 'Skinny' Gervaise, Roger Denhardt, John McCabe followed in the procession, their names occasionally graffitied in the latrines at Brixton Prison or in the police cells – too late a warning for most of their former colleagues.

One of the most prolific was Roy Garner, a former night-club owner who worked as a supergrass for more than ten years before becoming unstuck on a large deal and being jailed for twenty-two years despite being described by the police as having 'achieved successes in the war against major criminals far in excess of any informant in the history of the Metropolitan Police'. Garner came to prominence because of his association with former Detective Superintendent Tony Lundy, who retired from the Yard in 1988 on health grounds, following a series of internal inquiries into his methods and allegations of improprieties. Nicknamed 'Top Man' by his colleagues, Lundy claimed that he was the victim of a smear campaign coordinated by criminals and a group of journalists, and said he had helped jail 300 top criminals for more than 3,000 years because of the way he worked his grasses.

The formula for the informer was simple: remission from the sentence or a smaller sentence to start with; sometimes a new identity – Lowe received a new face under plastic surgery; and a secure wing in prison if they had to spend time inside. They usually ended up along with other grasses, with 'nonces' – the sex-offenders who are a normal target of other prisoners – and ex-policemen in for corruption. Having served their sentence, some informers just disappeared from view, others poked their heads up again. One grass had not only pleaded guilty to fifty-seven robberies but had killed a man; he was charged with manslaughter rather than murder.

O'Mahoney, having unburdened himself to the law and in print, was less than happy with the treatment he had received from the police. He phoned up a reporter at the *Guardian* and told him, in language which seemed to indicate he'd been reading too many headlines about himself, 'I've risked my life giving the police information. Now they've dropped me flat. The canary that fell from his cage . . . suddenly the armed coppers who had been looking after me disappeared and last week I was told I was not getting any more money from a special fund and that I should go and look for a job. I might as well commit suicide as expose myself like that . . . I'm running scared and in fear of my life every second of the day.

They've fed me all this bullshit about helping society, got all they could out of me, then shit on me.'

When it was suggested in *Time Out* magazine that one of the people he gave evidence against was someone he had a grudge against because he had removed O'Mahoney's trousers when the latter was a shy youth, he was less defensive. He phoned up and threatened a knee-capping.

One grass, Alan White, did not get the opportunity to explain his case. His body was found wrapped in a tarpaulin and dumped in a lake in the Cotswolds in 1989. He had been given a 'panic button', linking his supposedly 'safe house' with Stroud police station, but apparently never got an opportunity to use it.

What puzzled criminals most was that the 'staunchest' people seemed to be informing. And what also became clear was that, far from having contracts taken out on them and the backs of their heads blown off, most grasses could slip quite happily back into the world, maybe moving just a few miles out of their old stamping grounds.

Soon Roger Denhardt, a top armed robber who had assured friends in Brixton that he would never, ever, ever inform joined the list. So did John Moriarty. He was a big, popular man known as The Target because he had been hit so many times. When I arranged to meet him for the first time to talk to him, well before he had become an informer, I asked how I would recognise him. He said, 'You'll know me.' I waited in a pub in Highgate Village. Sure enough a presence walked in. He was an outgoing soul. He explained how he took *The Times* regularly for the deaths column: if someone had died their house might be empty and susceptible to a tickle . . .

But he, like many others, made the calculation that being outside as a blackballed member of the old club was preferable to spending your life inside. Anthony Wild certainly thought so.

In his statement, he had told the police, 'It's almost a relief to be in the police cell and get it all off my plate. I am caught and am going to spend a long time in prison. When I come out I want only to spend the rest of my life quietly with those I love.'

To this end Wild continued informing. He suggested that Reg Dudley had boasted about killing Micky Cornwall saying, 'He went up in the fucking air, didn't he, boys?' Bob Maynard, he said, had remarked, 'I didn't know guys would squeal like a pig.' He said that Dudley had told him, 'We're Murder Incorporated' – one of the names, along with Legal and General, attributed to the people arrested.

Reg Dudley's own recollection of Wild is a bit different. 'We thought he was a poof and a bit odd.' The idea of him admitting to anything in front of a weird stranger – even if it had been true – was laughable, he said. He knew only too well of the practice of putting would-be informers in with remand prisoners.

But Wild was not deterred. Of Dudley, he said: 'He mentioned the Horse and Groom [the pub run in Brighton by Olly Kenny] and . . . he told me had taken a head to the Horse and Groom in a bag and shown it to the publican. He said the bloke nearly died when he saw it.' (Another account of this event had Dudley saying, 'I hear your beer doesn't have much of a head on it so I've brought one along.')

The big stage was waiting for Wild. At the Old Bailey, his former pay-roll-grabbing colleagues went down, with his assistance, for a total of nearly sixty years, then he returned to give evidence against Dudley, Maynard and the others.

He arrived like a star at a premiere. He carried a copy of Archbold, the legal bible, with him for reference and when Justice Swanwick told him to 'get on with it', he did.

'I think I have discovered why I am like I am – in the search for meat you have to eat bread and in the search for myself I had to continue to be the self I was.'

'Can you try and be less colourful?' Maynard's barrister, Felix Waley, asked him. Wild gave as good as he got. When Waley asked him if he was eating something he replied, 'I am eating wine gums. Like all the jury, all the defendants and half the police in court. Can I carry on?'

The defence barristers suggested that the accused had avoided him because they thought he was a homosexual.

'I am not, I have never been and I do not intend to be a homosexual. I could bring five hundred women here to testify to that . . . Do I look like one? Get stuffed.'

Dudley's barrister, Michael West, also cross-examined him and took issue with the way he conducted himself in court.

'Must you loll like that in the witness box?'

'Yes. Must you loll like that when questioning?'

'Your evidence is vital. Everything else is worthless and so are you.'

'Yes, yes, I'm a mad egotistical homosexual terrorist who wants to fit up these innocent people. Write it down.'

The beleaguered shorthand writer did so, along with hundreds of thousands of other words during the six-month trial. Maynard and Dudley were convicted. Wild, it appeared, was vindicated. He spent his time quietly inside. Within three years he was out. He moved back to Hove.

Graham Maclagan, a BBC radio reporter, has a vintage juke-box in his home, a collector's piece. One of the tunes on it is 'Whispering Grass' by the Inkspots, the song that some theories suggest gave us the word 'grass' for informer. (Other theories have it that 'grass' is the shortened rhyming slang word 'grasshopper' – shopper; a third is that the old Bow Street runners used to have billowing coats that made them look like grasshoppers.) He was also interested in the story of Wild. Having found out where Wild now stayed and knowing I had followed the case, he asked me if I wanted to go down there to see him.

On 19 August 1980 we set off for Hove. We were going to be late so we stopped on the motorway on the way down and phoned Wild. He asked for the registration number of the car. Partly this was to find out if Graham was bona fide – a villain might have stolen the car and forgotten the registration; and it was partly so that he could have the car checked out by his police contact so that he could find out if it did indeed belong to a Graham Maclagan of the BBC. We arrived in the early evening at his home in Hove. After checking to see if we were 'miked up', he directed us to a pub, just past the level-crossing.

Wild drank sweet martinis and lemonade and smoked rolled-up cigarettes in Gauloise paper. He said he was living with his parents and helping out with the security side of a firm that sold soft toys. He was curious as to how we had found his address.

We started off by talking about completely different cases. It was Wild himself who brought the subject round to the torso case. He said he had evidence which could get three men out of prison on something very serious which he couldn't talk about.

'I don't want to go near the centre,' he said. He talked about corruption but he said he had not been fitted up and most fit-ups were criminals getting their just desserts.

He said he had been presented with a version of events by the police and had agreed to give evidence on this version. So what about that famous evidence about the severed head? 'I made it up.'

He went on to say that telling the truth now meant there was nothing in it for him. 'You could put £50,000 on the table and it wouldn't make any difference.' He had all the money he needed and if he gave evidence for Dudley he would still have the villains to fear and the police would soon see him back in prison. He often referred to himself in the third person and laughed in a very exaggerated fashion. At the end of our two-hour conversation Maclagan and I headed back into London, dropping Wild off en route.

I made my notes and wrote an article for *Time Out* about it all. Following the appearance of the article, lawyers acting for Dudley and Maynard put forward Wild's allegations as new evidence and called for the case to be reopened. I was interviewed by the Serious Crimes Squad and made a statement saying what Wild had told us. By now, the man who wanted to spend the rest of his life with the people he loved was back with the people who loved him least – in Maidstone Prison. He had been arrested for another armed robbery. He was interviewed by the police but denied making the remarks to us.

A letter arrived.

Dear Mr Cambell,
My attention was called to your recent article in *Time Out* which I subsequently read with great interest.

The 'lay reader' of your articles might be persuaded to believe that you are the champion of the oppressed – your articles on supergrasses, R. Barron and myself. What is hidden from them is the link between your strident scribblings – a person with greater knowledge might, perhaps, with not too great a stretch of the imagination believe that you are on an 'earner' from certain interested parties.

Your magazine has a certain reputation for being anti-authority – no doubt it is an image that is sanctioned, if not encouraged in the editorial committee. However, in respect to the article that you wrote about myself I can say not only was it outrageous but it over stepped the line where one can make any sort of detailed criticism – you will surely understand what I am saying.

Good luck with your future 'investigator' journalism. I'm sure that your readers will be looking forward to some more exciting revelations from the champion of the oppressed. Personally I've never much been interested in fiction – reality may be that more boring but that is only my personal opinion and preference.

A. Wild.

His letter was passed to the solicitor who had taken over Bob Maynard's case for appeal, a man chosen for his reputation to win cases against improbable odds.

The Solicitor

Justice must not only be done, it
must be seen to be believed.

J. B. Morton, 'Beachcomber'

'It is like being in the company of larger than life figures. There's lots of money around, someone suddenly says, "Let's go to Brighton and have breakfast on the beach," and it's superficially a very attractive and dynamic way of living, at least in small doses.'

Physically James Saunders is slightly smaller than life as far as hundreds of these larger than life gentlemen – men accused of armed robbery, conspiracy, grievous bodily harm – are concerned, but there are few people they would rather have breakfast with on Brighton beach. For a start, he might save them a stretch in prison.

James Saunders is a solicitor. For about the last fifteen years he has been one of London's most sought-after criminal lawyers. He is not chosen because he has an in with the police, or because he is very expensive and therefore must be good, or even because he has a very old practice that's handy for lunch at the Wig and Pen. James Saunders' firm gets the phone calls because, quite simply, his clients believe they have a better chance of being acquitted in his hands and if they are not they will know that it was not because he couldn't be bothered or didn't want to rock the legal boat.

He is a small, droll man with glasses. He lives in a flat that he designed himself up in Ladbroke Grove. He drives a car that some of his clients wouldn't mind doing a burn-up in and he would eventually like to go off and just grow apples in the west country. Quite a few policemen would like him to go off and start growing apples right now. He has had a high success rate in winning acquittals for his clients on major charges, not a few of them involving the challenging of police evidence.

'I have been aware of the dangers of a criminal lawyer being associated socially with serious practising criminals and by and large I've gone out of my way to avoid it because I know that I attract a certain amount of attention and I know that it would be considered fabulous fun in certain circles of the Metropolitan police to compromise me, or worse. So I can't approach it in the way that, say, John Small-Villain might if he was invited into the company of larger villains.

'It has its sordid side as well. One sees quite a lot of death and desperation, kids brought up in a truly appalling fashion. It's superficially glamorous but below the surface quite a lot less so.'

But is there still a certain fascination in it?

'If I have developed a fascination for it, which I don't think I have, it developed from being persona grata in circles that I have previously regarded as being the dark side of the moon, something you occasionally read about in the Sunday newspapers. To be suddenly admitted to a circle which you regarded as, perhaps, very interesting but a million miles away is almost flattering and certainly is interesting. Frankly, I'm not really interested in the social side at all.

'There are odd people who, because of their immense charisma, I have associated with in fairly controlled situations. But, by and large, going down to the GBH Club and getting glassed and bombed with the lads is not a great objective in life. But as a working criminal lawyer you actually see quite a lot of what's going on. Not that you're not told a lot of lies, but obviously you learn to be reasonably efficient at working out where the truth and the lies are.'

Saunders grew up in Sheffield, a teacher's son, in a world where crime did not loom large. At Leicester University in the late sixties he studied law and learnt a few other lessons that were not on the curriculum.

'We all thought that student representation on the senate was a good idea. The authorities were appalled at the prospect of the consumer being involved in determining the nature of the product.' There was a sit-in at the administration building. 'We were attacked by seventy-two-year-old professors of classics wielding walking sticks.' The police arrived. 'I was politicised. Before that I was a wimp. Probably still am!'

It gave him a taste for a certain kind of confrontation.

'The real fascination of criminal law is that you get a big case with important issues and the evidence is that which determines which way this crucial vote is going to be taken. To be able to influence that by addressing scientific procedures to evidence, preparing cross-examination, researching people's characters and to be able to influence the outcome of something that is going to be reported widely in the papers – that is what it's all about.'

Had the young Saunders dreamed of a legal career?

'All the best criminal lawyers never intended to be lawyers and when they fell into the law they never intended to be criminal lawyers. Anyone who really wants to be Rumpole of the Bailey and sits there at the age of nine thinking, "I'll do that rather than drive a fire engine", is going to be a disaster. I'm only a solicitor because at the A level stage I decided I didn't want to continue with science and there was only one topic you could then study at university if you were a scientist who didn't want to read science, and that was law. I was very happy because it was so easy. After differential calculus, to have something that was very understandable, that you could live, was wonderful – so I immediately took to heavy drinking to celebrate.'

He qualified in 1972, after three years at university, two years in articles and six months at a 'legal finishing school'. 'I was interested in things outside the law and got into it entirely by chance so what I decided to do as a lawyer wasn't particularly related to any legal interest. Things were happening in criminal law, I enjoyed the thrill of the chase, thought the police were a jolly good enemy and could sleep lightly without worrying about whether I'd done the right thing by bashing them over the head and some, far from all, criminal defendants were very interesting people to be associated with in a work context. When I started it was local practice. Then I got known and was offered much larger work amongst heavy duty professional criminals.'

Why had he chosen criminal defence work?

'Lawyers who prosecute are a totally different breed. Motivation, attitude to life is completely different, which is not to say I regard all of them as failures or scum of the earth but it's a completely different activity.'

On one level, the job is straightforward: the arrested person approaches the solicitor, having been given the name by a friend or heard it on the grapevine. A meeting is arranged, either in police custody, prison, or in the solicitor's office if the arrested person has been granted bail. The accused then runs through his case to a solicitor's clerk. The clerk makes a detailed note for the solicitor. The solicitor discusses the options with the accused and a defence strategy is decided. A barrister, probably recommended by the solicitor, is contacted and hired. Witnesses and further evidence are sought, usually by the solicitor's clerk, an often undervalued soul in the legal process, who – if he or she is smart and conscientious – can sometimes swing a case by spotting gaps in the prosecution. As the trial approaches, the solicitor will arrange for the barrister and the accused to meet. When the trial starts, the solicitor is usually there – if it is a major case – for the opening and will then leave the clerk to keep watch until the closing speeches. There is the daily administration – 'I'm responsible for about 1,000 criminal cases at any one time and if you miss one you're taken out and shot' – which is less glamorous but vital. The families of the accused often use the solicitor like a doctor – 'Is he going to be all right?' – and usually with the same mixture of anxiety and deference.

In London there are probably nine or ten firms known for their expertise in serious criminal cases, scattered between a couple of west London practices, of which Saunders and Co. are one, a few in north London, a group in the East End and some long-standing south London firms. Poaching of the best criminal solicitors goes on. (There are a couple of other firms who are known for doing deals, either through policemen or ex-policemen, on behalf of their clients. They may have former, sometimes disgraced, officers working for them. One such firm recently saw one of its partners jailed. Some criminals, against whom the evidence is overwhelming, choose these firms as a last resort.)

The choice of barrister is reckoned as critical. 'Obviously the solicitor has chosen the bloke or lady because they would be good on the job. They've told the client that. The client's nervous so they've told him again. They have a conference and all goes well.'

Saunders is sanguine about the fact that quite often the barrister chosen is unable to take on the case at the last minute.

'You then come very close to the moment of truth which for the poor sod on trial is the difference between freedom and ten, fifteen, life, whatever it may be. And then someone says, "Oh, by the way, the bloke who was going to cut out your heart – hold the blood vessels while we get another one and put this other heart in – the man in whom you had confidence that you might live is busy in Newcastle on a seriously contested double parking but we've got this wonderful bloke called Joe Stranger and he'll do just as well." Or maybe you don't say it with lots of enthusiasm because you don't believe it.'

Which means that on occasions the accused would rather stay in prison than set off to bat with an opening partner he doesn't trust not to run him out.

'It's not altogether surprising that defendants sometimes feel it might be sensible in the short term to have a little hardship waiting in prison and delaying their trial to get the person that they have identified as most likely to secure their release. Beyond that there are a very small number of barristers around whom a certain mystique has arisen and, of course, they're always incredibly busy so the chances of an ordinary villain getting that person on the day are quite remote. I totally empathise with the client.

'In one case early in my career a good barrister that we had instructed said, "I've got too much on and I heartily recommend Ms X," who I didn't find out till very much later he was giving the treatment to on a nightly basis. She was absolutely dreadful. As the magistrate said, "But for the persistent questioning of your counsel the prosecution would have been unable to establish the crucial elements which they needed to have you found guilty. However in my view she elicited the missing elements and I'm left with no alternative but to convict you." What can I say?

'I have a rule that if a brief is returned by a barrister we will go to another set of barristers' chambers. It's a disincentive which I've adopted to barristers and barristers' clerks returning work. I know it sometimes happens for completely unavoidable reasons but I haven't the slightest doubt that there are some cynical bastard clerks who take on far more work than Mr Smith can handle any year on the basis that they'll let it run till desperation time, then say, "Mr Smith can't do it but we have got this complete drongo who is happy to stand in." As far as I'm concerned it's important that these people know that if they return the brief late it will not go to other people in their chambers. We have murders with barristers' chambers. Some of my better moments are listening to members of my staff sticking it to barristers' clerks when they phone up to smooth over these terrible things. They, by and large, couldn't care less about the individuals concerned, they've never met them, they're on ten per cent of whatever, but they're in total control. Warfare between solicitors and barristers' clerks would be an interesting sociological topic.'

His office is in Harrow Road but his work takes him to the various strange examples of British judicial architecture that are our courts.

'The Magistrates' Courts, which used to be really rather similar to abattoirs, these glazed tiles almost with channels for blood to run out, have now been replaced with large, extremely shoddy modern buildings so we operate in a superficially less Dickensian environment. And in Crown Courts that's happened to some extent too.

'Fundamentally what's happened in court hasn't changed so much. The characters are pretty much the same. The magistrates are gentlemen of the right pretending to be in the middle. The judges are, by and large, chappies and ladies from the right pretending to be only slightly to the right and juries are as bemused as ever.'

In the seventies and early eighties, James Saunders' clients were involved in a lot of cases in which the police were alleged to have made up confessions or near confessions – known as 'verballing' – for the people they had arrested. Many of the cases were thrown out by the juries.

'Verballing is still with us, although with more tape-recording of interviews in police stations it is less so. The police always take this very personally. A lot see themselves as being involved in a crusade of one kind or another. When they've got a target there's both emotional pressure on them to make it a good 'un and also executive pressure. Every month a committee of wise policemen sit down and decide who's going to be the target for next month. Squads are set up, DSs and DCs are briefed: this person is a terrible human being, he's committed this appalling crime and we've got to stop it. So they spend endless dull hours in Ford Sierras watching and waiting and ferreting around, extremely dull. Then there's this cataclysmic moment when the governor says, "Go!" If you don't bring home the bacon, what have you been doing? You've spent two months of your life smoking yourself to death, eating fish and chips, sleeping at three in the afternoon and being up at three in the morning. So the temptation to top it up is overwhelming.

'Oddly enough that's how they usually lose the case. They've usually got enough straight evidence on the videos, bits and bobs, to send them down. They then verbal them up. They don't quite get it right. That comes out in front of the jury and the jury decides that if the police were lying about what was said in the police station they can't be relied on to be telling the truth on anything else. Many's the time when impossible cases have been won because a verbal was exposed.'

The police suggest, though, that many a time an impossible case has been won because the jury has been nobbled, one or two of its members offered a bob or two to insist on a not guilty verdict until the others agree or weary.

'The jury nobbling stories are, by and large, police being bad losers. It's not a significant factor. As regards the dear old jury, it has as its most significant component what I call the x factor. Neither side really knows how it is going to work out. I see no more consistency or direction in jury results now than I ever have done.'

But Snaresbrook and, to a lesser extent, the Old Bailey have reputations of returning perverse not guilty verdicts which, suggests the police, shows that either there has been a spot of nobbling or the pool from which the jurors are drawn is hopelessly polluted with people who have fallen foul of the police in the past and who acquit on the basis of criminal solidarity.

'Snaresbrook and the Bailey, by virtue of the geographical areas from which jurors are drawn, are slightly more prevalent to acquittal. I would resent the suggestion that an acquittal is in some way a sinister event. It is for the prosecution to prove their case. If they can't do that to the satisfaction of twelve streetwise people drawn at random from Snaresbrook's catchment area then so be it. Certainly no reason to believe that the inhabitants of Snaresbrook are systematically corrupted by gangs of blokes with loads of money preparing them generally for jury service.'

Saunders has seen many people acquitted but probably many more go down. Is he affected by it?

'Very rarely now am I affected by a verdict. I've always tended a bit to the cynical and perhaps the criminal law concretises any instincts you might have in that direction. Also the fact that when it's happened to you a few times and people you like have gone down for ever, rightly or wrongly, you know that if you're going to continue as a practising criminal lawyer you'd better smarten yourself up. Because you can't do your job if the wrong result is going to be a major problem for you.

'You have to see it as a game. Any criminal lawyer who doesn't ultimately see it as a game is going to have personal problems. There are a few people who've gone down that I've felt quite sad about but you protect yourself.'

And the style of criminality has changed.

'The day of the large flash criminal group wandering around doing its business and everyone being in fear and admiration or whatever has by and large gone. The "omerta" principle [the Mafia rule of silence] has been destroyed by the supergrasses grassing and then the same supergrasses turning up at the Old Bull and Bush and no one shoots their legs off. It's perfectly obvious now that working in large groups is not a very clever way of being a criminal. The emphasis on heavy crime has moved away from big men with guns going after large lumps of cash.

'As regards gangland, take the Tibbses, for instance, who were nicked and sent down. The usual apparatus of the press invoked the idea that they were part of gangland which was ridiculous. It's just that there were a number of brothers who would stand up together and were quite photogenic and stupid enough, if they'll forgive me for saying so, to oblige the police and the press with the image that was required.

'The real gangland I've no doubt does exist but the successful gangland isn't chappies wandering around blasting away at things in pubs. Things are much subtler. That isn't the way to make money. It's the way to get the murder squad on your tail, the regional crime squad following you around. The real gangland is people who trade away in very dubious areas, and do fairly terrible things in moral terms. When someone complains too bitterly they go down somewhere, hand over a few thousand pounds and some mysterious figure comes along and does something terrible to the problem. The Krays were fairly unique. They were bound to fall because of the noise they made. But it was probably true that they could field more armed men in half an hour than the Metropolitan police.

'At any one time there are about 200 heavy-duty professional criminals in London. They go round about ten or fifteen clubs massaging each others' egos either by the conventional process of flattery or the less conventional process of shooting at each other. Some make some money and have a good time for quite a short period of time; most of them don't. To call them mugs would not be very fair but they are not the people who make the money. What are the criteria of success? We quite often deal for people who are fingered for this that or the other and as soon as the shout goes up they're over in Spain or Costa Rica or Brazil or wherever it may be. Almost invariably, within a comparatively short period of time, they come back to England. They don't need to for any objective reason but they can't live without the smell of drains, fish and chips and the taste of Watney's. These are the people for whom success is when they walk into a club everyone stands to one side, flatters them and allows them to buy a drink for everyone. Undoubtedly that is one of the major reasons for them to do what they do.'

And that is enough to risk fifteen years in establishments where all you can buy for people is a round of cocoas?

'There is also the excitement of robbing a bank, being out there on the pavement with a gun, the thought that D11 might be up on the rooftops about to shoot them. It is a slice of activity. Who am I to say that that is not the real gangland as against blokes who wear blue suits, drive around in quite expensive cars, deal more with accountants than contract killers and have enormous lumps in the Cayman Islands or Switzerland? It's a question of perception.'

Often the solicitor has to deal at length with the wife or girlfriend, since she is the one on the outside, trying to contact alibi or character witnesses, arranging the fees if the case is not on legal aid, trying to do the right thing by her man. But how often do women appear as defendants?

'In the vice end, dope dealing, obviously prostitution, human weakness, women are represented too. They are a bit like lady barristers, in that because they're a bit out of place in a traditionally male world they feel this terrible urge to be larger than life, more butch than their male counterparts. By and large they are used for carrying, looking after the more menial tasks. The women involved tend to identify themselves as the junior partners in the enterprise. I am struck with the image of prison visiting rooms with serried ranks of bottle blondes in fabulous finery with basketfulls of the finest food that could possibly be brought along for their man.

'One lady I remember from a case we did. The blokes went down for very long sentences and one has just come out. Lady stuck with him all the way through it. The day he was released she said something she'd been meaning to say for a very long time which was – "I've seen you all the way through it. You needed me to this point. Now I don't want to see you. I want to live my own life and you can bugger off and make your own life." I was extremely impressed in an odd sort of way by that.'

Crime is becoming ever more violent, according to the Home Office statistics, which show non-violent crime receding, while the other increases by around ten per cent a year.

'Most violent crime isn't planned. You go to a certain club and you're Jack the Lad and you look at a girl, whatever it may be. If you continue in that lifestyle, one day it's going to happen. I'm very suspicious of these statistics that are trooped out to show we are in a more violent society. A domestic which generally ends up with more claret on the wall than the average gangland affair is generally regarded as one of those things so classification is a serious issue.

'Armed robbery has changed from being the domain of a smallish group of men well into their twenties and thirties into being something that much younger men do. They're very crude. They're very inexperienced and more people tend to get hurt. I would have thought that one of the influences behind that is the hopelessness of people in certain circumstances – that the way forward isn't very easy to see – although there are many people in desperate circumstances who don't go out robbing banks.

'It goes in families. I'm sure that's not for genetic reasons. There is an area where quite a lot of major and minor crime my firm deals with comes from. It's an extremely poor area, very few amenities, a very hard nick. There are a significant number of what we would call animals operating out of there. It is a very harsh environment. The clans stick together.

'I sometimes feel it is quite tribal. Tribes of police in their uniforms, in their chariots, villains actual or perceived in their uniforms. There is an element of ritual in it. That area accounts for four or five times, maybe even ten times the amount of crimes than other areas from which we draw our clients. I begin to see it as something to which you can attach observable causes. They're poor, there's no prospects, there's nothing happening. Kids are on the street, big families, without getting into sociological crap, there are lots of boys and girls so they form units which smaller families might not do. Crime is started at a very early age, under ten, and it's there just waiting for the opportunity.

'People steal because they have some combination of greed and need. Usually need is in there. Generally speaking, people commit acts of violence because they're drunk and they're in the wrong place at the wrong time. The great truths about crime are not to do with magnificent figures involved in events of great moment, they're generally to do with rather sad people who haven't really come from anywhere and aren't really going anywhere, that're just involved in the milieu.'

And that is attraction enough?

'Most people lead extremely dull lives and the mere thought that someone has been able to burst out of here, grab a bag of wonga and have a good time is a great encouragement. Read the *Daily Mirror*. Myrtle Smith from Hartlepool won £10,000 in a bingo competition and is now going to get herself senseless drunk and go out with a gigolo and go on Concorde, this seems to be what it's all about. Most people lead such bloody awful lives that to know that at least hypothetically there are those who escape is uplifting. All the high moral tone about the train robbers is fairly pathetic.'

While we are on the subject of morality, what does he think about the coverage of criminal cases in the press?

'The crime press are bastards down to a man. Almost invariably inaccurate in simple facts. It's almost a matter of considerable amazement that they cannot report things as they are, because by and large they seem to be just as interesting compared to how they're actually reported. Almost without exception they have an arrangement with police whereby they place their office in a pub, some suitable watering hole and they're fed with information that the police want disseminated. They organise for the account of important trials to be restricted to the prosecution speech, juicy bits of evidence, sex or violence, judge's remarks in weighing off. If someone's acquitted, unless it's really heavy jelly, all the public will know about it is that on Day One Mr Fotheringham-Fitheringham alleged that and that against the defendant, and that possibly the judge in his summing up said, "Without wishing to give the nod to a blind donkey there's more than a little truth in this." Then that's it. Silence. Not even the fact of the acquittal goes in the papers. Totally disreputable activity.

'It's nothing to do with the truth. The criminals have got no credibility so, as the law of libel is that you have to be reduced in the eyes of right-thinking members of society to get a libel award, the crime reporters can trash the defendant's character, however inaccurate they are.'

James Saunders may have plans of seeing in the next millennium from a vantage point under an apple tree, but where will his potential clients be and what will the new generation be doing?

'Some villains decided with considerable reluctance that sticking guns up people's noses was a dated activity and they were going to get popped. In those early days making money out of dope was so simple. You could have a few morons move large amounts of dope for you. The attrition level was an acceptable expense. The Drug Trafficking Offences Act had an effect because it doesn't attack just the money you made out of trafficking. So people have identified that fraud is a much better activity. VAT has been a wonderful game, slightly less so now. "Long firm" frauds, property scams. I wouldn't be at all surprised if the various subsidy arrangements available through the EEC were not a source of considerable benefit.

'If I was careers officer for thieves' kitchen, to the big boys I'd say, "Go into Europe, move sheep carcasses to and fro across a border and collect £25,000." Or, as the Italians have done, produce more olives and tomatoes than the the land is capable of and crush them and throw them away and claim the money for it. Or construction: an institution has its officers, you give them £10,000 and they think they're Jack the Lad, take them out to the big boys' clubs, give them Sharon for a couple of nights so they give you a contract to build X miles of motorway or X block of flats. You do a truly appalling job for nothing and collect all the money. Transport: you're paid on tickets for the number of loads you take off site, you come to an arrangement with a ticket issuer and he gives you three tickets for every one load and so on and so forth. That's the future.'

And in it, no doubt, will be a place for the sort of solicitor who wouldn't be averse to the occasional Eggs Benedict on Brighton's pebbly promenade before he briefs a rising young QC.

12

The Barrister

Trial: a formal inquiry designed
to prove and put upon the record
the blameless characters of
judges, advocates and jurors. In
order to effect this purpose it is
necessary to supply a contrast in
the person of one who is called
the defendant, the prisoner, or
the accused.

Ambrose Bierce, *The Enlarged
Devil's Dictionary*.

It is one of those extraordinary summer days when even British people wear
shorts and talk to strangers at bus stops. In Hans Crescent, Knightsbridge, Terry
Venables, the Tottenham Hotspurs manager is being joshed by the Harrods
doorman, probably about the main story on the *Evening Standard* sports page that
he is about to buy the English striker, Gary Lineker. Further down the Crescent,
bored chauffeurs sprawl in their Daimlers, waiting for their employers to emerge
from the Food Hall, idly listening to Christopher Martin-Jenkins describing a
mild English collapse in the First Test at Headingley. At Number One Hans
Crescent a middle-aged West Indian called Frank Crichlow is watching his
barrister plead on his behalf and hoping that he can convince the slightly weary
and sticky jury that he is not guilty of drugs trafficking offences that could send
him to prison for about six years.

The barrister is addressing all his remarks very specifically to the jury – six
men, six women, ten white, two black. One of the men has a remarkable Abe
Lincoln beard, one of the women is distressed by the heat, now in the eighties
outside. He is taking them slowly through the evidence of the case against Frank
Crichlow, detailing how sixty or seventy police raided his premises at the
Mangrove Club in All Saints Road, Notting Hill, last year. He is suggesting that
the police had planted the drugs – heroin and marijuana – on Crichlow, a leading
figure in the Notting Hill black world, the best known face on the street, the
owner of the restaurant that has seen more raids than hot calaloo dinners.

'Take it slowly,' he tells them. 'Take it carefully. What is really being suggested
about this man . . . You think about it. I'm asking you to consider this as
thoroughly unreliable evidence. You can just be a little bit too clever when you are
fitting someone up for your own good.'

He pauses. Lets them take it in. Raises his right hand, which has a signet ring on the little finger. His style is conversational almost. 'Something funny is going on at Notting Hill police station,' he suggests. 'It's beginning to look a bit too neat.'

There is a polythene bag with heroin in it that is one of the exhibits. The barrister holds it up as if it is a dead mouse that has just been discovered behind his desk in chambers. 'Heroin is the one drug that conjures up the full horror of drugs. You may think there's a very good reason that it's there. It's merely allowing the world to think he's got heroin on him. Just enough. That'll do.' A member of the public gallery, a distinguished-looking bald West Indian nods at the point with approval.

He concentrates his attention further on the jury. 'I'm sorry it's a bit hot and a bit late and you've probably been listening to enough speeches,' he tells them. But he has some points he wants to make – why was Crichlow's home not searched, why have all the other trials completed in connection with this raid resulted in not guilty verdicts, why, why, why? 'The arm of coincidence is beginning to go all the way through. Seven other juries must have said to themselves that the officers you have seen are not reliable. At the very least.'

Frank Crichlow is pleased with his barrister at the end of the session. 'He is doing well, Michael,' he says. He seems confident of being acquitted. It is one in a series of many trials he has been involved in over the years but it is probably the most serious. He wanted a barrister he trusted to defend him. Hence Michael Mansfield QC.

'I'm the product of an American television series called *The Defenders*. It was a father and son team and each week they would take an issue through the eyes of the client they were representing. They'd prepare the case, interview witnesses and a lot of the programme was the build-up to the actual case. Then you got the case and most times they lost, so that hasn't changed.

'What I enjoyed about it all was that they had a deep sense of purpose, a commitment about their cases and I thought – this is what I would like to do. You could see something from beginning to end so you had a result. Secondly, the person or persons were getting a service and felt they were getting a service and you were helping them and even if they lost they felt they had had their case put. And thirdly, on the whole, you were doing it against the odds, there was this state machine which was bearing down on you which needed to be confronted. It had all those elements.'

He lives in Wandsworth now, not far from the prison where some of his less fortunate clients reside, in the house he shares with his companion, a film-maker, and their family. He has seven children, six from a previous marriage. She is in the process of making a film about the laundering of drugs money and a massive flash American car being used in the shoot is parked outside. He grew up in Lincolnshire, in the constituency which moulded the young Margaret Thatcher, in a middle-class Anglican railway family.

'I didn't come across the police when I was growing up except through my mother. It was an extraordinary case. She had confrontations with the police over parking and she got acquitted because a police officer had lied about a very simple thing. The police officer hadn't realised that my father, who was disabled, was in the car. She got to court and she called my father as a sort of Perry Mason surprise witness. She got the case dismissed.

'It got local publicity and at a very early age I remember her saying, "If men in uniform can do this what else is going on in the world?" Her whole attitude was coloured by this.

'That was my only experience but I did have a strong sense that you must question things because that is what she kept going on about. She said, "If my husband hadn't been there I wouldn't have been able to prove this. I'm not going to take this lying down." It was a strange example and I always remember that she fought it tooth and nail and thereafter the police could do no right.'

The law, like crime, has traditionally been a family profession.

'It's very difficult to get to the Bar. You do have to know people. I knew only one person, a relative of my ex-wife and without his help I would have had a poorer start; I don't mean economically but in terms of explanation. It's still an extremely closed profession. It's very difficult for young people to get on the ladder at all. There are just not enough chambers that allow people from different class backgrounds, colour backgrounds, to get in and there are still very few women barristers, although they're very effective.'

The twin hurdles to be jumped before qualifying are examinatory and digestive: Bar exams and the eating of dinners, an ancient custom, which requires would-be barristers to attend a certain number of dinners at the Inns of Court. It is a hangover from a time when the social niceties of the bar were deemed to be of greater importance than today.

'The exams are becoming more and more difficult and I don't think exams are very relevant at the end of the day. I think that even if you get through the exams you still have to work out the eating of dinners which everyone has to get through, the social-acceptability angle. You have to be vetted by benches, then you have to find a chambers that will take you for pupilage for twelve months, during which time you have no income – except at chambers like ours where we endeavour to provide funds. Then you have to survive for the next five years when things get a bit easier. But you're still not going to make a profit – if ever – because you're always paid in arrears. One is running on an overdraft from day one. I've only been in credit twice.

'I decided it was the sort of thing I wanted to do, but I did philosophy at University. I discovered I had to eat dinners and went and did that. I was at Keele and I commuted every term for a period of time in each term to eat the dinners. Then when I had finished the degree I had to do the law exams from scratch by correspondence course for a year. I failed God knows how many times then eventually got through it all.

'Then I had to find a pupilage so I went back to this relative and said, "Where do I start?" He said go and see so-and-so and I went on until I found a door that opened. I was going to emigrate to Australia but the right things came up at the right time.'

Michael Mansfield thrived. He became known as a defence barrister who fought for his client. Not all barristers enjoy that reputation.

Mansfield – along with a batch of around fifteen other bright young barristers of his era – was in demand from the time it took for his name to be passed around the prison grapevine. Some defendants would even sit tight in prison for a few months more until such time as he was free to take their case.

'The cases I take are decided for me in that solicitors over the years have got to know the kind of case I like doing. Secondly, it's determined by space, if it clashes with another case that I've already agreed to. All solicitors know that they're at risk. There is a third element which is that defendants get to know each other in Brixton or Wandsworth or wherever and one passes your name on to someone else doing a similar kind of case.

'I suppose it would be dishonest to say one isn't a bit flattered by being asked for and people being prepared to stay in prison until one's available, but one's concerned rather than flattered that people are prepared to wait, because in some cases it can be up to a year, and I'm concerned because at the end of the day it may not work out anyway.'

Cases may be only listed for trial at the Old Bailey or the Crown Courts at the last minute so the original choice of barrister may be tied up. The defendant then has to decide – or in some cases has no choice – whether he wants to be represented by someone he has no knowledge of or wait till his first choice is available.

'I think we have to devise a better system of listing cases for the benefit of defendants. One of the biggest complaints is that they don't get the barrister of their choice and that is often because they've come into the list suddenly and the barrister they chose is doing something else.'

Like every barrister, Mansfield takes part in the rituals of the trial.

'You go up to the robing room on the first day. At the Bailey they have senior and junior Treasury counsel and they have a separate room. There is a mess, as they call it, where you can meet and have coffee. Male and female don't robe together, they're next door to each other. It's a bit silly in my view but that's the way they've done it, maybe the women prefer that, anyway.

'A wig is about £150, a second-hand one goes for about £100. Mine was a very old one when I got it. I kept it till the hurricane. I was playing tennis and left it in the car . . . the police rang up and said, "Have you lost your wig?" and I said, "No." They said, "We think you have, because we've got it – and the brief." It had been found in the middle of the tennis court. Someone had broken into the car, got stuff out, got half way across the tennis court and thought we don't want all this and left it. It looked like a drowned rat so I had to spend a lot of money getting it rectified. They're very difficult to get hold of, the old ones, and the new ones look a bit naff.'

One of the rituals of the courts is the language: 'I try to avoid the archaic language but it's very difficult. I prefer to have an informal, chattier style.'

There is a disparate group of souls, mainly elderly, who as a regular form of daytime entertainment, sit in the public gallery at the Old Bailey and watch trials. It is cheaper than going to a matinee and livelier than the library. But while some are undoubtedly there on a ghoul's errand, some of them observe the proceedings like knowledgeable old buffers watching a cricket match at the Oval – nudging each other at the elegance of a point made in cross examination, nodding with approval when a witness is bowled out. Apart from the regulars, it is a motley crew: teenagers on a school project, nervous relatives, American tourists marvelling at the costumes and the language, illustrators who draw the sketches of the accused that appear on television news since cameras are not allowed inside the court. They seem most attentive at the openings when the story is told in abbreviated Reader's Digest style, they love the verdicts for their Laughtonesque drama, but perhaps the most consistently gripping *pièces de théâtre* are the cross-examinations. A good barrister can tie up a dishonest witness through good cross-examination, and the process is fascinating to observe.

Some moments provide their own drama. In the early eighties a man believed by the police to be a highly successful country-house burglar – indeed he would sometimes introduce himself as such to strangers – had eluded their clutches. He was eventually arrested, however, for a robbery of which he adamantly protested his innocence. Awaiting his trial, in mid-December, he invited two of the arresting officers to a mutual friend's house. He hid a bug in the Christmas tree and recorded the detectives discussing the charges and talking about money he was offering for them to tell the truth in court. When he duly appeared in court on the charge and one of the officers started giving his evidence, the accused man lent forward with delicate timing and handed his barrister a tape. The detective dried. For a moment you could have heard a jaw drop. The barrister asked him, 'Where were you on the night of . . . ?' The detective told the judge that he did not wish to answer in case he incriminated himself. The case was halted and the accused acquitted. The two detectives, for what it's worth, appeared on conspiracy charges: one claimed that he had never been to the bugged house and was convicted, the other claimed the money he received was a 'gratuity' and was acquitted. The first officer was freed on appeal.

Adam Mars-Jones, in his account in *Lantern Lectures* of the trial of Donald Neilson, the 'Black Panther', who kidnapped and murdered Lesley Whittle, explains how the defence barrister 'must give the impression of asking beady-eyed questions, do-you-really-expect-me-to-believe-that questions, without actually gathering new information. He is experienced enough as an advocate to sense latent masses of unwelcome testimony in some of the witnesses. He must force them to leave this unexpressed, by phrasing his questions with great care and warning them with great emphasis against the sin of irrelevance.'

Mansfield is a good cross-examiner in that he has the ability to ask seemingly bland questions that appear to be heading nowhere but finally lead the witnesses into saying more than they wished.

'But it is very difficult cross-examining a victim. There was a child in a kidnapping case. She was telling about fifty per cent of the truth and fifty per cent that wasn't true. She elaborated a bit because she had to protect herself against her parents so I knew why she was doing it. To get it out of her was a very difficult operation and I had to adopt a completely different tactic, being fairly gentle and fairly slow and not being too obvious about the questions so that she felt as though she was speaking. I was just gradually slipping in things that suggested this wasn't quite right and building up a picture so that she realised I knew more than she thought I knew.

'That is always the key to every witness – to let them think that you know more than you actually do. But you still know more than they ever imagined in the first place. They're not sure of the extent of your information and they don't want to be caught out.

'The younger victims and victims of robbery, if they've been shot, are difficult. There's been one case where the witness broke down and although the judge said, "You've got to carry on," I said I wasn't going to.

'One of the most important things is to have a pretty sharp recollection of what people have said. In the McKenney case [involving Harry "Big H" McKenney on a double murder charge] there was a witness changing his evidence within minutes of what he was saying and you have to be prepared for that.

'The public think, through various TV series, that one is sort of setting clients up as to how to answer but that's not how I operate. What I do do is to put them through what they are going to go through fairly stiffly. I do it about a week before or a day before they go into the witness box. I say, "These are the kind of questions you have to answer, this is the kind of cross-examination you're going to get. I'm going to pretend you're now in the witness box and I'm prosecuting. Right, let's go." For an hour, two hours, however long it takes.

'They usually say in the end that I gave them a worse time than they actually do get. But at least they're prepared. I don't tell them the answers, I tell them the questions. One, you're not allowed to tell them the answers anyway and number two, you often don't know them because you weren't at the scene of the robbery. Thirdly, you don't want them to be too stale. I leave it till the last minute so that the adrenalin's running.'

One of the most depressing eating places in the world is the canteen at the Old Bailey. It has the air of a shabby hospital waiting-room and food to match. Chain-smoking wives with desperately reassuring solicitors' clerks, journalists waiting for the tannoy to announce the return of the jury to Court Number Four, half drunk cups of coffee left on the table by 'all parties in the case in Court Number Ten'. The barristers are usually elsewhere.

'When we adjourn at lunchtime I often don't have lunch but that's a personal weight thing. I certainly don't drink. At the beginning of the day, because of short staffing or whatever it is, the defendant probably only arrives just before the court sits so you only get ten minutes. So now the only time you get to see somebody is during the lunch-hour. I make a point of seeing the client every day even if nothing much has happened, because if he's in custody he's worried, isolated. He needs somebody there.

'Obviously a lot of your friends will be barristers but you don't seek them out. Some go to El Vinos, not always the ones who are very good at their job because they drink too much. Other barristers think of themselves as in the acting profession so they'll join the Garrick, others who think of themselves as in politics will go to the Reform. Or possibly the RAC if they see themselves as anonymous but clubbable. I'm not a member, I've been to one or two once or twice.'

Some barristers both prosecute and defend, changing roles apparently without difficulty. But most stick with one of the two disciplines. Mansfield was always going to be one of The Defenders.

'The longer you're in the job the prosecution begin to see that you are not going to knife them in the corridors. They realise also that you're not exactly stupid at the job and you've got to get on because there'll be another case and another case after that. I put a lot of store by the fact that you've got to be able to relate to the person prosecuting because you're going to need his cooperation. There are going to be enough battles in court.

'Some prosecutors have a particularly prejudiced or jaundiced view of life, both from their political and social backgrounds. You have to try and overcome that. Because if you get into a personal battle, same as with the judge, you actually cut your own throat at the end of the day. Juries don't like it and I've seen it where the atmosphere is dreadful. So I try and avoid that but there are, like the judges, one or two entrenched prosecutors and they are rather difficult personalities.'

Mansfield has crossed swords with judges in the past. Some barristers do it unintentionally by their manner, others in veiled terms.

'I think we would all like to believe that if you cross swords with the judge it has no effect but I think it does. They are affected by battles in court and although it might surprise people I do try and avoid battles with the judge. Jurors are not impressed. A few years ago there were a number of judges who were difficult and biased against the defendant because, on the whole, they come from the ranks of prosecutors. You did have to battle to get minimal justice and the juries would see that. But that situation has begun to change. There are not so many entrenched judges. It's brought about to some extent by the fact that judges have children and the new generation is now educating the judiciary as to what is going on in the world.'

The barrister's set piece in his final speech. This is the moment when the press start getting interested in the case once more because the end is in sight. After a long case a defence barrister may spend more than a day on his feet running through the case. It is a skill. If the barrister just runs through the witnesses and the basic evidence, the jurors can easily doze off – after lunch in a court you can often catch three or four people dozing. On the other hand, the barrister cannot risk leaving out any evidence that may raise a doubt in their mind.

'I write the final speech in my mind at the beginning of the case so the cross-examination fits into the final speech – I know what I want to end up saying. It's a bit like a scientific approach. It's always thought that scientists are objective, I think they're thoroughly subjective, they know what they're looking for, they have their hypothesis. I'm a bit like that. There's a lot of preparation in the sense that I know the essence. So if suddenly you have to make the final speech because the evidence collapses you are in a position to stand up and do it, you've got all the headings and notes already. Some barristers actually cultivate expressions that they know will work as headlines.'

Some barristers also patronise the jury, being jovial to them, over-polite, like a politician on the hustings talking to potential voters whose support he desperately needs, but whose views he has no way of understanding.

'The way I judge whether it's a jury I can speak to is on the basis of, if I went into a room full of people, who would I pick out who I think I can relate to almost at a glance.

'It's absolutely impossible to tell from looking at a jury which way they're going to vote. Jurors who are nodding at you all the way may go out and convict. They're nodding because they're nervous or they agree with everybody or they're nodding off. Or you get a jury that seems totally disinterested and they're looking at the ceiling or doodling or they seem aloof – and they acquit.'

Traditionally the defendant has been allowed to challenge three potential jurors without giving a reason. In a trial involving half a dozen accused, this could mean that eighteen would-be jurors could be kicked off. The prosecution could also challenge. What all this tended to mean was that defendants would challenge military-looking types, elderly respectable women and people reading the *Daily Telegraph*. The prosecution would object to long-haired people, Rastafarians and blokes who looked a bit similar to the men in the dock. But by the end of the eighties those challenges, unless they were backed up by a specific objection, were being removed.

'I would only challenge on the way they dress or the newspaper they're carrying if the defendant instructs me. The jury system has to be maintained at all costs. I think its one of the biggest democratic rights we've got. Even more than the vote because the voter doesn't mean that much any more. To be able to exercise that right in a jury room is still one of the last areas where one can vote effectively, much more so than the ballot box.

'I think jury nobbling is extremely rare. It's being used as another way of attacking the jury system in order to, I think, abolish juries. I think that's where we're heading. There have obviously been examples but it's certainly not rife, certainly not the sort of thing that requires the abolition of the jury. Take the soccer trials which collapsed and the revelations in the *Sunday Times* about the average mentalities of jurors. The whole build-up seems to be trying to make the jurors out to be nobbleable, thick, therefore we can have a better system without them.

'Attitudes in the courts towards sentencing have not really changed very much and the amount of humanity expressed is still very, very low. There's very little time spent by barristers on aspects of sentencing and how you deal with people and how you address judges on how people should be dealt with. There's an idea being tried in the States that the punishment should fit the crime. So if somebody has committed a burglary they have to go back to the house where they have committed the burglary and meet the householder and spend a month or two or six months doing what the householder wants done. I'm not saying that's ideal but it's a new way of looking at things. We haven't got the barristers or the judges to do that.

'Mitigation is regarded as a five-minute job you do at the end of the case and a plea of mitigation always used to be regarded as a bit of a soft option. But someone's locked up for years as a result of this. There's very little training on it. I think barristers should be able to say to the judge, "Even if there aren't the facilities this is quite the wrong sentence and it's not my fault or your fault that Parliament hasn't yet got round to thinking about it but you should be making a statement about it."

'I get upset at the end of a case if we lose. Something I was advised to do right at the beginning was to distance myself but that's something I can't do. I've got to feel something for that defendant in order to communicate. I'm not one of those people who can be like a surgeon – here's another body and I can just cut it up. I'll obviously do cases where I don't feel very much but I don't think I do such a good job.

'We haven't really progressed very far at all. We have the biggest prison population in Europe; the whole idea is still on punitive deterrents. I'm far from convinced that locking people up on a punitive basis deters others – quite obviously it doesn't – and the conditions inside are pretty horrific. They're building better prisons but that isn't getting at the root of the problem.

'There's a whole area of – what is crime? I've always found that an extraordinarily difficult concept. Enormous resources are spent on catching people for miniscule amounts of money whether it be DHSS or takeaways from the local WH Smiths or a small offence, even a car offence, a lot of court time is taken up on these cases – OK, I'm not condoning it – but meanwhile major crime is taking place: dispossession of others by all sorts of people sometimes under the guise of legality, extraordinary things are being done in the City, and shareholders are being ripped off regularly.'

In early 1989, Valerio Viccei was jailed for organising the Knightsbridge safe-deposit box robbery. Mansfield was one of the defence team.

'Professional criminals are a very mixed bag. There are groups from very deprived situations, they've left school with very few qualifications, their families may have a string of convictions, fathers, brothers, they're all "at it". They're not used to any other way of living. I think gangland is dated. When I started there was a sort of Mafia that almost spread to journalists. There were police officers, known criminals, all working hand-in-hand. They knew their place; they all had little roles to play; backhanders going here, there and everywhere to get inside information. Since the break-up of the Krays and the Richardsons, there are many more much smaller groups which come together for a single crime. The same names crop up again and again, but they don't have the stranglehold that they once had. The police will now have target criminals as they call them, who they know are "at it".

'Supergrass trials have fallen into disrepute and supergrasses aren't used quite as much. But what they did was present to your stock gangland criminal a real threat. Gangs haven't stayed together because of that risk. The risk of being supergrassed got very high about seven or eight years ago. Then jurors started to acquit because supergrasses were being offered immunity or extremely low sentences, money was being offered or facilities in custody, so they died off. But meanwhile the confidence of the gangland people had gone because they now felt they were running a huge risk that one of their number might well be turning supergrass. That broke the stranglehold of many of the bigger names so now the situation is more fluid – you can't infiltrate because the gang doesn't stay together.

'Crime is international now in the way it never has been before. So many of the drug cases are international, crime doesn't pay on a local basis. The bigger money is moving into completely different areas. It's been drugs over the last ten years but the next one is going to be computer frauds and paper frauds that will involve a multi-million base and shifting money on an international scale. New technology has meant that different people are moving in – you can sit at home and organise, you don't have to leave the room.

'The Knightsbridge safe-deposit case is an interesting example: different nationalities, Italian and others. Another trial had one of the Angry Brigade at the English end, then there was an Israeli end to it and an extraordinary motley connection of people. Three or four so-called lads doing the post office at the end of the road, that's still going to continue though.

'Fraud is really the big area where the police are outnumbered and outsmarted and the frauds going on in the city are amazing, that's where the money should be spent because people are getting away with millions. These defendants are much better at providing themselves in advance with alibis or disappearing and evaporating. They are not even around to be arrested.

'I think the Robbery Squad have not changed a great deal and they're out of their depths, they are applying the same techniques to a league of people who are streets ahead of them. They need a highly-educated, highly-specialised, fast-moving squad of people because of the new kind of criminal. The Fraud Squad are understaffed, underfunded and I don't think they're even aware of all the technological ruses.'

In 1989 Michael Mansfield became a Queen's Counsel, something that barristers aspire to and that a young would-be lawyer might aim at. A few months earlier a young would-be lawyer might have been inspired by a television series about a group of radical young barristers called *Blind Justice*. The model for one of them, suggested many in legal circles, was Michael Mansfield, the Defender.

The jury return in the case of Crichlow at Knightsbridge Crown Court. They have spent a night in a hotel but they have not reached a unanimous verdict. The judge indicates that he will accept a majority decision. The jury retire and re-emerge with a verdict of not guilty on all charges. Frank Crichlow is delighted with his barrister. The judge awards costs to the defence. The barrister thanks the judge.

13

The Judge

I think a judge should be
looked on rather as a sphinx
than as a person – you
shouldn't be able to
imagine a judge having a
bath.

Judge H. C. Leon.

The taxi driver thinks he knows the house. It's the one with the statue outside, isn't it? On the front? He wouldn't be surprised if someone had knocked it off, it's quite small, a sort of nymph, came from the Town Hall, he thinks. But no, Canova's 'Dancing Girl' has survived, although some vandals have scrawled in pencil over the sort of places that vandals inevitably scrawl.

A small lift takes us to the first-floor flat where Judge Bernard Gillis and his wife live. He greets us with all the courtesy and self-assurance that comes from half a lifetime of presiding over matters of life and death. He is a natural talker.

'I never had an ambition to become a judge, but from my boyhood I had a passionate desire to become a barrister. History was my subject at school. I failed in mathematics, I wasn't interested in science, I went to woodwork for five years and made nothing. But history gave me an interest in the law and from the age of fourteen I had a book in which I stuck down the faces of famous judges and advocates of the day.'

His home, with its glorious view over the Channel, is lined with such judges' faces and other legal drawings. There were no judges in his family although there are some in Canada, where most of his family went towards the end of the last century.

'I got through the appropriate examinations somehow, and through sacrifice, I suppose you could put it, I had the privilege of going to Cambridge and joined Lincolns Inn. Even today every time I go into the Inn I get a thrill at the privilege of being there.' (He had recently taken his youngest granddaughter there for her first day at the Inn.)

'The Bar, in my mind, pays you in two currencies: you have to get the necessary money to pay the butcher and baker and so forth but apart from that and, in a way, superior to that, if you can stay at the Bar you are all your life guaranteed a quality of life better than anything I know of. You meet with men of culture and learning. It matters not if they are the most successful barrister and you are just struggling on humble briefs.'

As a student he would come up from Cambridge to eat the requisite number of dinners at the Inn – a requirement for a call to the Bar. 'We used to stay at one of Joe Lyon's hotels, about 7s. 6d. each. Breakfast at the Strand Palace – cereals and kippers and toast and marmalade – you didn't want to eat for the rest of the day. You would listen to a case in the morning, in the afternoon go to a matinee, two or three bob in the pits, and if you had time you'd go to the Trocadero where there was very good tea and lovely cakes. Then to your Inn to dine in messes of four. The great thing was to find two vegetarians or Mohammedans whose religion prohibited them for drinking liquor or eating meat. You'd get them in the mess and see they were amply supplied with potatoes and carrots and you used to get a bottle of port or sherry and as much beer as you wanted, then you would sit down for your meal.'

His contemporaries included Lord Devlin, Selwyn Lloyd and the Archbishop of Canterbury, Michael Ramsey: 'He had a problem whether to go to the law or become Archbishop, but we reminded him that the days of Wolsey were over.'

He decided against following a career in the law of property or tax. 'I have always been interested, if I may say so, in human beings and so I was attracted to the world where human beings are to be found – crime, divorce, libel, slander, breach of promise of marriage. And in one's early years, as the youngest man in chambers, you got the crumbs from the table.'

He did not much care for County Court work. 'It was largely the court for the poor man and you saw him trying to exist sometimes under unhappy circumstances, the debts they couldn't pay. You'd have some man come forward and say, "I can pay two shillings a week off the bicycle I bought for my boy's birthday." It's much different now.'

In those days aspiring young barristers who wanted to build up a criminal practice put themselves on the 'Yard list'. They would be briefed by the Commissioner of the Metropolitan Police and do Magistrates' Court cases. It was one way up the long ladder to becoming a Treasury counsel.

'In my day, before the War, if within five years you were booking a thousand guineas a year you were well on your way. Of course, you could live as I did in Bloomsbury with someone making my dinners four nights a week on five pounds a week and renting a flat from the Foundling Estate at £6.15s. a month. Maples furnished it for eighty guineas as if I were giving them an order for a battleship or a hotel. My dear Mrs Gibson looked after me until I got married.'

After the war it meant beginning again, but a few years later he submitted his name to the Lord Chancellor for consideration as a Queen's Counsel. The names are announced on Maundy Thursday and in due course the name of Gillis was among them. He also applied for appointment as recorder. The recorder sat four times a year in those days to try minor criminal cases with juries, and to hear appeals from magistrates. In 1958 he was appointed Recorder of Bradford, which he enjoyed greatly.

'I was welcomed by the Lord Mayor of Bradford. In his very kind Yorkshire words he said, "Now, Mr Recorder, we're very pleased to welcome you, you'll find friendship in Yorkshire, we know you come from London and I'd like you to know that you're the second citizen by our charter of this great historic industrial city." We had a splendid lunch afterwards.'

He is concerned that the traditions governing the courts should be remembered and respected: 'The City of London, from historic times, was responsible for its own courts and the Old Bailey. The first court was built, I think, some time in the sixteenth century. The only covered part, I'm delighted to hear, was the Bench. There was so little work that the place was let out between sessions. You could hire it to give a party.

'I think the wig and the gown are very desirable. If you go without a gown, one man might come in with a brown jacket or a grey jacket or a black jacket. I was told that historically judges wore gowns so that no one should seem better than the other. The earlier judges wore a cap on their heads, not a black cap, and the wig came in 1600 or 1700 when all gentlemen wore wigs and the barristers' wigs had different curls from the judges' wigs and so it's remained. When I went out to the West Indies to do some cases I had a thrill – I would go into court in Trinidad or Barbados and there was the judge sitting in the robes, using our books and running it according to British procedure. Americans and Canadians would come to see us in the Old Bailey and say, "Do keep your wig and gown."'

Critics of judges often suggest that they appear to have made their mind up about a case almost as soon as it has started. How much do they know about the details of the prosecution before they enter the court?

'All you know about a case that comes before you is a copy of the indictment and the depositions of the witnesses taken down before the magistrates. The usher will come and tell you everyone is ready. The City is responsible for the safe conduct of Her Majesty's judges. The alderman representing the Lord Mayor would come in robes at the beginning of each session with the under-sheriff and they would conduct the judge to the court. The under-sheriff was the only one who would be allowed to carry a weapon. That would be a ceremonial sword, there was nobody else allowed to carry a weapon in the presence of the judges – you can't walk in with a revolver! The usher would go in first and call "Silence!"'

He describes the scene so vividly that you can almost hear the word echoing through the panels of the court and see the clerk's back stiffening.

We pause for a lunch of smoked salmon and cucumber sandwiches on a tray while the Judge enquires whether these miniature tape-recorders are satisfactory. It is winter, but outside is a clear blue sky over the sea. What about lunch as a judge?

'The tradition in London is that the Lord Mayor and the sheriffs entertain the judges for lunch. You go down and you're offered a drink, most have a soft drink. The lunch is by no means sparse but not a gross meal. The traditional midday lunch survived: you start perhaps with grapefruit, have a chop, maybe fish, a piece of cheese. Wine was available but people took it or didn't take it according to their ability to sustain themselves in the afternoon. You discuss the cases if you have a difficult point of law, you don't discuss the guilt of the man. A dear and lamented friend, then Common Sergeant of London, he would drink a large glass of Guinness with his lunch every day. He was in the Chambers of "Khaki" Roberts QC.

'"Khaki", as we called him, was the most powerful prosecutor in fraud cases. Defending, you would get the defendant to go through balance sheets and auditor's report and there would be a pile of papers in front of him when you finished your examination. I can see "Khaki" now standing up and saying, "My Lord, would the usher remove all the papers and books." The usher does that. "Now Mr Jones, will you tell the jury what you know about a cheque for £30,000?" "Well, my company dealt in millions . . ." "Usher, show the defendant exhibit 56 . . . To whom is the cheque payable?" "I can't say." "Do you mean it's payable to cash?" "Yes." "Look at the signature. Do you recognise it?" Observe the skill of the short sharp question, so different, if I may say so with profound respect, to the form of questions with which the Prime Minister is confronted from time to time.' And the judge recounts how 'Khaki' coolly tied the defendants in knots and left them dangling. These cross-examinations, he says, are what the jury recalls when they adjourn to make their decision. 'Even in the longest case there are several, say six, fundamental questions which if the judge does his job properly will decide the case.'

And when the day's hearing ends for the judge?

'I would go home and my faithful dogs would be waiting for me after dinner for a walk. I didn't mind working, say, till twelve or one but one started to get tired then. In the summer I preferred getting up at six. In the long cases one didn't accept social engagements if one could avoid it, except on a Friday. I wasn't capable of going to a cocktail party from six to nine and doing my work the next day. The late Sir Sebag Shaw, dear friend of mine, he was able to do that because he didn't require much sleep.

'On Saturdays I used to go out with my dog – I lived in Totteridge, the last village in London in my view – and I used to walk on the fields for a couple of hours and the dogs somehow knew it was Saturday. I had a golden retriever and before that labradors. My wife had a Kerry Blue. One time we kept ducks and chickens, great fun.'

Most judges take a full note during the case, not as full as the beleagured shorthand writer who scribbles or taps feverishly away in the well of the court, occasionally appealing to the judge to ask people to slow down, but the Judge makes a full one none the less. He would look at his note in the evening and then rely on it for compiling his summing up, which usually lasts, in a sizeable case, two or three days. Judge Gillis' longest summing up was five and a half days. 'In the summing up you have to tell the jury the story, it's very tedious for them if you just go through the evidence.

'In the long cases you live in the case. If you find you're not concentrating, you adjourn. The public don't realise that what they see of a judge is not an elderly gentleman sitting in a chair dozing. He's not, and he spends many hours off the bench on his work.'

He appreciates good counsel and good closing speeches: 'I used to find it easier and, in some cases, delightful to hear a man make a speech in good grammatical English. One usually found he had had some sort of classical education.'

Defendants – and sometimes defence counsel – complain that on occasions a judge is biased against them, has stressed the prosecution case and left little doubt in a juror's mind what he thinks of the defence case. Would he accept that this happens?

'There was one judge, been dead many years, who was known for over-zealously putting the prosecution case and rather timidly putting the defence. He suffered from an unfortunate physical idiosyncrasy, saying, "ahem ahem", like a cough. It was notorious. He would say, "Now the defendant says, members of the jury, he was not there, ahem, ahem. If you believe that, ahem, ahem, then acquit." Anyone who did not know that the judge was in all sincerity giving way to a physical idiosyncrasy would think he was suggesting a different view because it so happened that this idiosyncrasy didn't manifest itself when he referred to the Crown's case. One counsel who suffered from this felt, "This is awful – I know the judge is an honest man but the jury may think he's laughing the defence out." It wasn't a very important case. It was a case of receiving stolen property but terribly important to the man concerned. This young barrister said to his opponent, all friendly of course, at the bar, "Look I'm going to make a star against every time this blasted coughing happens because I think it's unfortunate."

'They went to the Court of Criminal Appeal, in the days of Lord Chief Justice Hewart. He was a very fine classicist but not so good as an unbiased judge. He said, "What are you complaining about, it seems impeccable." And the young man said, "Well, my lord, you didn't hear what the jury heard." He said, "Do you mean something is missing?" He said, "No, my lord." Then this young man went through the summing up of the defence: "If you believe he wasn't there, ahem, ahem, then acquit him." They saw the point and they started to smile. Knowing the judge was a classical scholar and had a knowledge of the Bible, the young man said, "My Lord, what I complained of was that the voice was the voice of Jacob but the hand was the hand of Esau." The appeal, I'm told, was allowed.' There is a twinkle in his eye as he tells the story, which leads one to guess who the young barrister might have been. 'You might guess, but speculation is a danger.'

Judges almost invariably treat juries with great deference and politeness, even when they are unable to come up with a verdict after two nights in a hotel. But what do they feel about them, do they feel they do a decent job as a rule, that the system works?

'In the olden days in civil cases there were juries of various classes: there was the common jury – it doesn't mean they were vulgar – then there was a special jury in which a man had to have certain qualifications – I'm afraid to use language that might be misinterpreted. The ordinary English citizen is as good as anyone, but special juries usually had a property qualification. I'm in favour of the retention of the jury. People say why not have a judge alone. I don't think the judges would want that. Why not have assessors? But who would they be? Retired accountants or trade union officials? You couldn't expect people active in their careers to come and sit as an assessor for six months. Then there's always a danger of a person sitting who is not a judge – and the judge comes with a fresh mind to each case – becoming case-hardened. That's why I prefer the jury. The recent legislation [which reduces the number of challenges to jurors without giving a reason], in my humble opinion, brings in useful changes. But the jury's part is not a ceremony. It's the vital part of the trial. Who better can decide if a man is dishonest than twelve people?'

Often potential jurors who are reluctant to try a long and complex trial offer excuses as to why they should be stood down. One plea which caused laughter in court was that of a middle-aged woman who said she would be unable to be a juror because she had to get her son's tea for him when he came in. The son turned out to be twenty-four and the judge felt he would be able to make himself something nourishing for a brief period in his life without too much discomfort. Others try more outlandish methods, like saying they will acquit come what may, or appearing not to understand what is going on. Some are genuinely bewildered.

'If you were about to start a case that was likely to go on ten weeks and you saw a wholly respectable old lady being called to the witness box, what I would do before she was sworn – and counsel would see what one was doing – I would say, "Madam, I understand that the case which is about to start is likely to take a few weeks. If you find that is longer than you can devote I will hear any applications." No one objected.

'In a very long case which I tried, there were about eight counsel in the case and thousands of pages of documents and when I was addressing the jury I had to have an usher next to me to lift the volume I wanted. I would say to counsel, "Mr So-and-So, there is a letter in which the defendant says he was in Manchester. I can't find it." A voice from the jury: "Volume Three, my lord, page 95." And I looked and there was a plainly dressed man aged about fifty to sixty, with a little black beard; he wasn't a person of foreign origin, not that type of beard that some men wear, and counsel looked, as I did, and he was right. That would happen at least three times. When the trial was over I was anxious to check what his profession was and I always give my friends an opportunity to guess if I tell them this story: what occupation do you think this quietly dressed man had, an obviously careful person who sits there, and never made any notes? There he was . . . would you like the answer? He was a blacksmith and if people read their poetry, "Under the Spreading Chestnut Tree", you see the blacksmith in the village knew what was going on and often was a wise man.'

He believes that as crime has become more profitable so have attempts been made to corrupt juries. 'I've no doubt that in some cases paid persons sit in the gallery and look around the jurors and if they see a man who looks particularly shabby someone might follow him, if he goes into the bar to have a drink. I have sympathy with the police, who in their view have their cases interfered with. By and large it doesn't happen. Nor is the ordinary man taken in by the blandishments of persuasive personality.

'The jury looks with great suspicion – that's where the ordinary man comes in, leave your experts outside – if a man is a supergrass or grassing on his pals. "Well, he must be a so-and-so to start with," they think, and by nature they look on him with double anxiety and suspicion. But the late Mr Justice Avory, perhaps the greatest criminal judge in my day, used to say there's no such thing as honour amongst thieves and we shouldn't encourage it. We should encourage thieves to break out and speak against one another so that then we can try them and send them away.

'In one big robbery case, the evidence varied against different prisoners. The only evidence against one man on two counts was the uncorroborated evidence of an accomplice. On that the jury are in law entitled to convict if they are utterly convinced it is truthful and it is the duty of the judge to give them the fullest direction, to tell them that usually it is desirable to have the evidence of an accomplice supported by other relevant material. A man can't corroborate himself. In that long case, I summed up for five and a half days; fourteen barristers, and seven or eight defendants were involved. In my view there was evidence there which would entitle them to convict and I gave, I believe, to use Lord Hewar's phrase, "impeccable guidance". He was convicted. He was one of the middle division of the group, he got about five or six years and not unexpectedly went to the Court of Appeal. They didn't complain at all of my summing up, I'm delighted to say. No one said that the trial judge didn't put the case fully, no one said he didn't give them ample directions on the danger of convicting on uncorroborated evidence. But nevertheless, under the statute an appeal should be allowed if the Court of Criminal Appeal feel it's unsafe and unsatisfactory. Now if I'd been sitting I would have rejected it. But I think it was Lord Justice Lawton, a very distinguished lawyer, if I may say so with great respect, of vast experience, who presided, and that court felt it was unsatisfactory and they allowed the appeal.'

He recalls the *Lady Chatterley's Lover* case and the question that was raised in court by a counsel prosecuting as to whether one would allow one's servant to read it and thought that this must surely have alienated the jury. 'I don't suppose any of them ever had a butler, some of them may have come from East Ham, others from London. I've never had one . . . yet. Perhaps one day someone will leave me enough money. The jury might think of the barrister, here is a very charming fellow, just and fair man, firm, never unfair – but does he come from a world where people have butlers? That wouldn't have endeared him to the jury.'

One area where judges receive most attention – and often most criticism – is in their sentencing, whether it is judged to be too lenient or, less often, too strict. How are the decisions made, what tariff is used?

'For sentencing the prosecution counsel calls the officer in charge of the case then the court is told the man's record. The judge has to be alert that no witness spills evidence of his previous convictions before this. So you will hear something like, "Married man, my lord, left his first wife because she was a drunkard, he first came before the court . . ." and so on. Defending counsel asks some questions, "Is it right that it is nine years since he was before the court? . . . true he's left his wife but he's been living for the past five years with Mrs Snooks, looking after her, she was a widow with two children?" He might call a witness. I used to feel terribly sad when the mother of a convicted man was called.

'I remember a very serious case of conspiracy to rob banks, throwing something into the eyes of the cashier, driving away and almost killing a child playing in the gutter. There were five men convicted. One man called his mother. Try and picture the scene. Old Bailey court, crowded, I used to try to make them feel at home. As soon as she was brought in I would say, "Usher, help the lady to the witness box." She came from south London, a respectable old lady in great distress. I used to turn to her using a specially quiet conversational tone, "Would you like to sit down?" She sat down. Then the counsel asked the questions. "I would ask, now is there anything else you would like to say that would help your son?" "Oh, he was a very good boy. At home he would often take old-age pensioners across the road and when he was a lad he would run errands. He got into bad company, his father never recovered from the fact that his son went to prison." I would say, "Usher, help this lady down." That man was sentenced by me five minutes later to fourteen years in prison. When he was asked if he wanted to say anything, he said, "Yes, my lord, may I thank you for the way you spoke to my mother." Now there's some good in that man somewhere. It's a very arrogant judge who says he's not affected by pleas of mitigation.'

And he tells another evocative tale of mitigation, which seems to – and does – come from another era.

'The son of a famous family in the West End had got into the wrong hands. Young man, about twenty-eight, he was in the dock charged with obtaining money by false pretences, £200 or £300, before the war, of course, when £200 or £300 was worth more than today.

'It was a heavy task to try and win that case and Norman Birkett (later Lord Birkett) would advise a plea of guilty. He was committed for trial and came before a judge who was a great friend of mine; he had told me about the responsibilities of marriage when I was engaged. He had had certain sadness in his own life. He would not be unimpressed by an elegant lady, better than bringing in an old charwoman, and this man had a title, I won't tell you what it was, he may still be alive. Norman Birkett – it was a joy to be led by him – he gave the impression to clients in consultation that the Almighty had put him on earth for one purpose only and that was to defend them.

'It was quarter to four and Norman Birkett got up in his magnificent style and said, "My Lord, I'm anxious to call the prisoner's wife, the only witness for the defence, and it's true to say that her Ladyship has stood beside him in his dreadful hours and she wants to say something to your Lordship."

'We assembled again in the morning and Norman Birkett said, "Bring her Ladyship in." She was brought in on the arm of someone who called himself Colonel, with what right I don't know. She was wearing a mink coat which seemed a bit odd because it was a warm day in May – she may have suffered from coldness. As she passed me my face was more or less alongside hers and I formed a view. I got up and I whispered to Norman, "She's tight." I'd got a stench of gin and brandy and this was half-past ten in the morning. She didn't seem to be dressed as I would expect of a lady of aristocratic birth, some people might say she was rather loudly or flashily attired.

'Norman Birkett was watching her very closely and as she was about to mount the steps of the box he said, "Stay . . . My Lord, I fear her Ladyship is so overwhelmed I can't take the responsibility of calling her. Usher, conduct her out." She was tight. The judge had seen her and no doubt spotted the type she was. The prisoner had had the good fortune to meet her in one of the more notorious night clubs of London eighteen months earlier. He was bound over.'

But after the verdict and the pleas of mitigation and the examination of a defendant's previous convictions, how is the decision on sentence taken?

'It is difficult to sentence someone to twenty years. To take a man's liberty away and lock him up is a dreadful responsibility. And that is the duty of the judge alone. It's the hardest part because there the judge is alone and the Court of Appeal will only interfere if the sentence is excessive or otherwise unfair or unjust.'

Some men who have been sent down object to being lectured by the judge as he passes sentence.

'When sentencing I might say this: "John Smith, you have been convicted by the jury on overwhelming evidence" – that was a word assisting the court of appeal if they wanted to know what my opinion was – "of this dreadful offence, knocking down an old lady outside a post office and robbing her of her pension, an offence which is all too prevalent. The sentence passed on you is x years. Take the prisoner out." I'm not there as a lecturer or a moral crusader. And anger in a judge is bad but, human nature being what it is, sometimes one can't avoid it. A judge is very unfortunate if he lets himself be angered.'

But some do, don't they? Or at least some have personal feelings about particular crimes?

'In the old days Sir Montague Sharp, now deceased so I can mention him, was the popular chairman of the Court of Sessions in Middlesex. He lived in Ealing and we used to think that a burglar who committed burglary in Tottenham might get twelve months but if he did it in Ealing he got eighteen months. And the usher

would say, "Well, Lady Sharp has got a beautiful garden and she's very nervous."
He was a charming old boy.'

And afterwards, does he ever come across men he has sentenced? How would
he feel if he bumped into one on the promenade at Hove?

'I was once invited to a most luxurious party. I knew the host and hostess, very
successful, reputable people. At the supper table, about thirty of us, was a man
whom I had sentenced in a fraud case. I was introduced to Mr Snooks, said how
do you do, and of course never made any sign: the man was quite unmoved.

'The ordinary criminal, if you give him a fair trial, he won't worry about the
judge. There are scoundrels of course . . .' He recounts how he had had police
protection on one occasion and had asked the police not to let his wife know lest it
alarm her. They agreed but then phoned Mrs Gillis to tell her not to worry about
anything as there would be a policeman outside her front door.

If sentencing is the hardest part of the judge's job, what does he feel about the
prisons in which the guilty man will serve those sentences?

'The state of prisons now ought to cause the citizen great anxiety and in my
case I feel a sense of shame. It is to do with overcrowding and it is the biggest
source of, I won't say shame, but regret. When you send people to prison their
punishment is a loss of liberty not their degradation. How many thousands are
sharing cells that were built for one? And when in those cells there are no internal
sanitary arrangements and the men have the indignity of washing out – they go
with their gerries which are used overnight in a procession to a wash-house point
on the landing – I think their punishment shouldn't include that. I think all the
authorities are conscious of that and are doing their utmost to limit the number
who go to prison and increase the accommodation, and wouldn't place a
schoolmaster or clergyman who's gone wrong in a cell with hardened criminals
but, allowing for all that, it is a sad feature of our public life.'

But are there people doomed to end up inside a prison cell, a 'criminal
type'?

'If you have a father who is a drunkard, a wife-beater, and a mother who is a
drunkard, not doing the ordinary things the ordinary mother would do, and the
boy is brought up in that atmosphere, allowed to wander about, it's not surprising
he gets into bad habits. My wife has a bee in her bonnet about this. She says the
duty of a mother is to be at home when the children come home from school. She
knows in some circumstances a mother has to go out to work, but often they are
going out to work so that they can have more holidays or tape recorders or bicycles
and a higher standard of living. The result is when the children come home they
often have a key on a string around their neck and often until the mother comes
home they're playing in the street. My wife had an opportunity of assisting her
sister in her distinguished fashion salon in the West End but she preferred to be
home and, if she was out, she would hurry home. Better not have a bicycle and
content themselves with a fortnight at Southend-on-Sea rather than go to
Spain. But it's not for me to lecture people. If you want an opinion you must

ask probation officers or social workers and they'll tell you if what I talk is rubbish.'

He had had some experience of the early gangland trials. 'A man I once defended fell out that way and he was murdered by his ex-friends and his remains were put in a flyover in cement. I don't know if that was true. He was in one of the East End gangs.'

And he has observed a change in public attitude towards the police. 'In my early days at the Bar, if the only evidence in the case was of a police officer it would be believed. But as time went on the value of admissions to police, in view of certain cases where the police had acted illegally and therefore undermined the confidence of the citizen, got less and less. When there was an admission in the early days that was the most serious thing in the case. Not today. Because prisoners often say, "It's all a pack of lies." And in some cases, unfortunately, policemen have committed perjury and been convicted.'

How affected are judges by what they read in the papers about their cases; what papers, in fact, do they read?

'In most cases the press coverage of trials is very fair but in some cases outstandingly inadequate. We all read *The Times* because of the Law Reports. We once, at tea, were discussing which part of *The Times* people read first. Carl Aarvold, you know, who got his blue at Cambridge, played for England, said 'Naturally I look at the sports page." He was a splendid judge, he was the Recorder of London, Carl was. And somebody else, theatrical person, said, "I look at the reviews." I said I always look at the quotation from the Bible which was at the top of the page of *The Times* before it disguised itself in its present form; it was very interesting, one day the Old Testament, one day the New. Then I used to go to the obits to see if I was still alive and then I would turn to the Law Reports and by that time my tube train was at Liverpool Street.

'I think judges have a right to complain about journalists who comment adversely on the sentence without knowing all the facts of the case. They rush to "Another light sentence for rapist . . ." as a lead, but unless they know the facts, how can they call it light? People say that to me when I'm out at dinner – how did that judge only give that sentence? I say I don't know the facts. I think newspapers would do well to realise that criticism of judges, when ill-founded, is a denigration of the judicial system. And some of us say that there is a policy of certain papers to denigrate the established order of society, I would hesitate to make that allegation myself. And an example is the way the newspapers dealt with this man Biggs, the train robber, who got away, now in South America somewhere, as a sort of folk hero . . .' (Indeed, the same month, Biggs popped up again in the papers, on a beach in Rio de Janeiro, grinning and tanned.)

So where do judges swap notes, talk about how the press handles matters, how juries are behaving?

'Lots of judges belong to the Garrick Club; I don't. I'm the member of one club, the RAF club, a very good place to meet your wife because you know she'll be safe in the drawing-room, rather than meeting in the public room of a hotel. Judges don't meet up all the time, some chaps might meet either shopping or playing golf. We talk when we meet at our Inn or at Court.'

Which leads on to the nature of judges. It is said of them that they come from a narrow stratum of society, that their backgrounds are so different from those of the people they try that they cannot comprehend or empathise with what they see in front of them.

'It might be said that most judges have come from comfortable homes, went to good public schools, then Oxford or Cambridge, then into good chambers. But among judges I've known who've tried crime – one or two I can remember seemed very remote from the standards of living of most people, but they are very few. The late Mr Justice Horridge, was a very distinguished King's Bench judge; he used to go to Monte Carlo a lot for his holidays, when you went to him to make an application in chambers he would speak to you as a Victorian marquis might speak to his indoor servant but he was a very fine judge.'

He feels that most judges come up by their own efforts, unaided by family money. 'I think judges ought to represent society and as women and people of different colour are forming a larger part of legal society than they did I am quite sure the Lord Chancellor will bear this in mind. I remember we had on my circuit a charming chap; he wore a turban instead of a wig. He became a judge. Judges are ordinary people. They don't claim to be more. I once had a very strange experience.' And we are off again on a richly drawn tale.

'I was defending a woman about to be tried for stealing a gold cigarette case at a well-known and highly-respected night club, long before the war. When she came into conference – when you meet your client – she was about twenty-eight, she said the man gave it to her, that he was drunk and was carried home with her assistance. She mentioned the first name of the man who would be the presiding judge – "He comes occasionally to the club, brings a lady with him and dances." What do you do?

'I happened to know that judge personally, a bon viveur in a way, for very good reasons. He was very hospitable and often on the way home from chambers I would call in at his flat and have a glass of sherry and I thought what the hell are we going to do. It was February, a rotten night. He said, "I've just come back from a lovely holiday into this snow." I said, "You're looking a bit peakish to me, come from a hot climate suddenly into the cold" – he was living on his own – "you should be careful, you could catch a chill." He said, "What's your case about?" I told him. I said, "You know these people get hold of names," and I told him that she had referred to him by his first name, and said he was a very popular fellow, has champagne; the lady who's his friend is a well-known actress, they have a dance and go away. He said, "I know the club, it's a nice place, the Prince was seen going in there occasionally." I said, "You know how these people talk when they get hold of names, they chuck them about . . ." I was saying goodnight so I said, "You know, judge, it may be the light but you're looking a bit green. You should have a hot toddy tonight or you might not be in court tomorrow . . ." Got down there next day and waited and we were told the judge had got a chill . . .'

He has another story about the indiscretions of the judiciary. 'Another judge on circuit was entertained by the barristers at their own club and he enjoyed himself very well and had a few drinks. Then he had a few more. So the barristers got a bit worried and one said something to another – who later became a member of the government – and he went out for a few minutes and the judge said, "Right, I'll go back to my own lodgings, I came in my car." And we said, "Yes, we know that." So we all went out. He said he was sure he had left the keys in his car but couldn't find them, so we all searched, couldn't find the keys. Someone said, "Look judge, it is only a couple of miles, so, Charles, drive the judge to his lodgings." Of course, the keys were found under his car the following morning. It works, doesn't it? Provided judges and barristers can trust each other.'

It is related, like all his stories, with great attention to detail, with pauses in the right place, a perfect radio story-telling voice. What does he read for pleasure?

'All of Dickens and, for inspiration, the Prophets and the Old Testament and the Book of Psalms, which is common to Christian and Jew. You find it reproduced in the Moslem faith and you only wish men would follow it a little more precisely. The words of Micah which I used in the speech when I said farewell at the Old Bailey were: "What o man does the Lord require of thee but to love mercy, do justice and walk humbly."

'Observe the language,' he says, and he repeats it, underlining with his voice the words 'do justice' and 'love mercy'. And, after an enquiry about the times for the next train back to London, the court rises. He bids farewell with the genial, self-confident nod that must be remembered by the many hundreds of defendants who have appeared in front of him, and by their wives watching from the gallery.

14

The Widows

But the waiting time . . . is the
hardest time of all.

Sarah Doudney, *Psalm of Life*

'He walked down the drive flashing a torch and calling the dogs. That is not a man
going out to do something. He never sneaked out. If he had thought there was
someone out there the first thing he would have done is take a shotgun; we had
nine in the house,' says Brenda Noye.

'You see a man in a balaclava and camouflage suit – you don't say, "Excuse me,
before I hit you, are you a police officer?" If that person had been a rapist or some
evil person my husband would be a hero, he would be up there on a pedestal.'

But the man in the balaclava hiding in the bushes in the twenty-acre gardens of
Kenneth and Brenda Noye's Kent home in January 1985 was not a rapist or some
evil person. He was Detective Constable John Fordham, a member of an
undercover squad watching Noye because he was under suspicion in connection
with the handling of £26-million-worth of gold bullion stolen from the Brinks
Mat depot at Heathrow airport in 1983.

Noye's Rottweiler dogs had sensed someone in the grounds and started
barking. Noye had come across the man in the balaclava and camouflage jacket
and had run into the garage and grabbed a kitchen knife which he had been using
to scrape the battery terminals. Fordham, presumably because he did not want to
blow the undercover operation, did not identify himself as a policeman. The two
fought. Noye stabbed him to death.

The police, aware of having lost contact with Fordham, swung too late into
action and headed for the Noyes' home. Brian Reader, a friend of Noye's and his
partner in their current enterprise, was inside the house. On the run from the
police for another charge, he fled but was captured on the road. Kenneth and
Brenda Noye were arrested and told they would be charged with the murder of a
police officer. Reader's wife, Lyn, was also held. Over the next months, Brenda
Noye and Lyn Reader were to watch their husbands appear in two of the major
post-war Old Bailey trials: the first for murdering a policeman; the second for
their part in the largest ever bullion robbery.

In the murder trial, Noye, represented by John Matthews, QC, argued that he
had been defending himself and his family; that he had walked down the drive
with his dogs in a way that was not 'surreptitious or bent on evil intent'; that

Fordham had gone for him and had never identified himself as a police officer. Fordham's widow and young son sat on the benches in the body of the court. The gallery was packed. The jury deliberated. Noye and Reader were acquitted.

But they immediately faced charges connected with the handling of the Brinks Mat bullion. Their wives, elated with the acquittal, visited them once more in prison and waited for the next trial.

The evidence against them did not appear hefty. While it was clear that both Noye and Reader were engaged in very sharp practices in the movement of gold it seemed to their families that they had been charged with the wrong thing – there was clearly a large smuggling and tax fraud involved, but there was little evidence of involvement in the Brinks Mat case in the evidence that was emerging as far as they were concerned. The two wives lunched in the sandwich bars and wine bars near the Old Bailey, the difficult trial seemed over, they were almost light-headed. The jury decided differently. After a long spell in a hotel in St John's Wood they returned with guilty verdicts. Kenneth Noye was jailed for fourteen years and Brian Reader for ten. Brenda Noye and Lyn Reader, who have always protested their husbands' innocence, became prison widows.

There is a popular caricature of the woman associated with criminals: the gangster's moll, the prison widow, all mascara and sunbed tan, teetering to the steps of the public gallery and smiling devotedly at the man in the dock. Like most caricatures it has no shortage of genuine role models. And when the Knightsbridge Safe-Deposit Box robbery ended in 1989, up popped one Pamela Seamark, the former girlfriend of the main robber, Valerio Viccei, to tell her story to the *News of the World*: 'Sultry Pamela Seamark lay naked on her lover's bed and felt her skin crawl as she looked down at the £4 million plum-sized diamond nestling in her navel. It was part of the treasure Italian Stallion Valerio Viccei had stolen in the Knightsbridge Safe-Deposit raid. Now as she lay dreading Viccei's kinky lust, former convent girl Pamela . . .' and so on.

But the old caricature was confronted in the mid-eighties with a successful television series called *Widows*, written by Lynda La Plante and received with both popular and critical acclaim. It told the story of four women whose husbands or lovers were villains who had been killed while planning a major robbery; the Widows then took the job on themselves. Its star was 'Dolly', played by Ann Mitchell, who had deliberately chosen to tackle the notion of what people reckoned was the typical criminal old lady: 'As a child I was fed on movies in which the working class were portrayed by middle-class actors and it was very funny. Working-class speech and locations have become synonymous with violence, lack of intelligence and criminality. That is the cliché about the East End. The reality is very different.'

And the reality for Brenda Noye and Lyn Reader, despite the way they were portrayed during the trials, was also very different.

As the sentences were passed, so one paper reported, Lyn Reader cried out, 'I'll wait for you, darling,' while Brenda Noye 'cursed' from the public gallery.

Noye was described as 'the crooked Midas . . . bullion king . . . 24-carat rat';
Reader as 'the principal lieutenant . . . the burly minder'.

'I think if I'd actually said "I'll wait for you, darling", Brian would have jumped
out of the dock and punched me on the nose,' says Lyn Reader, sitting in her
Orpington semi-detached. 'And I was too flabbergasted to say anything,' says
Brenda Noye. She is less flabbergasted now.

Brenda Noye, *née* Tremain, is from Erith, the daughter of an ultrasonic
engineer and a computer worker; Noye was the son of a GPO general manager
and the manageress of Crayford greyhound stadium. The two met as teenagers,
fell in love, got engaged at eighteen, married and had two sons. Noye became
successful, very successful.

'People ask how he came to have money,' says Brenda Noye. 'When I first met
him he worked at night in the print and by day as a tipper driver. He would take a
couple of hours' sleep and go out to work. He did that for about two years and then
bought his own lorry and eventually got a fleet of about a dozen lorries. He
bought a yard, sold a third of it for the price he paid for the whole of it, dealt in
watches and jewellery, did property deals in Kent and got a place where the
children could grow up without roaming the streets and sniffing glue.' Noye
prospered, became a Freemason, gave to local charities, bought the dream house.

'We worked damn hard to get that house. We had six holidays, I think, in the
eighteen years we've been together and two of those since he's been away. He was
a workaholic. When he came home he would sit down and get his work out and
see how many lorries he had on the road and hope to God they didn't get a
puncture in Birmingham with this load.'

Lyn Reader is from Dulwich and met Brian Reader, then a haulage contractor
from Greenwich, when she worked for a turf accountants. They have two
children, Joanne, a PA and Paul, who worked as a Barbican stage-hand before
going into the motor trade. Life in the early days seemed sunny, there were
holidays abroad, Lyn's work as a riding instructress.

But by the end of the seventies, Brian was in trouble with the police. An
informer, Micky 'Skinny' Gervaise made statements about Brian and others. He
was charged with robbery and jumped bail. The family fled.

'We went to France, then to Spain. I hated it. I thought – you can't go home
when you want to. People think it sounds glamorous but it was awful changing
homes all the time. I used to get plants and flowers whenever we went to a new
place to try and make it look like home,' says Lyn Reader. 'Then I got a message
that my mother was ill so we had to come home. But we still had to keep hiding
because of what Gervaise had said and have different identities.'

But the police had already clocked the returned Reader and his relationship
with Kenneth Noye, who was banking large sums in Jersey and Dublin. The
surveillance team was set up. They watched the movement of gold. Then came
the dreadful events of that cold January night.

'When I was first arrested they took me down to Swanleigh police station and they took all my possessions off me – watch, wedding-ring, everything,' says Brenda Noye. 'Then they took me to Dartford police station and I was kept there and they came in and handcuffed me and said I was being shifted. They put me in a police car and took me at a ridiculous speed down to Gravesend police station. The next morning they took me back down the road to Dartford. You lose track on days.

'I've got to say some of the Kent police were good. There was a policewoman outside my door and she was a very nice woman, trying to comfort me, get me to eat something. She even said, "I'll send out and get something for you. I don't blame you for not wanting to eat the stuff they dish out here." When I was in there I asked two Metropolitan officers for some clean clothes. They came back. It was absolutely ridiculous. I asked one of them to bring a tracksuit because that was the safest thing. They came back with the top of one and the bottom of another. Two odd shoes. No socks or tights.'

The children, then aged ten and twelve, had to be kept moving about because by now the press was after them, waiting for them outside school. They went to their grandparents and aunts. Brenda Noye went to Holloway prison for the next two months.

'I had a job working as a cleaner and I met several old women in there for shoplifting. I was amazed how many people are in there who have not got a living soul to write to or turn to. I was charged with murder. When it came to the committal the magistrate asked what the evidence was. One of the police officers said there was blood spattering all over the place. I shouted, "That is a lie," and was told to be quiet. The magistrate threw it out. Then as I walked out of the door I was charged with conspiracy to handle gold bullion. Out of the kindness of their hearts they offered no evidence against me at the Old Bailey.'

Brenda Noye gave evidence at the murder trial and was portrayed by the prosecution as a cool customer. 'For a woman who had gone through that experience, I thought she was particularly cool,' said Flying Squad detective Kenneth O'Rourke. 'You went in there to bully her,' said Noye's barrister. 'I don't think she is the type of woman who can be bullied,' replied O'Rourke.

Did she not know that her husband was involved with illegal gold?

'I never thought about him being arrested because you don't know what's going on. You're at home doing the housework and they're getting on with their working life. All Ken has ever said about it is that he was smuggling the gold. I knew what he was like for avoiding paying his taxes, he could be a little bit of a bugger for that, but when it all came down I thought at the end of the day they'll sort this mess out and he'll probably end up with two years for not paying his tax and that is it. I never ever even believed it would get to court or anything like that.

'When he was acquitted on the murder, I said, "They're going to get you, Ken, aren't they? If they don't get you here they're going to get you somewhere else. You're never going to live down the fact that you walked out of court on the murder." I think the keeping of me in Holloway changed his attitude. He thought

– Bloody hell if they're capable of doing that to her what the hell are they capable of doing to me?'

Kenneth Noye soon found out. 'Mr Gold ... the crooked millionaire' appeared on the front pages of many papers, dapper in a DJ and velvet bow-tie, looking every inch the sort of smooth operator who could arrange the disposal of millions of pounds worth of gold via smelting works and far-off bank accounts.

'That photo they kept plastering of him in his dinner suit, I suppose he's only worn it half a dozen times in his life. That was one of the last functions we went to before it happened. The police must have found it. I would have given them the ones of Ken in his working gear. He was such a scruffy sod. He was always in his black cords and check shirt, working boots, some tatty old jumper. He used to go out one night a week to the George at Bexley, the King's Head, sometimes on to a disco-cum-night-club in Bromley but every other night of the week he was at home with me. He used to go down the squash club once a week. Saturday evening we might go out to eat but probably only once a month. His home was his kingdom.'

There were stories of Noye the womaniser.

'To be quite honest I haven't read all the stories about him. I know there's one about a woman. What can I say? They say Princess Anne had a lover! Ken relates very well to women but he's no Casanova. If he had a girlfriend ... well, I've been with that man since I was fifteen years old and twenty-three years we've been together and he's slept with me every night and come home to me every night. We've got a good marriage and the children are stable and there's not many could go through all that and come out the way they have.

'The person in the papers is not the person I know. He took a man's life and that's something he has to live with forever. They make Ken out to be someone, because they've slagged him off so much – he's not that person. There were lots of people out there wanting to put a knife in his back because of what he achieved in his life: from nothing to something.' Lyn Reader was offered £1,000 by one paper if she could give them a picture of her husband drinking champagne.

Brenda Noye and Lyn Reader now have lives that revolve around the familiar prison widow routine: the letters, the visits, the efforts to find new grounds for appeal, the legal bills; dealing with men growing older inside and impatient with the years ahead in Durham and Parkhurst; keeping the family together; holding the head up as the neighbours water the lawns and nod at those scarlet ladies, the ones that were in the papers; the daily reminders ...

'I am aware of the police being around now,' says Lyn Reader. 'Different cars parked outside. There's a man on the corner, part of Neighbourhood Watch, who makes a note of the numbers of all the cars that come to visit and hands it to the police. When people phone they sometimes ask, "What's that noise?" and I say, "Hang on, they're just changing the tape".'

The four children they have between them deal with it in their different ways.

'My children's attitude has changed very much,' says Lyn Reader. 'Joey gets so uptight, she tries so hard but a couple of times she has really broken down. Paul gets so much stick over the Brinks Mat gold. People find out who he is. They start chatting to him so they can say to people they've been speaking to Brian Reader's son. I'm lucky I've still got them living with me because they've been a power of strength to me.

'Joey took me to see *Buster*. Half-way through she said, "Oh, this is the worst thing I could have done," because it's all about being on the run and wanting to have English things to eat when you're abroad. And I said, "Well, at least I didn't ask for steak and chips, did I?" In the last scene he's going to give himself up and he's in this little council flat and there's 101 police cars outside, she turned round and went "typical". Any other member of the public most have thought it was daft.' It reminded Lyn Reader of her own arrest.

'When they arrested me there were about ten of them. They were like a crowd of cowboys. One was drunk as a sack. They were screaming at me, "Has your husband got a green Cavalier?" I just screamed back at them, "What's all this about?" They got a message on their radio that a green Cavalier was approaching and one of them stood with a gun pointing at the front door. When they had me in the cell they were all screaming at me and saying that Brian was covered in blood and he'd murdered someone. I said, "You're a liar, you're a liar." I've got the clothes back now – there's not a spatter of blood but inside in the pocket there's been a hole cut and there's sellotape with gold dust in it. You don't carry gold bars in your pocket. There was not an inkling of blood on his clothing.'

Meanwhile, the Readers are staying put. The Noyes, who always had the higher profile, are not.

'I'm moving into a new house to try and get away from the press and try and put an end to the last four years for the sake of the children's sanity. I thought very seriously about changing my name and if it was just me I'd move to the other end of the country and totally change my name and just cut off every lead. But how can I expect my children to do that? I have told them to stand up, look people straight in the eye and say, "My dad is innocent." I can't keep back-tracking.

'They take a lot of stick at school. I say to them, "Don't get into fights. You start trying to fight your way out of it, it won't work. Come home and take out your anger on a punchbag or a football or something, don't retaliate." How can you say that to a boy that's going to grow up into a man: stand there and take it, for the rest of your life take it, because if you put one foot wrong you've had it.'

Getting rid of the house has not been simple. Amongst the 'prospective purchasers' were journalists and ghouls, there was enough talk of the place being 'cursed' to put off one potential buyer. Brinks Mat – who want money from Noye – have also sent their people down to inspect and inquire whose Range Rovers are parked in the barn, where the pictures have gone.

'I blew my top. I said, "The Range Rovers don't belong to me and I'm just housing them for people because I've got a damn great barn and they don't use them all the time," gave them the names of the people. "As for the paintings, they haven't been hanging up since this whole thing happened," I said. "How on earth do you think I paid for my husband's defence?"'

There have been black-edged cards sent, threats to kill the children. There are odd calls.

'I had a call from a man one night who said, "I've just lost my father." I said, "Oh, I'm very sorry." Then he said, "I always wondered why my father sold his land to your husband, now I know . . . I've got a tape recording of your husband threatening him. I'm going to the police with it." I said, "Well, you do that, I don't know what you're talking about." He said, "I'm going to take it to the police and he'll get another four years." He was on the phone every night.

'I thought if I go to the police the press are going to get hold of it. So I waited until I saw Ken and he said, "I only ever bought land off one old person and I got him rehoused and bought him a colour television and a video and Christ knows what else." He said, "Just front it out and take it to the police."

'I said, "I'm not going to because it'll just go to the press and they'll make it out the worst way they can." The funny part was that it was always on Ken's office phone. Finally he phoned up and he said, "This tape, how much are you going to give me for it?" I said, "You're sick, you're really sick and you need treatment." He said, "You're not going to look so pretty when your husband comes out by the time I've finished with you," and then he really started going on. I hung up and he never phoned back.'

The new house may erase some of the old memories but the details of the case, the trial and the appeal linger, picked over again and again and again. What were the jury talking about that kept them out for so long? Were they all paying attention? The judge's summing up had been fair but how much did everyone remember of Kenneth Noye the man who had stabbed an undercover officer to death?

'I analyse it every night when I go to bed,' says Brenda Noye. 'After the murder trial I was totally instructed by barristers and solicitors to say nothing, to not retaliate in any way, to be the quiet demure wife who was just happy it was all over. That is the greatest regret I've had in my life. I should have screamed and shouted and hollered about what happened and not accepted what the lawyers said. They're interested in you not rocking the boat. I should have started campaigning from that day on when I was given a chance.

'They told me right from the start, "You're wasting your time, you're fighting society. You're not in a position to fight it or get anywhere." I said, "I will prove him innocent and when he comes out you'll all bloody well kiss his feet." They give you a sympathetic pat on the shoulder and say, "That's life." I can understand that. They've got their living to earn. They can't be buggered about worrying about someone who's been put away. They're worried about their next case.'

Lyn Reader allowed herself to believe that the men would be acquitted: 'Even those old whatdyoucallits, the old people who sit there all the time said, "They've been charged with the wrong thing, love, don't you worry." As for the trial itself

. . . to me it's all actors on a stage and the best actor wins. They don't put it in laymen's language so that the jury can understand it.'

When John Palmer, who appeared later on Brinks Mat charges, was at the Old Bailey, Brenda Noye went to watch the case: 'The next thing I get in the press is that I've been accused of nobbling members of the jury! The last bloody thing I would have done. Then I was supposed to have been seen inside the court downstairs. You can't get in there without identity. In the end my solicitor had a thing put in the paper about it. That's the sort of thing we've had from them and it never stops. I would love to go and listen to every single case to do with Brinks Mat because, as far as I'm concerned, I might pick something up, but I can't go because I'm too frightened.

'During the last trial a man came up – he was a go-between – and said if we didn't give him £10,000 he'd tell the *Mirror* that the jury was being nobbled,' says Lyn Reader. 'We found out that he'd just come out after being inside for fifteen years.'

There is a bitterness there that Brenda Noye acknowledges: 'It stripped me and it's made me into a person that I'm not. I'm hard. I'm very bitter. It's something that grows in you and you can't stop it.'

It spreads to the rest of the family. 'My parents wouldn't have said a bad word about the police ever. We lived next door to some Welsh people and the woman used to say what the miners were going through in Wales and it wasn't all their fault, the police were provoking them, they were brutal buggers. And my mum used to say, "She doesn't know what she's talking about." But what happened devastated her. It destroyed every belief they ever had in British justice, in the country itself. How do you make up for a tragedy like that? My mother wrote back when she was called for jury service that she could not possibly consider judging anybody who came before the court because of the experience my family suffered.'

As far as friends go, some have gone. Some believe that Noye and Reader were indeed guilty men and their wives were either duped fools or loyal spouses going through the motions of a protest of innocence. Others had no desire to be seen rubbing padded shoulders with them any more.

'The ones I honestly felt I could lean on I never saw,' says Brenda Noye. 'The ones you didn't know that long came to the front. I am in debt up to here. I just thank the gods that my husband was surrounded by a lot of genuine businessmen who have helped me an awful lot.'

There are photos of younger laughing husbands on the mantelpiece, holiday grins and sunny smiles. Life was good, the risks seemed small. The two women are both still handsome. Passes get made.

'You get a lot of people coming up to you and saying, "We could have a whale of a time!" You don't know whether they're after the gold or us!' says Lyn Reader.

So the two visit, the long haul for the two hour chat. 'He's treated quite well because in the top security prisons they don't go steaming in because there are too many dangerous people around,' says Brenda Noye.

15

The Prison Officer

The misery of jails is not half their evil . . .
In a prison the awe of publick eye is lost,
and the power of the law is spent; there are
few fears, there are no blushes. The lewd
inflame the lewd, the audacious harden the
audacious. Everyone fortifies himself as he
can against his own sensibility, endeavours
to practise on others the arts which are
practised on himself, and gains the
kindness of associates by similitude of
manners. Thus some sink amidst their
misery, and others survive only to
propagate villainy.

Samuel Johnson, *The Idler*

'The perfect world, perhaps, would be if we deep-froze them all, hung them on coat hangers – take them out the day before they are released and defrost them. Then there'd be no problem. But that's not quite the reality of the thing.'

The reality of the thing is what Frank – not his real name since prison officers cannot talk for publication without the permission of their seniors – has just driven home from. He greets two small dogs and one larger son and puts on the coffee.

'I joined in frustration at being unable to progress in my civilian job. My father was in the job and he was always against the idea of any of his children joining. But I had a civilian job and was bluntly told that the age I was they weren't prepared to promote me for another twelve years. I was only twenty, a cost office manager, part of the Sears empire, so I applied to join.

'I was brought up as a prison officer's son. I went to a school in Acton where there was one end of the playground and the other end of the playground. Some have ended up in prison, some as well known singers – Adam Faith went to my school.

'I was no saint. Shoplifting we saw as good sport, talking to the shopkeeper while someone filled his pocket up with ready made quarter-pound bags of sweets they used to have in those days. Broke a few windows, got chased. But as an officer's son the family control was strict.

'My father's wishes are that my two sons don't join the job because it's changed. It's ruled by the Treasury now, people in pinstripes, it's all efficiency and money, money, money. But you can't work on the Marks and Spencers system. They're not all the same size, not all the same colour.'

Few parts of the judicial system feel as beleaguered as the prison service. Even the nickname for a prison officer – screw – seems harsher then the cozzer, brief, Old Bill and beak that describe the other links in the chain. They feel undervalued and underpaid. If they do their job well no one notices; if they do their job badly, there's a riot or a break-out and the world examines them. Their image ranges from that of a flat-capped thug to a bloke who couldn't get into the police force. They find their role is increasingly that of the faceless turnkey. They feel their skills are unrecognised.

'When I first joined, the test you took to get in was basic English and arithmetic. Now it's more a psychology test, putting squares into the right place, and an observation test: you're shown pictures of a cell with two people searching it and certain things are missing. There are two pictures, you look at the first and then at the second and there's a bar missing off the window and so on. If you're unsuccessful, you go home; if you're successful there's a very basic medical – urine sample, height, weight, eyes. They then sift through those results and you're called for an interview in front of three people: a governor grade, who normally chairs the board, an administrational grade, that's the officer side of it, and the working grade, a chief, the uniformed side. They interview you: why did you want to join, what are your desires, do you wish to help people, relate to people, work with people. After that you leave the room and they call you back and say if they are prepared to accept you.

'You always feel sorry for the new people because they've never worked in a prison and they're in civilian clothing with a cap badge stuck in their lapels. They're called NEPOs – New Entrant Prison Officer – and they're lumbered with that for eleven weeks.

'They then spend a fortnight at the establishment. In London it's Pentonville, Feltham or Oxford, usually a local prison where there's a variation of work going on so they can observe. Twenty years ago you had to be twenty-five to join, now it's down to twenty. So you finish that fortnight by being called and if they think you're not observant enough, you're not taking the detail in, they can finish you then. You are also expected to go to physical training to get into some sort of physical condition for contending with prisoners fighting and running for alarm bells. For a person joining at thirty to forty it could be a blessing. At the end of the fortnight you are sent to the training schools, near Rugby, in Wakefield and Leyhill. That's a nine-week period where you're taught the theory.'

Most of the schools take around 160, 170. The theory – how the gate should be worked, how escort duty is carried out – is taught. There are lectures and a first aid course, and the St John's Ambulance certificate has to be taken.

'You have physical training. It's not called self-defence, what we do now is a thing called control and restraint. This is an approved method where three people go into a cell and put a man under restraint, one on one arm, one on the other arm and one holding the head, to move the person. That has been the best thing to happen to the prison service because before it was grab an arm, grab a leg, and there were too many people involved and not only the inmate could be injured but the officer could be injured too. With this method it's a blessing, it really is. They also get psychology training, relationships with ethnics, relationships with other officers.

'It's like being a schoolboy, like university. You meet people you've never met before, from all walks of life. In the wing I work in now, I have an ex-carpet fitter, ex-mechanic, two ex-ambulance drivers, a man who's come out of the forces after twenty years in the RAF. You've got a completely mixed bag, office workers, ex-police, ex-Special Constables. All these people meet and form friendships. You've also got female officers at the school and that has led to permanent relationships . . . so it's very much like a university. One day you've never met anybody and the next there are another 159 people.

'You'd have exercises where you had to move a vault box across a chasm sort of thing so you had to work as a group. They tried to build that sort of relationship up because there may be an incident at work where there's a riot and you're trapped with three or four of you to try and get out of the situation.'

Half-way through the training school, the officers are given their postings, which can be for junior establishments, fourteen to seventeen-year-olds, or young offenders, seventeen to twenty-one-year-olds, or local prisons. The tasks vary – Brixton has a heavy commitment to the courts; Wandsworth takes convicted prisoners and sends them off to training prisons; Coldingley has a large workshop where they make the big motorway signs and a laundry for outside work; Maidstone has a whole wing of sexual offenders, who are kept under Rule 43, which means they are separate from other prisoners; Pentonville has a reputation as the dossers' prison because of the large number of drunks doing sentences of less than six months. For some of those, the very routine is an attraction.

'On a basic day, the staff come on at half-past seven and carry out a roll check to make sure that what's supposed to be on their landings are there. They then get out the people who are required for discharge and court for transfer that day. We then go through the mundane things: slopping out, the plastic bucket routine. I have yet to meet anyone who enjoys that. We then take all their applications to see the chaplain, for education, to apply to be on classes, for exercise books, drawing material, to have property in their possession, to see the governor with personal problems like to get married, to get transferred to other establishments, can they make phone calls etc.

'We then breakfast them all. Normally a boiled egg, as much bread as they want, a portion of butter, porridge or cornflakes, sometimes bacon or scrambled egg, cup of tea or hot water so they can make their own tea. They are then locked up so that searching can be carried out. Then they're exercised.

'Every inmate may also apply to see the doctor if he's not feeling well. There's no appointments – if a man applies to see a doctor he will see him that day. He can apply to see an optician, to see a dentist. They go to classes – English, maths, sociology, art. You also have classes for people who can't speak English – we have someone from Vietnam at the moment and a Pole who only knows two words: "Bounds Green".

'Their dinner is normally a three-course meal: soup, choice of one or other, vegetarians are catered for, the Jews are catered for, the Muslims are catered for, the vegans are catered for – egg-free, cheese-free, we've even got people who don't like potatoes who can have rice. The other day it was chilli con carne or meat pie. It's all cooked in a very large kitchen by inmates under the direct supervision of staff. They normally get a sweet: duff and custard, the old school food, rice and semolina, or a trifle, or jam tart and custard. They also get a cup of tea. After dinner we then slop out again and we send about thirty inmates to the gym, another fifty will go on association where they can play pool, do a bit of ironing, watch a video film and associate with each other, and others get to classes.

'The afternoons: once a week is bathing, twice a week is canteen, where all inmates are given what's called wages which fluctuates between £1.50 for those with no job and up to nearly £4 for those in jobs like reception, kitchen, canteen workers. Tea is bread, butter, tea and then a meal. Quiche, pizza with beans, bacon, egg, beans, a tea and they're given a cake – it's called the supper cake. That's the wing for people awaiting trial.'

Matters have been simplified by a change in the prison rules in 1988 which ended the practice of food being brought in for unconvicted prisoners awaiting trial. Although the rules were complex – only two items of each fruit, no yoghurt, no tins – the food parcels were an important part of the visiting ritual. Wives and girlfriends were expected to cook a meal and bring it in wrapped in tinfoil, and countless little treats – a half pint of beer (but no Special Brew), a half bottle of wine, tobacco – were eagerly anticipated. All these items were ticked off on a form by a prison officer and the inmate could then check that all his tuck had been delivered. He could then eat it or swap it or share it. But as drugs became more prevalent in prison, the food became the natural way for smuggling it in: a banana could have its top delicately lopped off and a sliver of hashish slipped into the fruit after which the top was gently replaced, lumps of dope could be hidden in stew, oranges injected with vodka. The then Home Secretary Douglas Hurd announced the changes, to the disappointment of the inmates and the relief of the prison officers and, quite possibly, a few prison widows who were released from the responsibility of providing home cooking for someone who was never home. But if the food privileges had vanished, inmates still wanted some relief from the tedium of life inside.

'On the convicted wing up to a hundred can be on evening classes, pottery, art, creative writing, yoga, chess. Once a week there's a church class and also the gym is available for weight training, indoor cricket, football. We have outside teams come in to play indoor cricket, basketball, five-a-side football. Sometimes a celebrity comes in, the ones that come to mind are Frank Bruno and Trevor

Brooking. Brooking met a few prisoners, signed autographs and took part in five-a-side matches. Bruno issued some photographs, signed autographs, spoke to some inmates and then gave a demonstration of his workout which was very impressive. Invariably it's an invitation. There's not been many refused – Kevin Keegan's been, Sharon Davis has been. It could be curiosity, no one can say that they're not curious. We even had Georgie Best – but as an inmate. He was a novelty value and didn't last very long before we sent him to Ford.'

The Famous Prisoner has a special role inside. Lester Piggott discovered this during his sentence for tax evasion: the advantages are that some privileges will be slipped in his direction by people anxious to share his company, the disadvantages are that half the would-be pals are hoping to sell a story about the Famous Person as soon as they get out. Some of these stories may be true, most are exaggerated. Many revolve around suggestions that life inside is a doddle.

'They're allowed radios, board games, matchstick model making, the newspapers, the magazines and the books. Any newspaper lasts eight or nine days, people grabbing it to read even after that time. The books are not predictable, one would think they would all be horror, westerns, but they're not. The variation is quite astounding, anything they can get their hands on to read.'

Anything to escape reality. But what is the reality of prison for the officer?

'*Porridge* is probably nearer the truth of what prisons are like than anything that's ever been shown. The public image is hobnailed boots, uncaring, lock 'em up and keep 'em behind that wall. It's a tragedy that a lot of people who do a bloody good job don't admit they're prison officers. If you meet people socially there always seems to be a look: how can you go to work locking up people behind those walls, rapists, murderers, drug addicts, AIDS victims, how can you do that job?

'The fact is that you may have a family, that we go fishing, play sport, some of us are councillors, some do charity work, one of the most generous groups in charity are prison officers. The girl from Liverpool, with the growth on her face, officers cycled to the west country to raise money for her, sat in the forecourt of the prison and allowed people to throw wet sponges at them, had discos, dances, did crazy things around the country.

'If someone asks me what I do at a party I tell 'em. And I wait for the reaction. And it's not long in coming: who do you have? It's got to be juicy, it's got to be something they can understand. I went to a party once and when I said how prisoners had colour televisions, had gym equipment, how we took them outside to play other teams at sport, there was horror. They seemed to have the idea that it should all be hard labour and lock 'em up and don't let 'em out. It's not that easy. They're human beings, they're all different, no two are the same. But people can't see that and that frustrates me at times.'

There are many frustrations. They are aired frequently in *Gatelodge*, the Prison Officers' Association magazine, where officers complain of being treated like 'serfs' by the management and make jokes about the prisoners soon being given keys to their cells. What also frustrates prison officers is being called warders, a word that still appears in headlines about prison disputes.

'We're not warders, we're prison officers. We spent nearly thirteen weeks training and it costs between £6,000 and £7,000 to train each officer. There are officers with university degrees, A levels, they're not all from the dole queue. There are a lot of very hard-working people who believe in what they're doing and enjoy it, who become very frustrated that as soon as there's a row or a riot it's always the prison officer that got it wrong. What we find hard to accept is that we work on the landing with the prisoners; we get that smell of bodies who've been in a cell for fifteen hours and stand and watch while they do the day's slopping-out routine.'

The sheer familiarity with their charges, the fact that they see them at their worst and most vulnerable means that they also get a closer insight into the working of professional crime than many on the outside who only see the criminal with all his defences up.

'As regards "gangland", there are definitely still groups of individuals that work together, have an order together. It's quite fascinating that at the moment we have two people who have an awful lot of respect given to them by the other 200 and yet as individuals those two people could walk past you and you wouldn't give them a second look.

'In the old days you had the one father figure in the old gangs or the two who were the main people in the families in the seventies. There was normally one senior member and the rest. There don't seem to be families any more, there seem to be groups. There's often reference to what they call the coloured group, the Yardies. There seems to be more connection with foreign crime figures. You still get "I'm from the north of London so I only belong to a north of London crime group", "I'm south London", that still seems to exist. But the leaders are more at the back. In the old days it was the main figure who led from the front. Now it's like a pyramid that's been stood on its head, the central figure is at the back and you've got to get through the soldiers to reach the general.'

But it's still very clear how the pecking order stands.

'Those who are prepared to commit the violent act and be aggressive in their crime, be it murder, be it GBH, can get an awful lot more respect than the petty thief. With the pickpocket, the mugger, it's always considered, well, you've crept up behind somebody. But the person who has committed a big fraud case, has used his brain, can also have a lot of respect.

'The lawyer who's gone bent will have all the prison clientele he wants. Or the person who has carried out a really outlandish crime, who's made the headlines. The documentary on the Flying Squad showing them in action meant that there's been a lot of "he arrested me". In this prison there's six who were arrested by those officers, so suddenly they're able to get a lot of attention because they're able to say, "Oh, I remember when he arrested me – he put the gun in my eye and said to me 'Don't move' . . . I remember those two, we had them."

'The Knightsbridge gang who carried out the safe deposit box robbery, people say, "Oh, I knew them . . . that bloke who's just got eighteen years, I knew him." It's to try and build themselves up because their own crime may only get them a small sentence. They think, "Because I mixed with him I might be a bigger criminal than you think I am."

'The professional criminal – you always say to him, "You got caught, you weren't very successful. It's your job of work to be a criminal, it's my job of work to keep you locked up and the policeman's job to catch you. Two have been successful and one failed." And he'll say, "Yeah, all right but what about the three I got away with." So you have a bit of repartee between you. They'll say, "The money's there when I come out, it's the only thing I know . . . I haven't got a trade, this is my occupation. While it was going on I had a nice car, I lived well, I had good holidays and I've got life-style and this is the price I've got to pay, reluctantly."'

Prisoners are well aware of the fact that prison officers are not well paid. The introduction in 1988 of Fresh Start, a system which abolished overtime in the prison service and introduced a fixed wage, meant the end of the chance to work round the clock and increase the weekly take-home pay. So they know there may be temptations.

'They offer you money – how much are your keys worth? Can you take this letter? Can you get a bottle of drink for Christmas? Extra tobacco? A hacksaw blade? And rewards are offered. Normally they never come out with a figure, it's pay you a deposit and the rest later. You often get the tentative enquiry.

'The biggest mistake you can make is to discuss your home life with them because they say in all innocence one morning, "You look worried, governor, is everything all right?" And you'll say, "Oh, no, the missus is gone," or, "The kids want to go on holiday and I haven't got the money." Then they might say, "I can help you out." If the bloke's really desperate he'll fall for it. But if they get you once, they've got you without any shadow of doubt. It's the spider in the web syndrome because after that they won't pay you. Some of the sums they've caught officers for are ridiculous – £1,000 or as little as £300. One officer who was caught had only been offered sexual favours.

'Twelve years ago I was offered money to let a Borstal boy out early from a minimum sentence. I reported it and it was noted. The father was seen on his next visit. "Me not understand. Me foreign. Me haven't been in this country very long." Very interesting to see how quickly they lapse back into their native tongue.

'I meet quite a few I knew as Borstal boys when they were fifteen or sixteen, and here they are ten years later and they're twenty or twenty-six and all that's happened is they've got older and I've got older but their attitudes and their crimes are no different. Obviously some have progressed from the theft of a car to becoming a getaway driver, the GBH has become a robber, the conspirator to defraud the post office becomes a bank robber. That progression . . . so when they become lord of the manor and start strutting around I've always found a simple word of "remember when you were fifteen" soon stops it. It can be quite amusing.'

Everyone loves a good escape. Everyone outside that is. When in 1987 there was a spectacular helicopter escape from Gartree Prison in Leicestershire, normally law-abiding people watched it on television and chortled. The prison officers were less amused.

'They have got away lately more than we care to admit. It is of concern to us all. Over the last eighteen months we've lost seven over the wall. You're always a little bit concerned – have you got a bad apple in the barrel? You think – I'm doing my job, there's ninety-nine of us doing the job, who's the hundredth one who's not doing his job?

'Most successful escapes are in the hours of darkness so the bells don't go. You do get the daylight ones when observation isn't so intense – breakfast time, tea-time, early hours of the evening. You get the spectacular escapes – the helicopter, over the wall, highly organised, lot of money spent – who ever expects a helicopter? It was very well organised. Each officer on the yard was isolated. It's not a physical isolation – they stand in such a way as to leave you under no illusion at all that as long as you don't move nothing will happen. I don't care who you are, you can fight one on one, but if there's ten which one do you fight? So you push your bell and hope someone responds.

'We had two recently going over the wall and we managed to get one, the dog handler appeared, but the other managed to get up the rope first. Others we've been able to prevent – we've found the bars cut, dummies in beds. The classic was a prisoner who had been up all night sawing the bars and had fallen asleep. Everyone laughs about it but we were lucky.'

Often escapers are found within hours or days. Too often they have returned to the wife or the girlfriend and the police merely watch the loved one, knowing that that is one of the strongest pulls that will take a man over the wall. Sexual frustration and ambiguity inside is high.

'There's no way round it, homosexuality exists. He can be the biggest macho man you ever met in your life, if he's locked up for x amount of time his sexual frustration has got to be channelled either into containing himself, diverting his frustrations by throwing himself into the gym, pumping iron, punching the punch bag, doing the circuit, becoming a monk in training and trying to blot it out. Or he's got to learn masturbation, with whichever magazine he can, and relieve himself that way, or he turns to the other thing which is something he may have never considered before. There are the weak in prison, the homosexuals who are available. He may not become involved but he will use that homosexual to satisfy his needs and he satisfies the homosexual's needs.'

But people who have offended sexually against children are kept separate, the pariahs amongst the pariahs, fulfilling the function of being someone that everyone can look down on, both prisoner and prison officer.

'For Rule 43, firstly a man has to ask for it. An officer can ask him if he has informed. There are some who ask for Rule 43 so they can get a single cell and are quite disappointed when they find out that's not available to them because there's quite a high number of them now, the child molester, the informer, those who have informed on other prisoners, the child batterer, even those who have mugged old women or raped old women, you get that variation.

'The officer has got to treat them as another prisoner, same rules and same rights, but everyone is human. It can be a very lonely existence. It does happen that they are beaten up. It does happen that when they arrive the person receiving them has said quite loudly what his offence is and a cleaner has heard it. It's not encouraged but then again it could be a notorious thing that's been in the press and an inmate will see his name. They'll very quickly click who he is because the person will be looking nervous. Amongst the Rule 43 prisoners you get this acceptance of each other – "If you're on Rule 43 you must have committed an offence . . ." The numbers are increasing as people become more aware of it.

'You will always have fights between prisoners, you will always have the law of the jungle, you will always have the one who wants to rule and those who resist it and you get a fight. Some of the fights are over trivial things. On the other hand, you will get the case where a prisoner's radio goes missing and he'll find out who stole it and he'll confront that person and a fight will occur. You will have two people on exercise, one from north London, one from south London, supporting rival football teams and they'll have an argument and a fight will ensue. The biggest problem is boredom and once they become really bored small things become major things. He may have had a Dear John from his wife, she doesn't want to see him, another prisoner may make a remark about her, is she still running around, not knowing he's had a letter and a fight will ensue.

'Today's present fear is hepatitis B, blood flying around. You are wary of what you can get – you may not know if that person has hepatitis or AIDS. No one wants a fight and we try and avoid them but they do happen. There's always a theory that we enjoy them but we don't enjoy them, we don't go looking for it, running for it. We try and stop them and try and contain. We would rather they came to us and talked to us, but with the convicted population the routine doesn't give you the time to talk, it's a constant keep them moving.'

For the ones they can't keep moving and who buck the system there have been two very separate approaches tried; in Barlinnie Prison in Glasgow, there was the Special Unit, made famous by its best-known former inmate Jimmy Boyle in which the men were trusted, allowed far greater freedom and given more time by the officers who worked with them than they have ever had before. The other approach, which was adopted in the seventies in England, was the Control Unit. Neither system operates now.

'There are those of us who reckon they should take all the known troublemakers and put them in one place and then you would have an explosion. The other theory is you mix them up amongst the rest so they are not mixing with a group . . . but do they spread their poison? What's the perfect answer? It worked when you sent a man to the Control Unit but it took an awful lot of people's time to do it, the hours and time devoted to it. It drains a lot of people off.'

The prison officer's most public face is at visiting time. They know it. And many make an effort, joking with the wife, spoiling the toddler, trying to defuse the atmosphere with a 'Good morning' and 'Come along, ladies'.

'With visitors you get two types: the girlfriends or wives who have come from the hard areas, have lived with crime all their lives, fathers, uncles, brothers were involved with crime so they find it easier to adapt. Then you get the other type who have never seen a prison before, have never been involved in prisons before and are very distressed by the first experience of it all. In the old days when they were allowed food in you would get the wives and girlfriends coming with food they'd taken a lot of trouble to prepare – soup, cold meat, biscuits – and making sure they got cigarettes.

'The most difficult thing was when a husband or boyfriend had offended against the prison rules and wasn't allowed that privilege of food and the wife turns to the child in the pushchair and says, "Daddy's been a naughty boy he can't have his food, we will have something to eat." They were keeping the peace by making sure the person inside had something to eat even if they went hungry. However hard you are, to hear any female turn to their child and say that does affect you.

'We've had boyfriends hitting girlfriends, husbands hitting wives because he's heard she's been unfaithful or because she hasn't been to see him. "Where have you been?" "I've been ill." "I don't believe you." A row starts. You have some girlfriends who are quite relieved when you tell them the time's up. Some of the men are very demanding: where's that money I wanted in so I could buy a canteen? Where's that clean shirt, that pair of trousers? They're very selfish some of them, very selfish.

'Food not being allowed in has stopped a lot of drugs but it's like a prisoner of war system – if there's rules you've got to beat them. So the visitor makes a solution of the drugs, soaks a T shirt, irons it, presses it. You have a visit, you hand out a dirty T-shirt, she hands you a clean one, you take it back to the cell, soak it in a bowl of water, and you have a drug. How do you stop stamped letters where the drugs are underneath the stamp? How do you stop a man kissing his wife goodbye where she puts a drug inside a contraceptive and it's swallowed? He is then gambling that it won't burst, which has happened – fortunately the man's life was saved – he then carries out his bodily functions and he has the drug in his possession. He'll gamble that after the visit you won't find it because he's hid it in his underpants or his shoe. Or he'll have long hair and hide a reefer under his hair. These are just some of the ways. It can be thrown over the fence, a red band, a prisoner not regarded as a security problem, who works on the yard will pick it up, pass it on the way.'

Some prisoners say that staff turn if not a blind eye then certainly a hooded one to the smoking of cannabis inside, because they know that a stoned prisoner is less likely to be disruptive.

'No, they don't, they're looking for it all the time. Yet you can walk into a cell and they've been at it. They're not with you, they're not even with the Woolwich to use a phraseology. Their eyes are glazed. They could be aggressive, or very quiet. But you haven't the proof. Without a sample, how can you prosecute? If they hear you open the door they throw it out the window. On the side of a wing of 300 people, which cell did it come out of?'

Older prisoners go for the more traditional escape route of home-made alcohol, using everything from emptied out fire-extinguishers to slopping out pots as their distilleries.

'Good old-fashioned hooch. They get oranges and apples. Not everybody likes apples or oranges so they sell an orange for a cigarette. One man could end up with twenty oranges or apples. Bowl of water, throw the fruit in, bit of sugar, leave it in a bucket. You've got hooch. Birthday is coming up, Christmas coming up, you need a drink. They're not worried about the risk they're putting their brain cells at, they need a drink. Then you play a game. If you can smell it fermenting you have got to find it. They're very clever. They'll hide drugs in the buckets. Who wants to check a bucket of urine for what's at the bottom?

'With the coloured inmates, there's a very quick defence syndrome: "You're only picking on me because I'm black." The biggest chip on the shoulder . . . you never hear a white man say, "You're only picking on me because I'm white." We have coloured officers, we have Asian officers, we even have female officers now. Are we going to have the homosexuals shouting, "You're only picking on me because I want to be a female?" You get the words flying around. The prisoner is more ready to complain than the officer.'

One delicate task is the censoring of letters, those exercise-book lined pages that are posted off in Dartmoor and Parkhurst and Durham often without enough news to fill the four small sheets. The ones that come back can be no more inspiring as the years pass and the common experiences dwindle.

'The criterion of censoring mail is to try and pick up if he's had a letter coming in from a wife or a girlfriend saying she's going to end the relationship, that someone in the family has died, things that may cause him distress, witnesses or friends trying to arrange his case, arranging things to be brought in for him. On the outgoing track it is people arranging things to happen. So censoring is difficult, not the most thrilling of jobs but one that is considered part of the task.'

One source of resentment within the prison service is the recent disparity between the salaries of police officers and prison officers and the status of the two roles.

'The police come in two groups. With the uniformed side we both accept we have a job to do. There is frustration that they can't understand our rules and regulations and we become frustrated at the difference in rates of pay; they get overtime still, a high rent allowance. But the basic relationship is very good. With the detective you can be swayed by what you hear from prisoners, allegations of officers taking bribes. You can be quite impressed with how smartly they're turned out sometimes when you consider their income. It would be unfair to judge all on a small group but we don't have a lot to do with the non-uniformed side. We meet them when a prisoner says, "I want to see him, I might have something to tell him."'

But if there are ambivalent feelings towards police officers, other parts of the system evoke different emotions.

'Judges are very good with prison officers. They form a good relationship with officers, especially from Brixton prison where the officer may be with the same judge for twenty weeks. That works well. If you regularly attend the same court that works well, too. I worked at Brixton for five years and worked with Carl Aarvold, a gent, a real gent, a pleasure to work with. I had the pleasure of working with Widgery, Lord Chief Justice Widgery, for two weeks. Peter Mason. Greenwood. Terrific man. You can run the names off. Great people. You can get to know them and they know you because you have been there for a few weeks.

'The old barrister, the wig is a bit tatty, well travelled, he knows the prison officers; then you get the young ones who are out to make an impression and he'll start this "warder" business and the hair goes up on the back of our neck because no one likes being talked down to. Solicitors – they wouldn't have a job without crime.

'As for the probation officers, we very much resent a person arriving, who may have years of practice outside, they arrive at ten, finish at four. They're very well-meaning, very dedicated but I can make a phone call, I can ring a parent or a girlfriend and tell them Johnny's in prison can you bring some clothes. I can do that and it would give me more variation. But to be told by a social worker that I didn't know what I was talking about when I have had months of looking after that person can be very very antagonising to me. I think those probation officers could do a good job by training up prison officers sufficiently to do *their* jobs.'

More and more of the charges they have to deal with are hardly professional villains. 'With the population of mental hospitals dropping you get people who've been in a routine in a mental hospital and now they're in prison where there's a warm bed. They don't have to think, three meals a day. If they're drunks or junkies, you're drying them out.

'There are very heated political discussions about all these kind of things amongst officers. Every political party you want to name from extreme right to extreme left you'll find amongst officers. One of the most militant people I know is a young officer who is not unionised and someone else I know belongs to Tribune group. You get a lot of debate.'

And a lot of resentment at the way they are portrayed in the press, a universally disliked group amongst prison officers.

'There was an editorial written in the *Express* about one of our disputes and I couldn't believe how hard it was to get hold of the person who wrote it. If he's so convinced of what he's written why doesn't he put his name to it? I know it's not the editor who writes it. When I finally got hold of the one who wrote it he was absolutely fuming that I had the affront to find out who he was and ring him and ask him to prove his editorial. He was fuming.'

And part of what Frank wanted to convey was that the prison officer no longer has any role, if he ever did, in helping a prisoner to prepare for what is meant to be a 'good and useful life'.

'My basic job is to contain. I enjoyed Borstal work, the old Borstal work. They got a sentence of six months to two years where you aimed them towards course work, education to try and get something out of it. You had a group of boys you worked with like a father, an uncle or aunt.'

If such relationships are now impossible inside, prison officers, like any group that sees itself as under attack, tend to stick together outside. 'We socialise as a group. The biggest tragedy is that most prison estates on which most officers live are next to the prison. They work together, walk home together and the social clubs are on those estates. And where they build prisons is never near public amenities so the officers get forced towards each other. There is this tendency so that if there's a major problem in the prison they can get hold of the staff readily.

'There are drinking problems. You have your secret drinkers. There's not many drink at lunchtime. It's not like the police where your shifts finish at two and you're off till the next day.

'A lot of us are divorced. Marriage is a very, very difficult thing to sustain in the prison service because you become so drained at work during the day that you have a tendency to come home and not face any problems at home. You want to collapse in a chair, you want your meal. You hope you don't fall asleep. If you've been on since half-past seven, the last thing you want is someone to start giving you the earhole about their problems. So the argument will occur and the wife becomes annoyed and feel neglected – there's the accusation, "You're married to the job not to me" – and the row starts. It seems to be very popular that officers live with people and never marry them.'

But Frank will probably stay in the job. He has his friends, his current girl-friend is a good-looking prison officer, he has his union work, although the sons are unlikely to follow him and the rest of the family have chosen careers elsewhere.

'One brother now works for London Transport, one's dead, one is a ranking clerical officer in the civil service, one is a housewife and happy in that role, good luck to her. One has finished work because she was fed up being robbed – she was in the banks.

'I unwind by walking the dogs. The hardest part of being a prison officer is not only physical. It's mental. We have one of the highest casualty rates from stress and heart trouble. The constant thing of thinking, will an alarm bell ring, what happens when I open this next door, is anyone trying to escape?'

16

The Escaper

Anyone who has been to an
English public school will
always feel comparatively at
home in prison. It is the people
brought up in the gay intimacy
of the slums . . . who find prison
so soul-destroying.

Evelyn Waugh, *Decline and Fall*

The front page of the *Daily Mirror* of 11 October 1958 shows, next to its 'Forward with the people' logo, a remarkable photograph of a good-looking, sharp-featured young man at the wheel of a car. Behind him, with his arm in a lock round the young man's neck, is a burly plain-clothes policeman. The expression on the young man's face is of startled bewilderment. Above the picture the triumphant headline reads simply 'CAUGHT!'. The sub-head explains: 'Police Trap Angel Face'.

The story below, told in gripping detail by the *Mirror* Crime Bureau; explains that '"Angel Face" Walter Probyn, the prisoner who escaped from Maidstone Gaol a month ago, is held in a neck lock by a detective after walking into a police trap in Hoxton, last night. In this exclusive *Mirror* picture, "Angel Face" is about to be handcuffed after being bundled into a police car by detectives. Last night twenty-seven-year-old Probyn was in a cell at Stoke Newington police station. He had been charged with attempting to make use of a firearm, or imitation firearm, with intent to resist arrest.'

'That picture's like an old nightmare. I seemed to be swept along and I just wasn't able to cope with it,' says Walter Probyn, still in Hoxton, east London, more than thirty years later. The features that won him his nickname are still as sharp, the hair is combed forward and there is no sign of twenty-nine-years' worth of stodgy prison food on the slight frame in its skin-tight black jeans. 'I had been betrayed – I was a bit naive. I was set up by a reporter from the *Mirror*. Because of what had been in the press about me the day before, I got in touch with the *Mirror* and said I wanted to put the record straight. I agreed to meet him in order to talk. I said, I think, that I was prepared to give myself up but not in that sort of atmosphere. When I went to meet him he had set me up to get that photograph. It destroyed my perspective of these reporters.'

It also brought an end to his latest sniff of free London air and saw him return once more behind familiar bars, familiar since he was first arrested as a nine-year-old for stealing a tin of peas from a bombed-out cafe in wartime

Shoreditch. His probation required that he attend a local Roman Catholic school. He truanted, ran home to his cabinet-maker father, mother and five brothers and sisters, was apprehended and dispatched to an approved school.

'The first I heard of the nickname was when it was given me by the press, when I was fourteen or fifteen. I think they had been fed this by the police, and the police and the reporters combined together to create an image. They both have an incentive: the police in order to denigrate the person they're actually dealing with and enhance their reputation – instead of catching someone who's done something that's quite mediocre, it's represented as something that's startling and dangerous so obviously there's a reflection on them as to how brave and courageous they are. The press has the same reason – they're not going to get a very stimulating story if it's about mediocre people so they go along with it.' It could have been worse. One arresting officer referred to him, rather tortuously, as The Dimpled Demon. But it was the activity for which he became best-known that earned him the third of the names that have been hung on him – the Hoxton Houdini. He acquired it in the course of escaping from different penal institutions on a total of sixteen occasions. His creed became With One Bound He Was Free.

As a teenager in a remand centre in Shepherds Bush he stole a set of keys, but could find no occasion to leg it. He duly handed the keys back to the governor who, gratified by the change of heart, wound down the surveillance. He escaped. Sent to approval school in Carmarthen, he had his clothes confiscated so that he would not try and make another getaway. He shinned out naked at night and made a midnight escape on a bicycle, pausing on his way back to London only to steal a pair of shorts and some women's shoes.

Twenty years later one of the magistrates in front of whom Probyn appeared, Lady Wootton, was to propose his suitability for parole. She could still remember Probyn even though he had appeared in front of her so long ago: 'There is something significant about the fact that I remember this, as during my twenty years in the metropolitan juvenile courts I must have dealt with at least 8,000 juveniles and necessarily few have remained in my mind. But I was greatly struck with Walter Probyn as an unusually intelligent and sadly maladjusted child. I have often wondered since whether we dealt with him wisely or whether damage was done at that early stage.'

But when he appeared on a charge of assaulting a policeman with a penknife at the age of fifteen, the bench had little doubt about the wisdom of punishment. He was jailed for four years.

The grown-up prisoners required different escape techniques. In Wandsworth he swallowed carbolic soap which gave him a high temperature and added credence to his claim that he had appendicitis. It was easier to get out of a hospital than a prison and that he duly did, in his pyjamas, from St James. He married Beryl and when he heard she was being given a hard time by another man he escaped again, this time from Dartmoor. A friend gave him a .22 American Star target pistol and when he saw a group of men closing in on him, he told the court later, he reckoned they were heavies connected with this man and opened fire. Justice Melford Stevenson was not impressed by his claim and jailed him for twelve years. He refined his methods of unofficial departure.

'When I was a boy, escaping was for rebellion. Later, when I escaped from Dartmoor it was a real challenge. When anybody escaped they used to lock everybody up for three days while all the screws went out and set up roadblocks with the police. When they caught them the screws would come back crowing. There were thirteen caught before I went. Sometimes people would escape, fall in the bogs and come back asking to be let in at the gate.

'What I found out was that all these hardened criminals were petrified of the dark. I had a brother-in-law there who used to go around putting the cosh about and snatching money bags, really doing damage to people, a big hard thug – he wouldn't escape from Dartmoor because he was frightened of the sheep and the cows and the darkness. He nearly tore my bollocks off one day going over a barbed-wire fence. Some cows appeared and he grabbed hold of me in fear and tried to pull himself over while I was straddled over a barbed-wire fence. It was just a cow with great udders!

'The reason most of them got caught was because they wouldn't go across the moor. There's a right myth about the moor, even the locals if they're caught in fog – because the fog drops down in seconds sometimes without any warning – they say they just sit down, they won't move. But if you follow the roads you come into a roadblock so it was really a challenge.'

He admired the legendary escapers. Harry Brett was one. He escaped, casually robbed the prison officers' mess of drink and tobacco, and rambled about the village where all the officers lived creating mischief. He spent his first night of freedom asleep in a hut at the bottom of the local policeman's garden, only making a run for the moors when he was disturbed.

'It was lovely,' Walter recalls, 'I really enjoyed it. You can't move about in the day. The army has got a range there and they do survival exercises. But they're armed with all sorts of equipment, compasses and so on and if they don't reach a certain point at a certain time they have search parties so they're not really on their own. When there's an escape the army get involved, so you're pitted against the police and the army. You've got to avoid all the high Tors because you know they're sitting there with powerful binoculars. It's a real game of wits.

'Whenever you look out at night from Dartmoor it looks absolutely pitch black but when you get out on the moor it seems to have its own light. In the daytime, you get immersed in the cloud in no time. When I escaped it was brilliant sunshine and within a few minutes it was thick fog which was fortunate for me as I got chased immediately. I think the only people who get away are the people who enjoy it.'

But the preparation, the planning must take great patience?

'You don't need a lot of patience to plan an escape because you've got nothing else. Something like that is something to cherish while you've got it, it's a labour of love, something you really enjoy doing so you take your time doing it. It's like a hobby.'

Like many people with an absorbing and totally fulfilling hobby, he felt a sense of puzzlement that others did not always share it.

'It is amazing that very, very few people would escape. In places like Dartmoor, because it was so old, sometimes the wall would fall down but no one would run away.' Sent to Durham jail he met up with the only other genuinely dedicated escaper that he knew of. Usually Probyn's escapes had been solo but he thought in a place with Durham's forbidding reputation he might need assistance. There were repairs going on and scaffolding all round the main wall so an escape was definitely a possibility. But it required the help of half-a-dozen other prisoners who would assist in tying up the six or eight officers in the exercise yard. Although some were facing thirty-year sentences none was prepared to join the venture.

'I found it really hard to understand. I don't know if they had become totally institutionalised. When me and Johnny McVicar escaped there was a guy, a young bloke doing life. He had been involved in some fascist group and he stabbed somebody. But during his time inside he came right the other way, really left wing. He was in Wakefield, he had tremendous loyalty to his friends. He was friends with somebody in F wing, a young prisoner and there was also an incorrigible bully there. The guy was a bit of hard nut and, eventually, he stabbed the bully and, not intending it, killed him. So he was doing two life sentences. You would get the impression from that he was a nasty bastard but he wasn't, he was one of the nicest people I've met and despite the fact that he's killed two people he was a very gentle sort of guy. So when Johnny and I were going I offered for him to come. And he wouldn't go. I couldn't understand it. He's got two life sentences and it's possible that he would never get out.'

Harry Roberts, who had shot dead two policemen, was another puzzle. 'Harry was constantly plotting in Parkhurst to escape. He's never going to get out and he knows he's never going to get out. I took him seriously because I was a perpetual escaper. It kept me alive. He would come up with incredible ideas, a lot of them impractical. Anyway we eventually worked out how we would get out.

'We were in a top security wing, really the tightest one that there is. Alarms, cameras, a prison within a prison. You have the outside wall and then a separate wall. Getting out of the block itself was the problem because there was an electronically operated door and you had to go through a hermetically sealed box connected to a control room, with an inch and a half thick bullet-proof glass which they look through. They had a screw permanently placed in this box. The door wouldn't open until the other one was shut. And that can't open unless the guy in the control box can see that everything is OK. So we're on the inside and we have to get through one door into the box which is electronically operated. We can't. Even if we got in there there's no way we could persuade the screw to open the other one. But they've made one ricket that they didn't realise: the roof of the box, part of it, was on the landing. Although the main part that jutted out was concrete, that part was the landing slab and they had overlooked the fact that you can lift the landing slab up and drop through.'

He describes the technicalities in such detail, with hand gestures to explain what door opens where, that it is hard not to imagine a fellow prisoner agreeing to it all and immediately dropping a postcard to his girlfriend telling her to expect a surprise. What was needed before the door could be breached, however, was to overpower one of the officers.

'We were going to get the screw to go and get something out of the greenhouse for us – because there was a garden outside. We would let him come back in, drop through the landing, tie him up, then we could get out and nobody else could chase us. All they can do is phone through to the main wing. But they couldn't get out because we would leave the door open which means the inner door can't open. It would have worked.'

The plan was to hang a rope out of the window and drop into the grounds. Then they would have run along a wall, over a large hump by hoisting each other up. They would have still been on the Isle of Wight but the most difficult part would have been accomplished.

'We made replicas of Lugers out of wax and cotton reels and they were absolutely perfect. We had photographs of the Luger from Harry's case so we copied them. But then Harry got into a panic over something and put the guns in the toilet so the screws found them and knew something was on. They gave us all a spin and in the leg of my bed they found an Ordnance Survey map of the island and a naval map of the Solent, which I had had for about six months. We had been waiting until the clocks went back, it was September, because we wanted the dark nights. The next morning I got ghosted [moved without warning]. They came and dragged me out and took me to Durham. I did two escapes from Durham and I came back to Parkhurst. And although about twelve months had passed Harry hadn't used the escape. I realised then that he was living in a world of fantasy. He couldn't face doing the bird he was doing. He's doing forever, he's got nothing to hope for, he's going to stagnate – and the only way he could survive is the thought of escaping. That was the only way I could survive. But I really meant to escape whereas Harry didn't. It was just a game. He was pitting his wits against the screws to find ways, but it was only in theory – he didn't want to do it in practice.

'Then I gave him some hacksaw blades which I brought back from Durham. On my previous escape I had had hacksaw blades concealed so when they gave me my property back they unknowingly gave me the hacksaws, too. I had a black folder with a plastic cover with a label of "Probyn versus . . ." over it. I had taken it apart and put the cardboard back with a hacksaw shape cut out of it and a hacksaw sealed inside. Then I just sealed it back up. So when they gave me back my case papers they handed me the hacksaw. I also had some small hacksaw blades in a bottle of sauce and they gave it back too. But Harry never used them.'

So Probyn settled down to finish his sentence. He had little respect for the prison service, although he believes a strong governor can make the difference between a brutal regime and a fair one.

'A particular prison gets a bad name for brutality, then a governor comes in – which is very rare – who won't tolerate any brutality at all and he threatens to have people prosecuted. And it all stops. That happened in Pentonville in 1962/63. The place was really notorious. The governor, a Quaker, came into the prison and he laid the law down. He had all the screws lined up in front of him and told all the screws in the chokey block, the punishment block, that no prisoner who was brought down who had injuries was to be received by them. They were to direct whoever had control at that time to take them to the hospital and that if they didn't they would be held responsible and be prosecuted. It was miraculous, the violence just stopped dead.

'That big minority of screws that behave like bullies, they're in a rut. If they weren't in there as guards they'd probably be in there as prisoners – they have the same sort of characteristics. There's not much difference between them and the prisoners except they go home. They get institutionalised, they sit there barking and snarling at everybody and they have the problem of re-adjusting from screws to human beings when they go home at night. I've spoken to their wives when I was at Dartmoor on the outside party, when you go into their homes doing repairs. They've told me things about their husbands: they're nasty to them not just physically but psychologically.'

What made Probyn finally abandon escapology was the realisation that the escapes merely meant longer sentences and, with his marriage over, there was no urgent domestic reason to get out anyway. In any case, an informer had been slid into Parkhurst and had become friendly with Harry Roberts who duly told him about the weak link of the flagstone. The route was rumbled and the flagstone replaced and reinforced with concrete.

The chance of an escape as spectacular as that of George Blake or Ronnie Biggs or, more recently, of the helicopter escape of John Kendall and Sydney Draper from Gartree prison in 1987, had slipped past. And by now Probyn was wary of such high-profile activities and the notoriety they brought.

'At the time of my escape with McVicar from Durham, McVicar meant nothing to anyone. Then the next day it was splashed all over that Durham walked in fear of Johnny McVicar. Nobody knew Johnny McVicar in Durham! Nobody had ever heard of him. I suppose all the prisoners were totally amazed the next day when they read that they walked in terror of him. Maybe they did after they read it!'

He emerged finally from Leyhill open prison after a long battle for parole on the grounds that he was a reformed character. The world of crime had changed while he had been away.

'In the early days crime was quite different. People used to be able to disarm burglar alarms. They used to be able to fit up locks quite easily and they used to be able to turn off the clocks of shops with skeleton keys.' Crimes were simplicity itself. There was the jump-up: a lorry loaded with, say, cigarettes would be followed from factory to warehouse to see its normal route. The robbers waited for the driver to pull into a café or a layby and then jumped up and stole the lorry. If they were impatient they would just stop the lorry on the road with an unofficial road-block. But improved communications, two-way radios, more sophisticated burglar alarms drove the locksmiths and the jump-up experts in different directions. The criminal as artisan became a rarer species.

Wally Probyn talks with admiration about one: 'He used to have an American science magazine delivered every week in nick so that he could learn about all the new developments. He was the first to use the thermic lance here, or so I heard from the grapevine. He was quite brilliant and became a millionaire. Yet he still used to go out. It was a compulsive thing. It was his life's blood, he liked it. He wasn't doing it for money eventually but because he liked the challenge. He used to be sought after to advise people. He would go and disarm a burglar alarm system and get a cut without even having to go in.'

But his respect for the expert is coloured by his feelings about the philosophy of the English criminal. 'They're much too individual. They don't take orders from anybody even when you're talking about firms like the train robbers. They weren't a proper firm. This job was tendered out to different people that I knew who rejected it when they realised the number of people that were going to be involved, because they felt that someone was going to talk out of turn and they would get unstuck. When they realised they couldn't get enough people together they went to different firms that they knew were operating. They went to some family firm in south London who wouldn't have anything to do with it, some from Hoxton, most from south London. It was amazing they ever got together because they're so argumentative, these people, they have their own ideas about how things should be done. So it's very difficult to get groups of more than five to six together to do things.'

He thought that the place of protection in the criminal portfolio was exaggerated, 'but it did exist even up to the late seventies, well after the Krays and Richardsons were inside. I had a friend who had a number of clubs and restaurants and I know somebody used to go down there and make his presence felt and I know this guy would not succumb readily unless there was a real threat. So if it was happening to him it must have been happening to most people in that business.

'The Richardsons and the Krays were the last of those sort of firms. But it was grossly exaggerated. The Krays lived in this area and I've lived here all my life and I met them once in a club they owned. I don't know anyone whose life they infringed on. I'd heard things about what was going on among the criminal fraternity. I know some people hated and feared them and yet still sought out their company because of their name. But it was only amongst the guys who were aspiring to be big criminals, tough guys. What they said about them holding the East End in terror, iron grip and so on, was absolute rubbish. The same with the Richardsons. They didn't hold everybody in fear. They went inside and they were no different from anyone else in there. If they have a go at someone they get a right-hander same as anyone else. There was the Tibbses in Canning Town – I've lived over there. But that was the same thing. It was only the criminal element over there, and just a select group, who were touched by it all.'

He is sanguine about organised crime. 'The most organised crime, I think, is that which has involved Scotland Yard. All the big crimes are always mixed up in it. The ten per cent racket originated from there.

'The ten per cent racket works like this: there was a period back in the sixties when all the old masters went missing, sometimes two or three times they went missing, but they were always recovered. The police would be working with criminals who steal and store the paintings, then give information so that the paintings are recovered. For that they need a body to claim the reward, which was ten per cent of the value of the paintings. If they're worth £1 million that's a hundred grand reward which is split up between the police and the people stealing the paintings. But it always means someone going down for it, so they always had to have a fall guy.

'I've spoken to people that were involved with policemen who were running the ten per cent rackets. I've spoken to a number of people because it wasn't confined to paintings, there was a period when they were doing the jump-ups – the lorries go missing and a few hours later or a day later the full load is recovered and there's ten per cent of whatever it's worth. It saves fencing the stuff out and the dangers of having to store the vast quantities of it. Since the police were in it there was no possibility of it coming unstuck. If something's worth sixty grand, they're bringing in six grand for nothing, just for transferring a lorry load of goods from one point to another.

'Another racket was gelignite: there used to be a fridge at the Yard that everybody knew about. When they nicked you, you knew you would get five years. They would get a piece out of the fridge, rub it round in your pocket, put it in a plastic bag, send it to the forensic laboratory with your coat. When the scientist came to give evidence he could do it with all honesty. He could say the traces of gelignite are the same as were found in the bag. That appears to be conclusive scientific evidence. People were going down like flies for that.'

Walter Probyn has had a fairly jaundiced view of the law from his childhood onwards. 'My first experience of straight policemen was in Bournemouth and I just couldn't believe they were straight. It was amazing. When they picked me up – this was way back in '57 – they thought because I came from London the first thing I was going to do was offer a bribe, which showed what their opinion of the Metropolitan police was. They warned me not to try and do any deals with the governor because he would go spare.

'I did have another experience, fairly recently in Hackney, when they picked me up on this job, stealing simulated furs, and they tried to get two young policemen, only eighteen or nineteen, to identify me as the man they saw. At the time they refused to do so. The trial took two years to come up and I was convinced that they would definitely have been corrupted by this time and they would change their story. To my amazement they didn't. I can only guess what it does for their career because the police badly wanted to nick me.'

It was a strange case. Part of the evidence against Probyn rested with a policeman who had left the force and whom the police seemed unwilling to subject to cross-examination. They said it was impossible to trace him. Probyn felt that if he could prove that the policeman was easy to find it would show that he had not been called for another reason, so he set about tracing him. Without much difficulty he found out that the ex-policeman was signing on in Finsbury Park, north London. So, with the patience that comes from months of planning escapes, he settled down in a van with a camera to await his prey. He repeated the same exercise at weekends, having discovered that his quarry played dominoes for a pub team, using a camera hidden underneath a sweater, operated from a line running down his sleeve. The photos, carefully dated, were produced as evidence when Probyn appeared in court and assisted in his acquittal.

This drove him further in his pursuit of authority. He formed the Shoreditch police monitoring unit, keeping an eye on the people who were keeping an eye on him. He admits it has become a bit of an obsession but says that it's his insurance against being put away again. He has his reasons for not wanting to return: he has met a young and attractive Irish woman called Valerie and they have between them three young children to look after. Angel Face becomes the family man. It has not stopped him from voicing his theories on crime.

'All they are, most criminals, is a fucking nuisance. What they knock off in a year is not what it would cost to put them on trial, nowhere near it. So in terms of finance the public would come out better off if they didn't put them on trial. There must be some way of cutting down the cost of a trial from £5,000 a day – getting rid of the judiciary and putting people there with common sense rather than all this esoteric knowledge. With big finance cases, the judges don't try to bully juries into convictions in the same way that they do in ordinary crime. I think it's because it's a class crime, the sort that's committed by their own classes.

'The majority of the prison population are incompetent, inadequate people. They start off stealing something because they can't get it in any other way. They can't cope with life, especially if they're been inside – they have a sort of apathy. They can't organise themselves, they can't wheel and deal even. So they go back into crime.'

He found, like others inside, that a lot of criminals yield nothing to the Monday Club when it comes to the efficacy of flogging and capital punishment, provided it isn't for anything they have done.

'They would have a go at sex offenders – "they should be hung and flogged". It was mostly the cardboard gangsters who would say that, wanting to show off. But I've met sex offenders who condemn ordinary criminals and say they should be flogged and hung! They're all against unions. Whenever anything happened, strikes – especially if it affected them like the mail or trains might affect their visits – they were vicious against them.

'I was in with Peter Kroger, the spy, and right-wing people like the train robbers there would use him because he was very educated and he used to teach people things and help them, even people who gave him a hard time. He was a lovable sort of old guy and even those who didn't agree with him politically admired him.'

After Probyn came out he found himself being portrayed in the film *McVicar* – about McVicar's escape from Durham – by the actor Adam Faith, whom he met on the set. He was unimpressed by the film itself: 'They could have had a message but they made it commercial. It didn't quite glamorise crime but it came fairly close, especially for someone impressionable – particularly the robbery scene. There are certain women that are attracted towards anyone notorious. At the party after the preview of *McVicar*, there was some posh lady going berserk trying to get hold of Johnny McVicar, she kept on coming up to me asking me to introduce her. She wanted to go to bed with him.

Probyn still lives right in the heart of Hoxton while his contemporaries have dispersed to Epping and Loughton and Spain. They have drifted out of heavy crime with a few exceptions: 'Ronnie Easterwood who's just got a life sentence. He's fifty-seven and he's still doing what he was doing then. He was involved in what they call a stake-out but it's a set-up, where they're waiting for them. It's rather difficult to condemn the police totally for that because they say that they were at it anyway and the only way they can catch them is to set them up. That's their rationale. I suppose some people swallow it. They get a grass and then plot up on them. And now there's been several where they've shot them. They use grasses for that sort of thing and some people are taken by surprise that people they know have become informers. I'm not. I don't have a very high opinion of criminals. I've never done any banks but maybe one of the reasons was because I didn't trust anyone.'

He mentioned the case of George Davis, freed after a massive public campaign that suggested he was 'Innocent, OK', then caught red-handed robbing the Bank of Cyprus in Seven Sisters Road: 'The police had the hump with him and that was a set-up but you can't have any sympathy for him because for all the people that stuck their necks out for him he didn't show his gratitude, he was stupid and got big-headed. It was only the campaign that made him something, he wasn't really anything at all. That damaged a lot of campaigns, because whenever someone gets a campaign up for someone who's innocent they can always point to something like that. It shouldn't work like that because George Davis didn't do the original thing that he was alleged to have done.

'I think the present climate is going to make people more likely to use guns. There's been too many incidents of the police shooting people down, which means that you can't afford to take a toy gun, a starting pistol, because they're going to shoot you whether it's real or not. Anyone that's going to carry one now is going to be prepared to shoot to kill themselves.'

He pours a Guinness from a bar stocked with spirits and decanters, offers some more sandwiches and goes to feed the rare fish, Koi, which live in an elaborate system of tanks in his ground-floor flat; they have more room and entertainment than most tanked fish.

'There's been things that have kept me in Hoxton but I would love to live in the country because of the Old Bill. We had an offer to move to Wales but I've got an eighty-seven-year-old mother and no one else does anything for her so I can't really leave. I couldn't take her with me because she's really eccentric. She stuck by me, she's the only one really.'

Not that he had any intention of being in trouble again. 'If I was going to get involved in crime again I would make sure I educated myself in computers. It's seen as permissible. It's all right in this society to rip off millions as long as you wear a suit.

'I know that people of eighteen or nineteen look up, if they're in it at all, to people they think are well-known criminals. People make that mistake with me. I'm not a big criminal and I've never been one, but young kids that know about me say, "Oh, yeah, yeah, Wally Probyn." I object to that. I don't feel flattered by it and I don't like the idea that they might use me as some kind of model. If they did, they'd come badly unstuck because I've not been a competent criminal. Mostly it's been motivated by rebellion which is rather incompetent because there are better ways and more efficient ways I could have rebelled had I had it over again.'

17

The Probation Officer

In nature there are neither rewards nor
punishments – there are consequences.

R. G. Ingersoll

'I never considered doing anything other than working in the public sector,
probably because that was the tradition in my family. Also, because we are black, I
think my parents believed that it would be really hard for the children in the family
to get into the law or any professional job, it just hardly ever happened.'

There has been a party in the flat the night before and a message is scrawled on
the mirror. It is south London, a divided house on a quiet street not far from
where Cynthia Payne caused a minor scandal by bringing libido to the luncheon
voucher and ended up in court. But the clients that Claudia Crawley has to deal
with as a probation officer are not going to have films made of their lives. They
have been arrested for thieving, or drug dealing, or robbing, or violence, and she
and her colleagues have the business of trying to keep them outside the prison
and inside the law. It is a Saturday and there is an air of weekend relief about the
neat rooms and the smart young woman sitting on the settee.

'When I became a probation officer my parents were incredibly proud because
it was like I had got somewhere. They know I'm a professional and that's very
important to them. The same applies to my brother, who manages swimming
pools for Hammersmith and Fulham, they're very proud of him. I've a sister
who's a secretary, others in the family are in the National Health Service. Nursing
runs throughout my family and it was always expected that I would do something
similar.'

In the chain of criminal justice, the link represented by probation officers is a
tenuous one – they are distrusted by the police, resented by prison officers,
patronised by the courts and barely tolerated by some of their clients. Like social
workers, they remain largely unthanked for their work; noticed when they fail,
unnoticed when they succeed. The pay is average for the public sector but,
compared with a job carrying similar responsibility in the private sector, it is low.

'I came straight from studying sociology and politics at college in London. I
wanted to work with people. I'm really interested in people and what makes them
function, the way they behave. And I had wanted to work with criminals, again my
interest in human behaviour, since I was at school. I used to be very left-wing, I
suppose I'm left of centre now, but I used to think that society was very unfair to

the majority of the people and I wanted to be involved in giving justice to people who I felt were getting a bad deal.

Claudia Crawley grew up in Wolverhampton. 'As a teenager, I knew a lot of black guys who were always being picked up, that was when the SUS laws were in operation, just picked up off the streets. When I was younger I was quite anti-police but I feel a bit different now. You have your property and it has to be protected and the police are there for that so you do benefit. But on the other hand I do see the effect of prejudice in terms of black people going through the criminal justice system.'

There are two main ways of entering the probation service. You can enter either as an unqualified ancilliary worker, doing court work, and anything else that needs to be done. You then go on and do a one or two year course for a Certificate of Qualification in Social Work – the CQSW as it is known. Or you could come in as a volunteer, actually working with clients, probably visiting them in prison and learning about the job that way. But the most popular way is the ancilliary worker route. In training, you are taught theory – social work theory, human development theory, psychology – and you get some practical experience: working in an office and another social work agency for five or six months each.

Many people think the job is mainly to do with young offenders, which it is not. A probation officer deals with men and women from seventeen and upwards, people on probation, young offenders, lifers, or those simply requiring prison after-care. Lifers are released on life licence, which means they have served approximately ten years of a life sentence for a very serious offence and are then subject to supervision by a probation officer, perhaps for the rest of their life, or until such time as the Home Office decides to suspend reporting requirements. But they will be subject to life licence for the rest of their life and could even be recalled to prison in the public's interest. Parolees must keep in touch with their probation officer – 'You find out if they have problems you can help with, finding work, a place to stay.

'With people on parole, it's more surveillance. With people on probation you make a contract with them: "This is what we will do." It may involve a drug addict going to rehab and so on. You also look at why they committed the offence in the first place. As regards the after-care, that is offered to people who may need help with accommodation or just coping when they come out.

'The job does wear you out, a lot of probation officers get burnt out. We deal with a lot of disturbed people and as we go in for more high tariff offenders – offenders who could end up inside – you get more difficult people. There's a lot of mentally ill people coming our way now and being sent to prison when they shouldn't be there. They wear you out.'

Although it is Saturday she is dressed smartly in good jeans.

'I always dress smart for work. I worked for two years in Holloway prison and when I first went there I used to wear jeans, very, very scruffy and I found out they started treating me like a prisoner. It was bad enough anyway because they didn't have any black probation officers in the prison. They just didn't expect it. I found out I had to start dressing up so that people would take me seriously. I remember going out and buying a whole new wardrobe for work. After that I started thinking about my image, because I work in court and I could be called into court any time and I can't afford to dress down. But I think some probation officers do dress very casually and I think some of that is not wanting to alienate the client. That was how I felt when I first came into the job. I didn't want to present an image of "I am superior to you" – I had that superiority in the role anyway.'

People have preconceptions about probation officers just as they do about prison officers and barristers and police officers. 'I usually don't tell people I meet at parties what my job is if I can help it because they always say, "Oh, that sounds really interesting – it must be really hard work," and that's the end of it. The other thing they say is, "Oh, that sounds interesting," and they want you to talk about it. I think those sort of people have definite ideas about what probation officers do. They think we deal with juveniles and we're like the old court missionary that kids come to see when they get into trouble and they give them a good talking to, like mothers and fathers, and send them on their way.'

Nor has there been a *Porridge* or a *Blind Justice* or *The Bill* to offer a benign stereotype with which people could identify.

'There's only been one programme on TV from the probation officer's perspective – *Hard Cases* – it was a probation office in the Midlands. It wasn't realistic at all: there were things in it such as clients having a probation officer's home number and calling them up in the middle of the night. That's just not on. People just don't do that.'

But surely clients do fall for their probation officers, want them as friends even if they resent their role?

'There's always a danger of relationships developing but it's not something I would encourage. I can see how it happens. There's someone interested in the defendant's life probably for the first time, a kind of dependency like a parent and child can develop. There are some people who don't want to have anything to do with us at all – they might have had a bad experience so they don't want to have anything to do with us at all but I think we're seen as the more humane side of the criminal justice system.'

Many offenders talk about how they can placate the probation officer just by telling them what they want to hear . . . 'Some of them try and pull the wool over your eyes; you don't have any proof, you just sense it. So you need to be careful and check out with the client what's happening.

'We sometimes get families where the father is known to the probation officer from ten years ago and the son, all the sons, get known, you get the whole family. I've been in the job since 1976 and I'm now seeing children of people I saw in the seventies. There's the peer group thing as well, kids from the same street.'

Do the clients have a notion of themselves as outlaws, as people outside the system doing something more romantic than serving cheeseburgers at McDonalds?

'I don't know if I'd call it romantic or if they'd call it romantic but for the younger offenders there is quite a lot of excitement in it. Their friends are doing it, they get accepted. There are some who don't have much hope of getting a good job, they end up on a training scheme and a lot of them say to me that the schemes are incredibly boring and don't pay much at all. When they don't have much hope of getting what television and magazines say they're supposed to get then crime is probably seen as a good alternative.

'In some families crime is a way of life, it's accepted and the wives and girlfriends wait and organise their lives around the man in prison. I often wonder what would happen if the boyfriend or husband came out and didn't commit any more offences, they would have to learn a new pattern, a new way of relating to each other.

'We provide the link with the outside for prisoners. I think prisons do something to the people there, not just the prisoners, I think there are a lot of depressed prison officers who get affected by the environment. Their job becomes one of just locking doors. I've spoken to prison officers who went into the job thinking that they were going to do some sort of welfare and then they find that they can't do that.'

So what does the job of probation officer actually involve?

'When your client is on parole you need to see them regularly. If there's even a hint that they're going to offend they can be recalled to finish their sentence. If they have a drink problem and that's the underlying cause of their offences and they start drinking again or they're taking drugs, you inform the Home Office, via your line manager.

'You have to lay down the terms quite clearly: "You're on parole and if you commit any further offences I have a duty to inform the Home Office and you may go back to prison." You lay it on the line. The parolee should understand what it's about so that if anything happens and you've explained then it's a little easier to handle that situation.

'If they're smoking cannabis, for instance, some might say, if they're not harming themselves and they're not harming others . . . they're breaking a law. But it may be better to have a word with them rather than see them go back to prison for something like that because I think prison can do a lot more harm than good.'

What about relations with the police?

'We don't see the police so much now because the Crown Prosecution Service has taken over. They regard us as do-gooders, they see us as being much more concerned with the client than the victim. I have normally found them quite cooperative, if they know why you're making contact.'

What does she do in her own time?

'The longer you're in the job the more you learn how to cope with it. I read a lot

– Gabriel Garcia Marquez, Isabel Allende, Alice Walker, Maya Angelou, biographies. I listen to music – Miles Davis, soul – and I go to the ballet (I used to do contemporary dance) and movies a lot, then I go to bed and think about all the work! The weekends are never long enough.

'I personally don't really talk about my job outside the office unless I'm mixing with other probation officers. All probation officers think about leaving but it seems there's not that much you can do with the qualification other than social work. Some officers do end up at the pub at the end of the night. NAPO AGM [the annual meeting of her union, the National Association of Probation Officers] – there's a hell of a lot of drinking there.

'As far as black probation officers go, the turnover appears disproportionate and I think that's to do with the amount of racism – from the clients or from the service itself. You get abuse, it's an accumulative thing. You have to try and not let it affect you. You also encounter racism in the courts – people don't expect to see a black senior probation officer. I'm seen as a defendant or if I'm seen in the office I'm seen as a secretary. Prison officers – they don't say anything, but it's so subtle, they might keep you waiting a bit longer to see your client. That all adds up.

'The NACRO report [produced by the penal reform group, the National Association for the Care and Resettlement of Offenders] said that there was a disproportionate number of black people going to prison, and at remand stage a high proportion of them who were found not guilty had been remanded in custody. I think the probation service has played our part in that, particularly the way we write our reports. I think something is being done about that and we're much more careful than a few years ago, but often stereotypes may appear in reports.'

What about the Yardies?

'I don't think a lot of what has been written about the Yardies is true, a lot is to do with racist attitudes. I'm not saying there may not be organised black criminal groups but I don't know if the Yardies are as prevalent as the newspapers make out.'

If a probation officer has a duty to be on the side of the offender, what does she feel about the victim?

'I got assaulted in the street, I didn't report it. I was almost mugged once and I stopped him. I was at a bus stop in Brixton and this guy was watching me, then he started moving up to me and was just about to grab my handbag when I shouted at him at the top of my voice. And that was it. But that did shake me up.

'One evening in Covent Garden, it was quite crowded, I was there to meet a friend. I was just walking along minding my own business and I saw this man coming towards me and you know you have a premonition that something is going to happen. He came and knocked me over and laid into me. He wasn't drunk, I don't know if he was crazy. He was really abusive and nobody did anything. That was the worst part of it. It was still light. I couldn't go up to Covent Garden for months after. I should have reported it, but I was so shocked.

'It changed my attitudes to the victims, I think. Made me much more aware of their experience. A friend of mine who lives in Hackney has been burgled three times in the last year. I used to work in Hackney and it could well be one of my ex-clients. It makes me angry when I think about that. But we have to distance ourselves a little bit because if you allow too much of your anger towards offenders to get into the relationship then it's very difficult to supervise somebody objectively. You have to lay your anger to one side but that doesn't mean you shouldn't try to understand what it's like for the victim either.'

18

The Victim

I was struck by the fact that
someone had made a film
about Buster Edwards with
Phil Collins and that we lived
in a world where the great
train robber is a star and the
poor old driver who got hit
on the head and
subsequently died is
forgotten.

Alan Ayckbourn

Somehow lodged in my brain was the remark of a janitor at Bristol University where I had gone for a National Union of Journalists conference in the early eighties. The journalists, in the days before even they started counting their number of 'units per week', had drunk the bar dry the night before and the janitor was remarking with a metaphorical shake of the head at their capacity. 'No one has ever drunk that much at a conference,' he told me with near awe in his voice, 'except for the Burma Star Association – and, of course, Victim Support.' The latter name conjured up a picture of driven and haunted people seeking the consolation to be found at the bottom of a bottle.

My own experience of 'victims' had been mixed: in 1983 the mechanic who had been looking at my car had been having a curry one evening with his workmates. One of them was a bit loud and had been asked to quieten down by another group in the Holloway Road restaurant. The mechanic, Barry Carleill, a big but gentle soul, had tried to calm things down to no avail. An argument developed. It turned out that the other party were off-duty police officers who duly summoned colleagues, arrested the garage crew and took them to Upper Street police station. 'On the way there,' said Barry, 'the driver of the van put a glove puppet over his hand and asked, "Who's been naughty boys then? Who's going to find out what happens to naughty boys?" It was very creepy.' He was taken into a cell and told by one of the off-duty officers, PC Brian Renton, to take his glasses off. He was then struck with such venom that his eye came out of his socket. Shortly afterwards, at Moorfields Eye Hospital, it was removed to prevent possible damage to the other eye. Since the other eye was already damaged from a welding accident, he was effectively blinded. Sitting in his hospital bed the following day he was still unable to believe that he had been attacked so viciously and mindlessly – his only explanation was that the policeman had objected in some way to the notion of him trying to take charge of what was happening. Renton, a Scottish ex-army boxing champion, was arrested and charged with grievous bodily harm. At the trial the two sets of families stood at awkward distances from each other. Barry's family had done their weeping. A young man with Renton's family – I presumed his brother – wept when he was jailed for four years. Barry was paid £120,000 in compensation after Sir David Napley had taken on his case. But what struck me most about Barry's reaction to it all was his extreme puzzlement that someone could do such violence to him for no reason.

In a very different case, the wife of a man I had met through work was kidnapped and held under threat of horrific violence for a £50,000 ransom in a chalet. Her husband had been involved in crime and the kidnappers knew he had lived well for a while. At that time he was in Wandsworth prison but was released in order to be seen to be doing a deal with the kidnappers. Money was paid over, £1 notes wrapped up in paper to make it look like £50,000, in a bugged briefcase and the kidnappers caught and jailed. The woman was released and, to express gratitude to the media for not breaking the news blackout requested in such cases by the police, gave a press conference from her bed. It was an extraordinary scene, with the haggard and exhausted victim in bed surrounded by blokes with notebooks and cameras asking her to look this way, love.

Like most people who live in the middle of London, I know people who have been attacked on the tube, punched outside pubs, robbed at knife-point, burgled and threatened. But those two events stuck out for their horror and pitilessness. There is no typical victim, of course. The very word 'victim', with its connotations of someone caught in the headlights of life, conjures up a helplessness that is often easier to ignore. And often they are ignored – by journalists, penal reformers, criminologists. There are other reasons why they appear but dimly in the media, of course. Securicor, whose drivers face the daily risk of armed robbery, will not allow them to talk about their experiences as a matter of public policy. When I asked why, their public relations agency responded, 'What's in it for them?'

One evening I was at home when an Indian-born teacher who lived round the corner knocked on the door. His ear was bleeding. He had, he explained, just been pistol-whipped and kidnapped. Jawid was a middle-aged, easy-going divorced teacher who looked after a bright teenage daughter. He was interested in local politics and in literature, he went to the National Film Theatre, liked cricket and led a far from violent life in academia. He had come from a reasonably well-off Indian family, been educated in England and stayed on. Tall, grey-haired with a roundish face and a fairly downbeat manner he had quite recently met and started living with a woman, Nina, who had fallen foul of a wealthy Rachmanite landlord. Nina had given evidence against this man at the Old Bailey when he had appeared on a massive fraud charge and he was convicted. Jawid noticed that heavy-duty characters sat silently outside the court while the case went on. Shortly afterwards one of the landlord's cohorts had appeared at her house as she was in the process of moving. He wanted money from her which he claimed was still owed – £200. If he did not get it he would beat her up.

'I was influenced by my girlfriend to think we could handle it quietly, we had had enough of the Old Bailey with the other case. I foolishly didn't contact the police. She had had various experiences with the police – she had been smoking dope at home and they came to the door and caught her with a joint in her hand. They said something and she punched one and was taken to court. Having been institutionalised all her life, convent, orphanages and so on she had that thing about authority . . .'

So the first – and what they both thought was the last – £200 was paid.

'Then one day he turned up when my dad was over here for treatment for an eye operation. I don't know what was going on in his mind. It seemed he was a vicious crook who was not necessarily all that smart and equated intelligence – and the fact that I had a job teaching – with money. I said, "Look, I can't put up any more," but he took some gold chains and said he would be back.' The threats and the visits and the demands stepped up.

'On the day itself, I was in my office in the afternoon and I got this phone call. There were more threats to beat up Nina. He kept on ringing me. "Have you got the money?" I said I hadn't. He said he would ring again in half an hour. He was asking for £500 this time. There had been already been £200, £300, it was endless. He rang back, again I said no and he said that I had to go to my bank and I had better have the money by half-past three.

'I ignored it and round about half-past three I went down to the students' refectory and bought myself a cup of milk. I'd locked my office and just as I was walking upstairs they were there. Three of them. The leader was about forty, another man, his brother-in-law it later turned out, about the same age, and a youngish nondescript sort of bloke. They saw me and said, "You'd better come with us."

'My mind started racing. There were people about, people at the reception desk, porters and so on. I thought, "Should I shout for help or run?" I felt no, I'm too much of a coward, they'll probably attack me in any case.

'I didn't know if they were armed although one of them seemed to have a cosh in a leather case. I knew the leader to be quite vicious because he always delighted, when he first came to issue his threats, to boast of what he had done – there was this West Indian guy who had borrowed something and not returned it and he delighted in telling us how he had done him over.

'I decided I would try and bluff. I suppose it comes with having some kind of confidence that I could actually talk my way out. So I accompanied them across the road. There was a Ford Granada or something like that and they got me in the back seat. They said it was very bad I hadn't got the money.'

It is a year or two since this happened but Jawid describes the sequence of events over a glass of wine as if it had happened the previous week. I find myself asking the sort of questions witnesses get asked in court, anxious for all the details to be filled in. What goes through your head if you think you are about to be badly beaten up and wounded, if you have no experience of violence and your own weapons are words, if you know that these people not only want money from you but probably hate you because you are an educated toff?

'I was frightened but I was concentrating on talk. We were driving past the site for the British Library in Kings Cross so I thought they were going to take me to a quiet street and beat me and probably let me go because they knew I hadn't got anything. But they didn't stop, they got me to direct them to my house. The girls – Nina has a daughter too – were at school; the house was empty.

'We went upstairs. The leader pulled out this gun, it looked like a little revolver and he put it to my mouth and said, "I'm going to shoot you there."

'Then he took it out of my mouth and shot it over my shoulder. When it fired I realised it was a pressurised air pistol because it fractured the glass on the picture we had on the wall. He immediately whacked me on the ear. I still have the scar. I decided it would be best not to show any emotion.

'I said, "Can you try and listen?" He said, "Listen?" and he hit me again, coshed me just above my left knee and shoved me in a chair. The other two had been downstairs and found things, gold necklaces, trinkets and things and he found Nina's pearls which were very valuable.'

At that stage Nina's daughter returned. The gang told Jawid to wash the blood off his face, make some sort of excuse and say that he was going out for a drink. They set off again.

They drove towards Aldgate, then Commercial Road and soon there were signs coming up to the Blackwall Tunnel. They put a scarf round his head, told him to put his head between his knees and not to raise it unless he fancied a coshing.

'The car stopped on what seemed like gravel and I could hear talking. They came back and said, "Drink this", and held a bottle to my mouth. It tasted of nothing but there was some kind of undissolved substance in it and they said, "It's going to knock you out." I was still blindfolded. They drove off, stopped again and put me in the boot.

'I was doing this kind of Hollywood B movie stuff – I'm not going to pass out, I'm going to stay awake – so I was digging my hands into things inside the boot to stay awake. But I think I must have passed out because when I came to someone was opening the boot.'

Two of them took him out and removed the scarf. Jawid was walked across the road and into a basement flat. He noticed it was a very narrow road, cars parked on both sides and quite a steep rise. He spotted a 53 bus and thought it very odd because the road seemed too narrow to be on a bus route.

He was taken down a long passage to a recess where there was a canvas chair and he was tied up with scaffolding rope. They threw a blanket at him and told him he was going to stay there. There were dogs around and he remembers one man taking out a knife and sharpening it.

Half an hour later the leader came and told him to phone his girlfriend. 'She didn't believe me, she thought I was out for a drink. I said you had better believe it, why don't you try some friends for money. That came to nothing.'

They decided to move him again and he was put in a different car and told to keep his head down.

'At some point I said, "Look, I have to have a pee." They stood beside me and I could see a signpost – it was near Brands Hatch. They then took me to a caravan site near a big pub. It was the night of the American satellite disaster. It was snowing and there was snow lying on the ground. They made me take my shoes and socks off so I wouldn't run away. They made me sit there until they were ready to sleep. There were some rifles, some shotguns and the main man kept demonstrating them. They gave me a sleeping bag and said I was to sleep there, the young guy got onto a leather Chesterfield and the leader went to another bedroom. They took my clothes off.'

He was given a coffee in the morning. In the hiatus he suggested that since it was the end of the month he might be getting his salary check in the post but they would have to return to his house for it. They somehow bought that. They drove him back but there was no cheque. Realising possibly that while they held him he had little chance of raising the money, there being no wealthy relatives waiting for a call, they decided to release him to allow him to try and gather money from elsewhere.

'I was told I had better not contact the police, because they said the young guy was very, very good at slitting women's throats and dragging their tongues out. They said they would do that to my daughter and my girlfriend.' But by now he was free.

'I had decided that I would no longer be terrorised. I would tell the police. My girlfriend tried to dissuade me because she still didn't want to be involved with the police. But I contacted them and met the DI and the Sergeant, who was bluff and plain and down to earth. They were sympathetic and they absolutely believed me.'

Two young plain-clothes officers went off with Jawid to try and locate the first place he had been held in what turned out to be Woolwich. The odd bus route and another landmark he recalled, a yellow dustcart, took them, after long trawls down narrow streets, to the basement.

Jawid knew the name the leader operated under from before so the police ran him through the computer and found he was on the run from a trial. He was arrested within two days. He was found with a variety of guns, forged passports in a number of different names and a small fleet of stolen cars.

Then Jawid had to identify one of the other gang members, the brother-in-law. This was done by the increasingly popular technique of having the victim stand with a policeman at the bottom of an escalator in an underground or British Rail station, Euston in this case, while the suspect is sent down the escalator along with ordinary travellers, a policeman following behind in case he makes a dash for it. The police find it more satisfactory on occasions than the standard line-up, partly because it is often difficult to get a dozen passers-by of similar build into a police station for an identification parade and, if the make-up of the parade bears little similarity to the suspect, a defence lawyer can make a point of this in the subsequent trial.

'He could see me. As soon as I saw him amongst all the regular passengers I pointed. It made me feel quite uneasy. His expression was blank.'

The leader was held in prison to await trial. The person in whose flat he had been held and the brother-in-law were given bail but told that they had to remain south of the river. The young man, who turned out to be a heroin addict, confessed. They were charged with false imprisonment, aggravated assault, extortion and holding a person against his will.

'It took a long time for me to accept that it had happened. The girls were absolutely terrified because the leader had made lots of threats and said he had someone who was very, very good at kneecapping. And I wondered what people at my workplace would think.'

Fifteen months later the trial took place. 'I wasn't looking forward to giving evidence. I had had a court case over the custody of my daughter so I wasn't looking forward to that kind of experience, where the defence have to say all kinds of things to you. But I decided I was going to give evidence because I started to believe that the things he had said, the threats he had made, were meant and they were not just for kicks.

'I was very angry with the police at this point because about a year afterwards they asked me to be free for the trial and then it had been put off. In the previous case – the fraud case involving the landlord – the police had done all the fetching of witnesses, picked us up in a car. That had been a fraud case and here was a different kind of crime that didn't somehow merit that attention, I felt. I was quite nervous going to the Old Bailey. I was walking up to the side entrance and thinking that anywhere here they could come up to me and do what they wanted. I felt quite unprotected. I had to sit outside the court with a policeman. They seemed to be more interested in getting their bloke – he was "their" bloke – while I was just the person who had helped them get him.

'The judge was good, she stopped a lot of questions and red herrings from the defence. They accused me of lying and said I had borrowed money and he was simply trying to reclaim it and I had spent the evening with him of my own free will. I had been told when I was in the custody case that I should look at the judge when I answered a question so I did that. I did get quite angry once or twice and on one or two occasions the judge did say, "Look, the witness has already answered the questions." I didn't think the prosecution was very thorough. That's why I wanted to go over it with the defence.

'The accused were staring at me. I think they were a bit taken aback that I wasn't as green as they thought when it came to behaving in court. I was quite calm in a way. That was very much to do with my experience in the divorce case when I was challenged in a very similar manner so I got used to thinking on my feet.'

He was not present for the verdict because he was working as a supply teacher and could not take the day off. In some ways he would have liked to have been there: many victims of crime – and sometimes even more so, their relatives – do feel a need to be present for the jury's return to see their own evidence vindicated. The police phoned him up with the verdict – guilty.

'I don't know what I felt. I certainly didn't feel safe because the police said that while the leader was in custody he was saying things like "I should have killed him" rather than responding to their questions, so I never felt safe. He got thirteen years. I felt yes, that was right, where else could he be monitored or supervised?'

The brother-in-law was jailed for four years, the heroin addict was released on condition he receive treatment. The man in whose flat he had been held was found not guilty on the grounds that he had been unaware that Jawid was being held by force.

'It all made me think about the law and the police. My first experience with them was when I was at school and ran away once and slept rough in the woods. I was stopped by a policeman and he struck me as very kind and paternalistic and so that was how I saw them. I didn't have respect or fear of them because I had grown up in India and they could have been working for my family.

'I had had a peaceful childhood. I had been a prankster and got into scrapes which I had got out of. One time I had challenged American marines by singing Cuban songs outside their quarters off Queensgate and I got saved by the sergeant from being beaten up when the marines came out and said, "Don't you fuck with the US marines, knock your head off," all that sort of stuff. But there was no real fear. What the whole business taught me was that on serious crimes the police will act. On other things they will choose which bits of the law they enforce and which they don't.

'It has also made me aware of all sorts of things – just the behaviour of people on the streets, which I wouldn't have recognised as necessarily aggressive, young people who shove and barge you off the pavement. I always walk my daughter home to where she's staying now. But that's part of a general unease about London, not just stemming from what happened.

'I don't know how I would handle it another time but I have a good network of friends and one who is into Polarity Therapy and he said, "Look, if you had told me what was happening, I have a whole group of people who are into kendo and they would have sorted the whole thing out, they would have been there in no time."

'But that doesn't make me feel easy. I still look when I walk down the road if there is anyone in a car – is he observing, has he got someone to take revenge, how long will it be till he gets out on parole, is he that vindictive and stupid?

'Our bedroom faces the street, there's a very low wall and I sleep nearest the window. I do sometimes think at night when I can't sleep, if I can hear voices . . . And it's just people walking past having a conversation.'

He has filled in the forms necessary to claim compensation from the Criminal Injuries Compensation Board but was still waiting for a result of this, three years after the attack. He had not been to Victim Support because he did not know of their existence.

19

The Victim's Supporter

These have-a-go idiots get everything they bloody
well deserve. He wasn't a hero. He was a nutter and
a suicidal idiot.

Message sent to the press supposedly by the armed
robber who shot a man who pursued him after a
raid on the National Film Theatre in 1989

Jawid had not heard of Victim Support. I wondered how many people had. On the
way to a party in a minicab I got talking to the driver, a middle-aged Nigerian who
worked around the clock, ferrying people around east and north London. He had
just been robbed by a young man who had put a knife to his throat, said he was a
junkie and therefore mad enough to do anything, and relieved him of his takings.
He had smacked him about a bit before departing with the money. He seemed so
bewildered by it that I suggested that he contact Victim Support before it
occurred to me that I had never met anyone who worked there. What were they
actually like?

The office where Joanna Woodd works in Lambeth is well-protected and has a
warning sticker inside the door, counselling against leaving doors unlocked –
'Don't let strangers in, use your chain'. Her small office is at the top of the
building and the eye catches *The Profession of Violence*, the John Pearson book on
the Krays, on a shelf. She's in her middle years, open, friendly, doesn't mind
being there on a bank holiday for a chat as she has some paperwork to do anyway.
So who are the victims?

'Anyone can become a victim but their reactions fall into two or three different
categories. Some are almost paralysed with fear and shock and I find that very
difficult. There doesn't seem to be a straight answer and it leaves us very helpless.
There are others – "Well, what do you expect, it happens round here, I've been
through the war, I'm absolutely fine, thanks very much." And other folk who
think they're all right at the beginning and then the shock hits them three or four
days later. Some are very, very angry.'

She became involved after she was approached by another mother at the school
where her children went. A trained nurse who had worked with lepers in east
Africa, she had also had experience in a hospice: 'Dealing with people who have
suffered feelings of loss is very similar to dealing with people who have suffered
from crime.' She was attracted by a job that she could do at home and was only
sixteen to twenty hours a week. But the job became larger as growing awareness
of the group's work led to greater demand, and with increased funding the job
moved into an office.

On an average morning she goes to Brixton police station and collects the referrals from them – residential burglaries, street robberies, assaults and rapes. These are put on a card index system as they are not computerised. During the day the other police stations ring up with their referrals or the victims themselves may drop in unannounced.

Victims are contacted by a volunteer calling round or by telephone or letter, saying that Victim Support have heard from the police that they have suffered a crime against them and explaining very briefly what and who they are. Then there is the filling in of grant application forms, criminal injury forms for people, and meetings of their own members or with the local community police consultative group.

Volunteer workers – there are 6,000 of them, dealing with 60,000 cases a year – are told what commitment is involved and it is explained to them that their own fear may increase. Would-be supporters are checked on the police computer and most people with criminal convictions excluded. Those who are accepted are trained in a group of four or six, learning how to listen and counsel, through role playing and watching videos. An evening is spent with the police who explain their procedures and run through the different types of crime they are likely to encounter and a brief introduction to crime prevention. And the volunteers are taught about welfare rights so they know where to refer people, how to approach social security to get through quickly on the phone and so on. They are finally issued with an ID card and are ready to start.

'Some volunteers find it quite hard ringing up cold because people say, "I've never heard of you." But generally people are very, very grateful. We get quite a few letters saying, "Thank you ever so much, it's good to know there's someone out there who cares."'

Part of the work involves going along with the victim when the person who has attacked or robbed them appears in court. 'A lot of the victims when they're being cross-examined feel that they're the guilty party. If the person is acquitted that almost confirms the victim's own feelings of guilt so we need to spend quite a lot of time supporting them.

'One can sometimes see the barrister tying them in knots and you think, "Oh, help, are they going to go down this avenue trying to prove their person's innocence?" In one rape case they said the girl was drunk and no way was she drunk. In another case the girl hadn't been able to identify the person who had raped her. She had had her jaw broken, but the way the questioning was going was that maybe there had been two people in the house and I thought maybe they'd get the person in the dock off. Her neighbour, who had identified the person concerned, was a lass with a very strong personality and she was able to take a pretty strong onslaught from the defence counsel.'

It shocked her at first that the victims could be subjected to such a punishing ordeal. 'Then I had to realise that this was the way British justice was and try to prepare the victim for a tough time. I know one is glad when there is a sentence and hopefully British justice is right. But at the same time one hopes that when they come out of prison they mend their ways and lead a more positive life.'

Does the catalogue of inhumanity not sour her?

'It hasn't made me more bitter. I remember spending a lot of time questioning and thinking how am I actually able to forgive these people, as one had been taught as a Christian? Can I go on forgiving? I wrestled with that for a long, long time. I can't remember coming up with an answer. When one does see people with their whole lives absolutely shattered and changed for no reason – the attacks can be mindless or purposeless and often without any gain – you think, "Why?"'

But what about the victims? Does their experience make them bay for stiffer penalties, the rope, the noose? 'Most of the victims don't want hanging brought back. Even one chap whose parents were murdered . . . he's a fairly violent person as he says himself, he doesn't want to see the murderer hung.'

At the same time she comes across plenty of people who feel that the attention is tilted too much in the direction of the criminal.

'I've forgotten their names –' she gestures at *The Profession of Violence* '– the Kray twins, the wife of one of their victims came in and she was very distressed. She had umpteen newspaper cuttings about the Krays and some were very recent. She was saying that all the time she's having to read about what the Krays are doing and the money they're making from books and films while she was lost and forgotten and why should she go on suffering.

'Basically she seemed to want two things: one was a home of her own – she was living with other people – and the other seemed to be to have some recognition from the authorities about her plight. So I wrote to the Home Secretary and he finally – he took a long time – wrote back, recognising that she was suffering and saying that the Krays wouldn't get any payment from the papers, which I was surprised about, and that there wasn't anything he could do about the film. I sent her a copy and I didn't hear from her again.'

How hard is it dealing with people who have been suffering the death of someone through a murder or manslaughter?

'We come across some murders where the victims have been involved in something criminal, whether their families know or not. But they're always "very good boys". With the murder cases I began to question whether there was a cultural difference in the way that people reacted. But then I realised in some cases that we aren't actually needed, somehow they have their own mechanism, their own family network which is fantastic.

'Reaction to murder seems to vary almost as much as it does with burglary. Even the man who lost his parents, he still had his evening meals there, he has been slightly upset but not as upset as one might have imagined. And a Glaswegian family, so broad I could hardly understand anything they were saying, their daughter had been murdered. There was a question of whether she had been a prostitute, but that's neither here nor there.'

There is a theory, a controversial one, that some victims actually attract their crime; that an attacker can sense instinctively that fear and will act on it.

'With a few people there is a victim mentality, not many. One lady was being referred to us almost weekly, time and time and time again. I talked to Age Concern and the Social Services and decided she must walk down the road with her purse in her hand. I used to see her with black eyes and it wasn't her husband or anything. So we said OK, we aren't going to see you again and it just stopped. So maybe sometimes people, if they get all this attention, think it's worth it.'

Much of her work is with the police and the relationship between the two organisations is quite good, she says.

She had grown up, the daughter of missionaries, in Uganda, with a favourable impression of the police. 'My parents were on leave and we were staying with someone who told me how she'd been broken into and how wonderful the police had been, that was the impression of the police I was given as a small kid. Then when we were broken into once or twice in Blackheath when I was in my teens I remember ringing up and having some policeman try to chat me up on the phone and I was pretty disgusted with that.'

She had been involved in a project in Bermondsey with children who had a variety of problems with the law and worked quite closely with the home beat officer. 'He was a remarkable person, he'd seen people grow up and would point to someone in a Rolls Royce and say, "I nicked him when he was a kid." He had been around longer than any social worker and he was very supportive to work with and understood the aims of my work. On the other hand I suppose I've been hauled up once or twice for driving the wrong way down a road and then I think the police can be rather arrogant. I suppose I think they're decent people, but I recognise there are good and bad there as in any other profession.'

She has also been a lay visitor – someone who has access to the police station to make sure that arrested suspects are being treated properly. 'It was very interesting when one went into police stations because often before making the visit I would maybe have seen victims. Driving down to the police station I would be thinking "little rats" about the people who had carried out the attack but as soon as one meets them they're people. I didn't find myself so interested in what they had done but whether their needs were being met.'

She is puzzled by people's reluctance to help each other out in trouble. 'Even when they hear someone in the street or hear someone crying for help no one will go along to help apart from the odd one or two. The victims acknowledge their neighbours' fear, saying they might be attacked too, which is absolutely valid. But at the same time, one can feel sure that until the general public are prepared to step in the offenders are going to get away because no one's giving them any boundaries, no one's saying we won't tolerate that sort of behaviour.'

Her clients gain some satisfaction when the offender is caught: 'The son of two people who were murdered brought in the newspaper when someone had been arrested for the murder and said, "Look at this." He had always suspected the person but it took time for the police to pick him up and he would come in and blow off a lot of anger to me. He would leave, having absolutely blasted me out and say, "Thanks for the visit."

'This anger does not have an effect on me, I think that blows off and they go off and feel better. But the fear leaves me feeling so helpless. One can say to people just remember all the other hundred and one times you've been down the street and never been attacked but I don't think it's a very helpful comment to make.

'We're not that aware of organised crime but sometimes there has suddenly been a whole spate of crimes, and then it goes down and you say to the police what has happened here? And they say, "Oh, we've just picked up two or three from a gang," and you realise there is something organised.'

She doesn't like watching the celluloid versions of her clients although her children watch the police series, *The Bill*. She would rather watch a different, gentler kind of detective like Sherlock Holmes, or read historical novels or the classics.

And she does not necessarily see herself climbing up the steps of the Lambeth office forever. 'I wonder if I have enough time left in life to go and study law.'

She is married to the director of a voluntary agency and they have three children. 'When I was working at home the youngest one used to come home from school and maybe play with bricks up in the office. For various educational reasons we were round at the hospital once or twice to find out why he wasn't making progress and we were told that once he gave three wishes: that my mummy doesn't die, my daddy doesn't die and my family don't go away. All on loss. And I'm sure his feelings of loss were reinforced by the conversations he heard me having about victims. Just the other day the little one said, "I wish you didn't work for Victim Support then I could lead a normal life and I wouldn't know so much about crime." I think it has an enormous effect. Inevitably one does talk at home and inevitably the fear is increased.'

Their Peckham home, with its anti-tunnel rail-link poster in the window, has been burgled several times since she started at Victim Support. 'The last one really knocked me sideways, they took furniture, they took big stuff. We'd come back from a weekend and the next day going in to talk to victims I thought, "Help!" and I was really able to understand their feelings of sickness and the whole physical reaction to it. Also the feelings of vulnerability and being targetted.'

Does she feel that the offenders should be confronted with their victims, to make them realise what effect they have had on lives?

'There was a scheme here for trying to encourage the offenders to see the effects of their crimes. It was very good, the Junction Project. One time the victim verbally attacked the chap concerned – I think he'd taken his car and ruined it and his girlfriend had just passed her driving test and was looking forward to driving down to the pub on her own. He levied out [wrote out a list of what the offender had to do to make reparation] and said yes, you can come down and do this and this. Unfortunately there was a hiccup, they wrote to the magistrate and the magistrate said, "What's this dirty piece of paper," and tore it up and took no notice.'

All this rang a bit of a bell. It sounded very like the project that Bobby King, the ex-bank robber, had been involved with. Did she recall someone of that name?

'Bobby King, yes. He was a lovely person, super.'

She deals a lot with young police officers and feels that often the police don't recognise the effect of dealing constantly with brutality and despair in the inner city. 'I wish the police would recognise that they are more frightened. Some of the WPCs say, "I only go to get my car from the garage if I'm accompanied by a male police officer because I'm too frightened," or they say, "I carry all these various items in my bag for self protection." You think of murders and violent crimes and the whole effect that has on some of the senior officers. It's just non-stop. It calls into question what support the police force offer their officers.'

20

The Young Bill

It must never be forgotten that it is
the beat officer who is the key figure.

Gilbert Kelland, formerly head of
CID, Scotland Yard

'It wasn't a vocation. I thought it would be exciting and that and it was a way of getting the money I wanted at that time.'

Protocol demands that police officers should receive permission before talking to the press so we agree that we will call him Jim and I reassure him that he will not be identifiable. We head off to a local pizza house for a meal and just as the pepperoni-and-olive special arrives so, out of the blue and in jocular fashion, does a journalist I know. Jim, a tall, neatly turned-out young man, seems unperturbed. He is quite an unperturbed sort of person.

He had not had much experience of the police when he was growing up. 'I had my cigarettes confiscated by them, that sort of thing, and I was always scared of them. I always used to like detective stories but in the classic mould.' He joined up after packing in higher education and now works on a busy inner London patch.

'I've fallen very much into the mould of being a policeman now and it's hard to think of doing anything else. I certainly wouldn't have joined the forces and I wouldn't have got a job doing any sort of manual work. I shy away from manual work. My father disapproved of my joining at first. He thought all policemen were stupid because he's a staunch Labour Party supporter. My mother was quite pleased.'

Jim was quite pleased himself when he started out in uniform, people noticed him and reacted differently. 'You feel self-conscious but quite important. People are normally quite happy to talk to you. The ones I deal with mostly are middle-class – they've got a vested interest in liking the police because they've got property and possessions that need looking after; whereas if I was to go to a pub in the East End and try to make acquaintances they'd look upon it very differently. When you walk through an estate in uniform people shout rude things at you quite often.

'You can usually tell a policeman. Very broadly speaking, there's only three groups of people in London who still wear a moustache: squaddies on leave, homosexuals and policemen, they all wear different types of moustache.'

When he first started, he had lived in a section house where young officers have their own room and eat in a canteen. 'I can't imagine anything more unpleasant. It was like a half-star hotel. Half the people there you wouldn't want to spend your spare time with.'

In the news that week had been a jailed and disgraced Manchester policeman, one of whose less loveable hobbies had been organising degrading initiation ceremonies for new recruits, handcuffing them, scrawling words on their bare bottoms, that sort of thing. Had Jim had been through such rituals?

There had been harmless ones, being sent out to take a test-tube sample of the River Lee at midnight – it had to be midnight for the labs, they were told – that sort of thing. There was teasing of the new boys but not much more than that. Women officers had to put up with sexual innuendo – 'the same as any other job, I suppose'. It was only the 'macho' officers who objected to working with them on patrol. Since these types had a notion of themselves 'risking their lives every day for Queen and Country', it was a bit galling to have to acknowledge that a mere woman could handle the situation just as comfortably, sometimes more so.

Now he is a uniformed policeman although his current work involves much plain-clothes drug work, that being one of the boom areas in all levels of crime. Dawn raids?

'No, by and large drugs raids are carried out in the middle of the afternoon. Those are the times when people deal. Most drugs dealers are wise to the fact that the police have been doing dawn raids ever since the police began and so they don't keep drugs in their houses in the early hours of the morning. They get what they need to sell and then sell it through the afternoon and hide it somewhere normally away from their addresses.

'We go in, six or eight of us, we all rush in and each room is searched very quickly for people. Then there's a systematic room by room search in the company of the people there. A lot of people don't use hiding places; it's just on the table. But otherwise it's up chimneys, under floorboards, behind light switches, in the cistern, in the toilet, behind the panel in the bath.'

Most journalists are familiar with calls from people whose houses have just been turned over by a police raid and left in a fashion that wouldn't win a rosette at the Ideal Home Exhibition.

'We do tidy up after ourselves, as we're required to by the Police and Criminal Evidence Act. Ninety per cent of the time we do. The way I deal with people is I start off being polite and see how they treat me. If they're going to be rude and shout and swear that's going to affect my behaviour.'

Does that mean they would plant stuff on people who they thought had ditched their drugs?

'There was a temptation a couple of years ago to put things found at a party back in someone's pocket but I've never done it personally and it just doesn't happen any more. The police force has always been a lot more honest than people think and now it's sparkling clean.

'Then the prisoners will be taken back to the station and interviewed, all the paper work will be done and they'll be charged or released pending further inquiries. We normally average about two or three raids a week or we might put a whole week aside for surveillance. That sometimes involves a static observation on an address or group of addresses but more usually it would mean following a suspected dealer round London and finding his suspected supplier before hitting him.'

There is an image of the policeman, like 'Popeye' Doyle in *The French Connection*, waiting bored out of his skull, with a doughnut, while he carried out a drugs surveillance. Is it not a tedious task?

'Often you sit in a car for several hours waiting for something to happen but there's an air of expectancy about that makes it quite an anxious experience, not a boring one. When you're actually following someone about it's a hell of a job. You need three or four vehicles, all with good communications between them, to take over the following. Often we have to break a lot of traffic rules, go through red lights for fear of losing them.

'People working on the squad did get sussed recently and did pull away from a follow but it's never happened to me personally. On a raid we don't knock because that would be daft. The normal reaction is one of fear and shock because we go in very quickly, otherwise you lose the evidence. Sometimes it's, "How dare you do this to me!" and sometimes it's a very resigned reaction. More often than not people are resigned to the fact.

'We check out the doors first and often we use a sledgehammer. We've got people we can call in with other specialist equipment. It can take quite a long time to get through a good door with a sledgehammer but we've got good equipment that makes it a lot easier.'

Jim is a burly, athletic looking man. Does he throw his weight about on these occasions? It was rare that it came to anything physical, he said. He has been on duty in riots in east London, on marches when abuse and other more physical things are hurled.

'You do get frightened although no one says so at the time. It's all bravado afterwards, though people go back and tell their wives.' There were the odd pub brawls and street fights. He didn't mind them too much: 'It can be quite exhilarating afterwards if you've won.'

It was not the worst part of the job anyway – that was having to tell someone of a death. He had not had specific training in this though he said you were supposed to be sufficiently sensitive to break the news properly. 'There are jokes about it. "Are you the Widow Brown?"' He did not much like dealing with dead bodies either and there had been a few of those. 'I had nightmares after the first two.'

Sometimes the people he arrests have knives and bayonets although he has never been threatened. 'Sawn-off shotguns are still the most popular because they're easy to get hold of. Currently a shotgun licence enables someone to have as many as they want. People get paid just for looking after firearms – we had a case recently of someone getting £100 to look after firearms for a robber.'

So who are the dealers he arrests?

'We've had quite a few forty-year-old ex-hippie types who've been dealing in quite a large way intelligently. To my knowledge some of them have amassed quite large amounts of money doing that. Then there are addict dealers, young people in their early twenties and very desperate just to get the money to fund their habit. They're always heroin addicts because heroin is the worst drug in the kind of effect it has on people. Then there is the group of West Indians, they're working just for profit, a lot aren't even users of heroin. A lot of them deal in cannabis as well. We arrest cannabis dealers and we're happy to do it but it's not a great concern. Then there are Nigerians who bring in a lot of heroin and cannabis.

'It's very common for ex-armed robbers to go into dealing. It is a safer way of making a living and more profitable. Drug dealers have become more sophisticated, using car telephones and bleepers and sometimes their technology is ahead of ours and that never used to be the case. Robberies and burglaries are going to become increasingly less profitable as security systems become more sophisticated. Drug dealing is a safer and more profitable route.

'There isn't a typical professional criminal. I've arrested fifty-year-old lady drug dealers, eighteen-year-olds, they're all living from the proceeds of dealing. Anyone who has got the lack of morals and the courage to do it – they're the only criteria.

'What's happening now is that there's very small groups of very self-interested people who are willing to resort to violence and then there is the Yardies who are coming in a big way and deal a lot in cocaine and a lot of other things besides.'

A few years ago there was a highly promoted advertising campaign for the Metropolitan Police which set would-be recruits a few posers: what, for instance, would they do if they saw a mate or a mate's mate smoking a joint at a party?

'If someone was smoking a joint at a party that I was at, that wouldn't be a dilemma for me, I'd let them get on with it. But if someone was taking heroin I would nick them or arrange for them to be nicked. I can't see any problems in decriminalising cannabis but it's of no consequence to me because I'm quite happy to arrest people for supplying cannabis as long as it's outlawed. On a personal basis I can't see that it's more harmful than alcohol and I can't see anyone criminalising alcohol so why not legalise cannabis?'

He has to attend court a lot and he loves it, the favourite part of the job. Even when some clever dick barrister is trying to catch him out? 'Those are the best fun.'

Does he swear on the Bible, is he ever tempted to gloss the evidence?

'I swear on the Bible in court. I'm not a practising Christian but I'm not totally irreligious either. It's annoying if a defence lawyer accuses you of lying. A defence lawyer is meant to defend a case on instructions from his client but I suspect that it's often the case that a solicitor will tell the client what the instructions are. And there are certain solicitors who are known to be left wing and they are always coming up with the same defence. It's a disgusting way of carrying on really.

'I'm in the position that I always know the person charged is guilty but the judge would have to lend a similar amount of weight to even a fairly ridiculous story that a defendant came up with. I think someone would be morally justified in cutting corners when you know someone's guilty, but not in the eyes of the law. I don't think people get out and out fitted up. I think in conversations between a police officer and someone at the time of an arrest maybe the police officer hears what he wants to hear rather than what he does hear. Sometimes it can be done on purpose, sometimes by mistake. I think a few years ago it wasn't as reliable as it is now.

'Often you can tell from looking at a jury whether they're going to convict. I've seen a jury with three Rastafarians on it and by and large Rastafarians don't like the police and aren't disposed to believe their evidence. I've seen acquittals there. Juries have got to be checked a lot more thoroughly – there are random checks made by officers of the court and I don't think these checks have been done as thoroughly as they could be. I think they should be checked not just for their criminal connections but also their educational qualifications so that you can be sure they understand what's going on.

'Middle-class people are more likely to convict than working-class people because the middle class come into contact with the police and legal system, as victims of crime, and more often a working-class family, as well as often being a victim of crime, may come into contact with the police as perpetrators of it.'

He has been threatened by people who have been arrested by him and then convicted but he does not take them too seriously and allows himself a 'bit of a gloat' if they come on heavy after the case, pointing out to them that they haven't done too well so far. The ones who get off are usually so cheery that they don't make any remarks to him.

His work requires information from the public. On whom does he rely?

'Very rarely you might get a public-spirited person who gives you information. More often than not it's a prisoner who's been arrested and there are various inducements that can be offered . . . he might get bail or he might be promised a letter to the judge or magistrate at his hearing or he could be offered money from the informants' funds.

'Normally they're just criminals who've been arrested and are scared of going to prison. They can be strong types or weak types although some of the best are weak types because they are eager to please someone, for praise, because they don't get it anywhere else.'

And when his hard work leads to a conviction? 'I believe in punishment although it may not be a very enlightened view, for something like heroin dealing, or violent crime, or burglary in someone's private house. The longer they get, the happier I am, but I realise there has to be somewhere to draw the line. I don't think sentences are heavy enough but I don't think they're let off so appallingly easy, like some Tory MPs and the tabloid press think.'

Like most police officers he has strong views on the way the judicial system operates. He was against the right to silence. He was not a great fan of the PCA, the Police Complaints Authority, which some police officers claim stands for Prosecute Coppers Always. He thought they took two bites at a cherry, wanting police officers disciplined on offences of which they had been acquitted in court.

He likes the current top man at the Yard, Peter Imbert: 'He remembers everyone's name, he gets on well with people.' Sir Kenneth Newman, his predecessor, was known as ET for his slightly other-wordly appearance; he had tried to move changes through a little too swiftly, felt Jim. The one before him, MacNee, had been a 'prat'.

And when his work is done for the day, does he join the others for his companionship?

'There is comradeship in the force and a sense of looking after each other but that's just at work. There are a lot of heavy drinkers in the police and they get on well. There is some stress involved although it largely depends on the individual, most stress is self-imposed or comes within the hierarchy of the job. It's not so much the fear of violence it's just the management problems.'

What about politics?

'Most of the police are quite reactionary but that doesn't mean that they all love Mrs Thatcher – though they like pay rises. Most policemen, for instance, don't like all the cuts in the National Health Service but they'd like to see hanging brought back and longer jail sentences.

'I suppose the favourite paper in the Crime Squad is something like the *Daily Mail* but you get people bringing *The Times* and the *Independent* and the *Sun*. If I had to choose a favourite it would be the *Mail* or the *Daily Express* but only just. Most of the quality press report quite fairly – sometimes the *Guardian* is a little left wing and a bit unfair.

'The tabloid press sensationalise crime and cause more fear of it, fear of crime is far bigger a problem than crime itself and they show no understanding of the complex things involved in investigating crime. It's as though they think police-men ought to be able to pull criminals out of a top hat. They don't realise how hard it is to catch a murderer. If someone murders someone, they come along and stick a knife in them, the person falls down dead and they walk away. If no one saw it and there's no fingerprints it's pretty hard to find out who did it.'

Jim thought that *The Bill* is the most accurate portrayal of the police at work, even if it is 'wildly over-dramatised. If anyone was to make a drama series about what police work is actually like I shouldn't think a lot of people would watch because they'd see people sitting round with pens writing on pieces of paper for about ninety per cent of the programme.'

Does he feel, as some police officers do, that films romanticise crime?

'If you look at most of the films and series on television, it's the police rather than the criminals that are romanticised. I saw John McVicar on a television programme and he was giving his views on the penal system to a group of sixteen-year-olds and one of them said, "You don't deserve to be sitting up there, you should have died," so I don't think people see crime as romantic.'

What of the criminals themselves?

'We often get on quite well with them when we talk to them and quite often they feel they deserve what they get. A lot of the people we deal with, apart from the fact that they're criminals, are quite nice.'

Are there known gangs in his patch?

'There are certain families who are renowned and might be feared in a small locality but it's not organised as it used to be. There is one big family in this area who own a lot of places and made their money by armed robbery and, I think, drug dealing and now they run a lot of what appear to be legitimate businesses. They've never received any substantial jail sentences and everyone's frightened of them. There was a drug dealer in the area who had his legs blown away recently but it's just economic. They're vying for each other's markets and that's why it's happening.

'There is one estate where the Yardies have got a very strong hold and have lots of flats there and one of the flats is so well-fortified it hasn't actually been hit yet.'

Does that mean that the police assume that a black person with drugs is a Yardie or is more likely to be in possession of drugs?

'There is racism in the police but it's not as the left wing would have it portrayed. There aren't many instances now – there used to be more – where, say, a police officer will make a racist remark to a black man. A police officer might have racist views but he wouldn't voice them in that way although he might talk about them with his colleagues. In my experience most black people and certainly younger black people don't like the police and it's certainly hard for any group of people who aren't liked to turn round and like the other group. Dislike or hatred breeds the same.'

21

The Black Geezer

Freedom is something people take, and
people are as free as they want to be.

James Baldwin, *Nobody Knows My Name*

Breakfast-time in Brixton. Trevor Hercules – 'T' to his friends – has just been for a swim and fancies some beans and eggs on toast. He greets people on the stroll from his Stockwell council flat to the Italian café off Brixton market. He is thirty-five, broadly built, dressed in a green-and-white hooped shirt and shorts. He has spent seven years in prison for armed robbery.

Born in Paddington, west London, he was despatched with a younger brother into care after his mother left to go to America. He grew up in Sussex and Bedfordshire in a series of homes. He was the only black boy at the schools he attended, where he excelled in sport and got on well academically. He left at fifteen because that was what was required of boys in homes and found a job in London as an apprentice electrician, going to college one day a week and staying in a rough, grim hostel.

'I worked with an older guy, who was black and like a father-figure. There was never any resentment – if it was "go and get the tools", I went and got the tools. It was great. The managers at head office were terrific.' He was well paid, gaining experience, and despite having to stay in the hostel, was enjoying himself when he went out for the night with two other young men.

'They were both about twenty-two and I was sixteen. They took me out to this club in Paddington called the Crypt. There was a nice little young girl and I was trying to get her phone number. They said they were leaving and I said, "Wait a minute, I've got to get this girl's number, I've just come to London and I haven't got a girl." They waited for five minutes but as they were going up the road, I can't be sure, but I think one of them put his hand in a guy's pocket who was walking past. The guy was drunk and they started fighting. These two guys took part in the fight, it was nothing to do with me – I had a good job, my pocket's full up with money. Nobody had ever had a bad word to say about me. The man screamed and they ran off.

'I had only been in London a short time and I didn't run off because I hadn't done anything. The police arrive and the man points at me and says, "Yes, he's one of them he tried to rob me." I never touched the geezer. The police started bashing me, bashed my head against the van and took me down to the police station. There was a geezer at the police station slapping me round the face and saying, "You black cunt." They caught the other two and both said I had nothing to do with it. In court they said the same thing but they didn't listen to them. At the end of the day they gave me three years' probation and a £20 fine. And that day I said, "Yeah, you fuck with me, I'll fuck with you." That's where I got my bad attitude from. That's the gospel truth.'

His employers stood by him and came to court to give evidence on his behalf, saying what an excellent worker he was. But the firm ran into difficulties and he was later made redundant.

'I got another job and the people were terrible. After having such good employers I didn't know anything else. They were very disrespectful so it was either leave or get the sack. I was seventeen, me and another guy named Samson were working in Kilburn, as apprentice engineers. Some other guys, white guys, came in after us. The foreman asked me to sweep the floor. I swept the floor. The next day he asked me again. I swept the floor. A couple of days later, he asked me again. I said, "Excuse me, you've asked me twice to sweep the floor and I've done it and never said anything. Why don't you ask those geezers there, they haven't done it yet." He said, "I'm giving you an order. You don't want to do it, I'm sacking you." I said, "Give me my cards, you're not sacking me, I'm leaving." Samson said the same thing and we walked out.

'I thought – I'm not working for this country. I started robbing. I had nothing to do, I hated everything.'

He was arrested many times. A young black man driving a good car could expect to be stopped around five times a week. 'It was your attitude. Police know who you are; if you're sort of proud they know. There's a certain way that people carry themselves and they know.

'Nobody thinks they're going to get caught. When I was carrying out the robberies I wasn't frightened, I didn't give a shit. Because at the end of the day we wanted that money.

'Mind you, we wouldn't have shot anyone. Sometimes we had no bullets in the gun. Most of the time, in fact. We were in Oxford Circus once, running from the bank to the car with people chasing us, and we had no bullets in the gun! Why didn't we have bullets? Sometimes we couldn't get any, to tell you the truth, and sometimes we didn't put them in because we knew what could happen. Now, if I went on a robbery, I would have bullets, I would be serious, because you'll be shot anyway. Black people revere life very highly, more than white guys. You'll find more black guys get caught with bullets in their gun without firing a shot. The white guys are not worried about selling you guns, they don't give a toss.'

He ran around with a team of armed robbers. Sometimes they would rob a bank on the spur of the moment, having decided they were short of money. 'We would be sitting around upset because we had no money and someone would say, "Let's go and rob that bank over there, let's go, let's go!"' Arrest became inevitable.

'They never bashed me around when we got pulled in. They put some black gloves on a couple of times. I said, "Take a look at my record, you don't frighten me. What do you want to do, kill me? I'm not frightened of dying." I said, "You're a pussy," and the policeman just left me alone. He just looked at me and knew. He had a respect for me because of that. The robbery squad wanted to do me for about five other robberies that they wanted to clear up. They took me in a car and drove me around and said, "Do you know this place?" They took me to five different places – bank, post office, everywhere.'

He stood trial, was convicted and gave a black power salute as he was sent down. He had little respect for the court.

'To tell lies to the British court is within the rules for me because as far as I am concerned they are the devil – I'm just using the term. They are evil. I've got no obligation to them. They've taken everything from us and yet I'm supposed to be the thief.'

Most of his colleagues eventually went to jail. He found himself first in Wormwood Scrubs then Wandsworth and Gartree. Having been in an institution for most of his life beforehand, he found part of the life quite easy to adapt to: 'We were used to saying "Ssshhh, here comes the teacher."' He found ways to entertain himself.

'Police came from Birmingham and Manchester to visit me and ask me about crime. But I can be funny as well. They would say you've got a visit, a policeman from Birmingham. I didn't have to go but I wanted to go to get out of my cell; it was so monotonous, you want to get out of your cell and have a smoke and a chat with the others. I would see the two policemen and they would say they wanted to interview me about a robbery in Birmingham. I would say, "Fuck you, goodbye."'

He spent time in solitary confinement for similar conversations with prison officers, read a lot and studied black history.

'I was a Muslim inside because I don't eat pork. If you told them you didn't eat pork you'd still get it so that was one way to avoid it. Also it meant we had time to ourselves to discuss black issues; if we had told them we were black people and could we sit down and have a discussion together about it they would have said not, but as Muslims we could. They had to have the Iman in – because of the Arab oil, they couldn't refuse to let him in as there were Arabs who were real Muslims. If they had tried to stop him he would have been down to the Home Office – leave my boys alone kind of thing. Once we said we were Muslims we came under him. He didn't mind because he thought he'd got converts. And you have to remember that in many of these middle-eastern Arab countries a large proportion of the population are black so it wasn't like a whole lot of black guys suddenly turning up at a Christian meeting.

'Sometimes in prison the colour of your skin doesn't matter as much as it does outside. If you prove yourself one of the people, then you'll get accepted in a funny sort of way, although not necessarily completely.'

There were football games – Hercules likes football and cricket and the Test match is flickering in the background as we talk in his flat, which is decorated with posters of heavyweight champion Mike Tyson, Frank Bruno and some Ghanaian carvings. His wife is from Ghana and has returned there with his son; he is planning to join them. These prison football games would be between England, Scotland, Ireland and – the team Hercules played for – the All Blacks. They were needle occasions, honour was at stake and, when it came, victory was very sweet.

'It's got so bad now if I see a black and white cat running outside I want the black cat to win. I see two black birds and a white bird flying I want the black birds to fly the furthest. They've labelled me as the black geezer and the black geezers at the moment are the bad geezers. We know we haven't really got anything, we're at the bottom of the social scale.'

When he emerged after his sentence he found many of his friends had disappeared. He went to college, thought of trying to be a journalist but didn't like the way he felt even black journalists reported the news. 'I couldn't do that kind of reporting where you can't tell the truth. I see black people on telly reporting on black incidents in the same racist fashion as white people because they can't do it any other way or they'd lose their job.'

He started a business with a friend, bringing in artefacts from Ghana, and got back in touch with his family in Ladbroke Grove. One sister is a solicitor, one has a boutique, a brother is an accountant and another a dancer. He wrote about his time inside, sitting up for days and nights at a time, writing in longhand, took it to an agent in the West End and eventually found a publisher, Fourth Estate. He lives half in Brixton, half in Ladbroke Grove, but he does not remove himself from the other people he knew who went to jail too.

'I'm not out of that world, I'm not in jail but I'm not out of it. I've lived that way of life all my life and people who are into that are my friends. You can't turn round and say to people, "Oh, I'm not doing it any more, I don't want to talk to you."' He has his own theories about black people and crime and knows that he gets called dogmatic for expressing them.

'The over-riding factor as far as what is happening to us will always be colonialism, imperialism and slavery. I know I'm beginning to sound like a parrot because I keep saying it but no one can ever stop the black kids from getting in trouble until all that is dealt with. No matter how bad the government think they are and how bad the police think they are and how bad the army think they are, they can never stop black kids.'

He gestures towards Brixton. 'Just walk through there. There are some bad motherfuckers out there. The riots – uprisings we call them now – Toxteth, Brixton, Liverpool, Bristol. They must have a reason why they're doing it, they must have a cause. They feel they have a grievance. People who have been lied to throughout history – there's an African word, *gaberooned*, which means slagged off, given a bad name – that's what happens. White people have a subconscious superiority complex over black people because that's all they've been taught. So governments have to go back and say, "Listen, we lied, black people have a history, they are the first people on the earth," to show all these young black kids that they have something to belong to. Basil Davidson – I love him – he wrote about the black man in Egypt.

'I was a decent lad when I came here, an honest, decent lad but what I saw I immediately rebelled against. I spoke perfectly good English before I came to London and when I saw what was happening I didn't want to speak it any more. I started speaking in patois – "raas claat" – and I just changed my whole personality.

'There's going to be so much trouble. White people have to be re-educated so that they can understand they're not superior to black people; even when they say they know that, you can tell they don't from their attitude and their mannerisms.

'I've got no respect for authority whatsoever. If I can see people killing my people on my telly – my people in South Africa – because they're black, and the rest of the world still dealing with them, well . . . De Klerk, that evil man, comes over here and the Prime Minister takes him inside and talks to him – who's going to talk to me? After that who can tell me anything? Sorry, bit of a ramble.' He gets some pineapple juice from the fridge.

'But a lot of black people who have made it, or say they've made it are not being honest; they've got a lot of burning hate in them but they keep it under wraps.

'You watch all those athletes running for Britain, they're not British, no matter what they say, they're black. Afterwards when they ask them did you win the medal for England, they say, "No, I won it for myself."

'The thing about black people and why we're always in trouble is if we don't like something we say it – fuck off. If I don't like you, you don't come in my place, I don't talk to you. I like most Irish people and you find most black people like Irish people. If you ask them out of English, Scottish, Welsh and Irish who they like, they like Irish because they seem to have the same kick – if they don't like you they say it.

'The sixteen-year-olds round here are going to go to jail, that's inevitable. They've got guns, little kids out there have got guns, little kids with crack pipes smoking coke. It would freak you. People smoking coke and when they've got no more they'd be looking at me and you, looking at the watch, the ring on your finger, they'd cut the finger off. You can talk to the ones who want to dress up in a suit, pet gorillas, talk to them but the rest of them you can't talk to.'

Trevor Hercules is sceptical about the notion of black organised crime: 'Yardies – what dreadlocked Yardie could come into this country, into an airport, without all his belongings being taken apart, without being strip-searched, without his hair being taken apart, who can get in with any drugs? If they're running anything over here it's only because white men make them run it. What influence do they have over here? A Yardie is someone who comes from Jamaica. The idea of Yardies running things – it's a fantasy so they can kick in a black man's door, so they can justify it.

'Where did we get drugs from? White boys. Any kind of drug that we get in this black community comes from white boys, that's why I don't want to have anything to do with it. Who takes drugs? People at the lower end of the social scale to get away from their trials and tribulations. They haven't got anything to lose, who cares, who gives a toss?

'We've already agreed that there are black people out there doing shit but to say that there's an organisation that we can label the black Mafia is complete and utter bullshit. They haven't got the room to manoeuvre. They live in a certain area which is heavily policed. It's impossible – you can't hide yourself in a white community. You want to talk about this happening somewhere else but this is England. It's just an excuse to come and trouble people, as I know. I can go and get a white guy and say there's a white conspiracy to kill all black people – I can get two white guys and they'll say, "Yeah, it's true, we've got guns," and I can photograph them and get their story in the paper but that would be bullshit.

'The black people who came here from the West Indies to get money; they work all their lives and they still don't have any money. Their children aren't going to suffer that. So they're always going to look out for easy money. So they look around for ways – robbing. They've got no respect. It doesn't matter who you are. "What's your name? The baddest white villain there is? I can kill you so don't fuck with me." A lot of them have not got much hope because their parents can't even talk to them, such is their disillusionment with society and life and themselves as black people.'

But he sees the divisions between the young white and the young black being eroded.

'I like seeing the young white and the young black guys together but a lot of the time you know they're only getting together because they're bad news. Usually when you see it, the white guy is within the black community, they're not frightened of black guys. You get them going to school together and it's good if they're getting themselves together for constructive business rather than monkey business. But now if they need a lookout they send the white boy because he's not going to get picked up; if there's a black guy there for too long someone is going to tell a policeman and say what's he there for? White boy with a suit on, carrying a case, it's all right; he can chat to a girl, he can stand there for five days no one will worry about him. But a black guy goes there, everyone will be on to him.

'A lot of the people in America doing the serious crime, the violence, are black guys because they're not in it just for the money – it's the rebelliousness and the hate inside. If you hate too much it eats you away and a lot of black people hate and this hatred comes out in terms of frustration and violence sometimes to themselves, sometimes to other people, sometimes to people they love. Even when they get the money from a crime they don't put it in a business. People don't feel the contact with this place to do it. So it's get the money and spend it.'

He sees his future in west Africa. 'There's some nice things about this country and I've met some nice people but I've got to get away. I can't get away from the fact that I'm Europeanised. I know there are corrupt officials in Africa so I'll get on their case too, not just on white people's or the West's case.

'A lot of people who do commit crimes, a lot of black people, I don't hold them responsible, funny as it may seem, because I believe if they were in a different environment, their own environment, black people determining their way of life, they wouldn't be criminals, or they wouldn't be labelled criminals.'

Black robbers, Trevor Hercules reckoned, robbed to make a living and not, like some young white guys, for any thrill or notion of glamour.

22

The New Face

I'm in showbiz – only a critic can
kill me.

Legs Diamond, in Harvey
Fierstein's musical of the same
name

A letter came from Reg Kray, about whom I had recently written an article, saying that a young man called Pete Gillet was about to leave Parkhurst prison after serving a robbery sentence and was worth a story. I contacted Mr Gillet, found out he was hoping to launch himself as a pop singer and went down with a photographer from the late *London Daily News* to the house in Crawley where he was being looked after by his friends.

Gillet was a lad, dungarees and bleached blond hair and offering to strip off to his shorts to show the effects of his weight training. Gillet sang some of the songs he was recording – 'Closet Queen' and 'Masquerade', which had been written by Reg Kray. The first was sailing close to the wind since some of the papers had hinted that he was having a relationship with Kray.

He had come from a broken home, got into minor acts of trouble, been an Arsenal hooligan, a Gatwick airport mini-cab driver and had been arrested for conspiracy to rob after a friend informed on him. Inside he had been taken under Reg Kray's wing and had since become his adopted son.

It was an odd life: on the one hand he wanted to make his name as a singer and showbusiness personality and on the other he knew that it was the association with the famous Kray name which still opened doors without a shoulder being necessary at the hinges. Thus he already had a recording contract and an entrée into the music world.

Since that first meeting he had moved into a bleakish house in Crawley. His room was full of Kray paraphernalia and there was an Arsenal souvenir of the Double-winning side, a giant stuffed toy tiger on the bed, fires blazing in the draughty house, a vase with plastic flowers, a copy of a Roy Orbison record Reg had sent him, a Robert Palmer single and an Ansaphone. He also had some up-to-date photos of Reg in the weight training gear showing a fit body for someone of his age and other pictures of Reg in the garden at Gartree prison trying to smile: 'He's not very good at smiling, Reg, so it doesn't come out looking quite right. He's more used to not smiling in his pictures.' Outside was a Mercedes 190E D reg.

We lunched in the neighbouring hotel. He asked the waiter cheerfully for a hundred bottles of house white to see my expression and chose the prawn cocktail and the trout – 'See, I haven't chosen the most expensive things' – and talked about crime as the waitresses hovered past.

He had recently been sent by *Network Seven* to a tropical island off Sri Lanka with two other young men, *Brookside* actor Simon O'Brien and banker James Anthony, and the English tennis player turned television presenter, Annabel Croft. There they had to go through their survivors' paces for the cameras. He had pictures of himself with Annabel Croft, of himself and the chicken he had killed, and him larking with the other lads. He was a bit hurt that Annabel Croft had been quoted in the papers saying slightly uncomplimentary things about him. Not to worry, he was shortly getting engaged.

He puts his dirty washing into the machine, curses himself for having left the heater blazing, and expounds on the seduction of crime.

'One mate said to me, "I enjoy sex but there's nothing quite like going out on a bit of work and walking away with the prize – the cash bag." That's what it's like for some people.'

'I used to think I was untouchable – until I had my collar felt. Never underestimate the police. They may come across as being as thick as shit but basically they're straight criminals.

'I do know one or two criminals who have never been caught. I suppose the secret is never do the dirty work yourself – there are the chiefs and they send out the Indians. The police just nab the Indians most of the time. But as long as a civilian isn't harmed and they're not taking from poor people I don't see any harm in it.

'If we had planned things properly there's no way we would have been caught. But we thought it was such an easy task. You have to take precautions. It's like having sex with a woman, if you don't take precautions you are liable to make her pregnant. A very crude comparison but the principle's the same.

'With hindsight, not enough planning went in to what we did. But I was involved with two absolute dickheads. It was my own fault. They hadn't got a clue, wouldn't have been able to fiddle a gas meter let alone a bleeding bank.'

Gillet talks about crime in a matter of fact way, describing its component parts as though he were delivering a lecture in Applied Robbery.

'The first thing has to be the escape route. Two or three cars if you're doing a robbery. Our attitude was, "Oh, so simple." Go in, take the money, drive off, spend the dough. The real pros – which I am not, although the bloody press have put me up as one – all the blaggers I know, plan the escape route and if they can't plan that they don't even plan going in. On a big one, it's handy to have someone inside. Just like you have spies to find out what another government's doing. Most people move quick once they've decided to do the job.

'Some bank robbers get other people to get the cars for them because cars may not be their game, fiddling around with keys and that. They've got the bottle to pick up the gun and go, "Worr! Give me that money! Don't look at me! Get on the ground!" Average car thief wouldn't have the bottle to do that.

'The average nine to five guy saves up for his holiday, saves a few quid each week. The average criminal doesn't want to do that, too much like hard work. They want the holidays right away. I have the same attitude. I don't buy anything on HP.'

Gillet wants to be known for his music rather than the Kray connection and although he visits both brothers he has not slipped into their old world, zipping off to Spain where some of the former cohorts are busying themselves with large helpings of paella and the small print of extradition laws.

'I haven't been out and met the people in Spain – no disrespect to them but I wouldn't want to get involved in that. I could meet a lot of people through being Reggie's son but I don't want to use the position I'm in. I don't use it in any way. There's no one I've gone up to and said, "You toe the line or I'll get the firm onto you," or shit like that. Initially I was called gay and "Reggie's toyboy" but that's all over. I am his adopted son, he idolises me and treats me accordingly. He's not gay, neither am I. I've never knocked on anyone's door and asked for money as a friend of Reggie's. Other people have, I don't. Just because I am close to a well-known criminal I do not see that as a natural progression to be close to every other criminal in the world.

'Women get a kick out of being involved with a criminal. You get women that like to be around villainous type guys. They enjoy the adrenalin and being seen with the faces. I don't want to seem a braggart but I'm talking about personal experience. When I came out of jail, I was in the papers and on television. I got besieged by them, one came up and grabbed me by the bollocks and said, "You won't have had sex for four years" – wallop. I freaked right out. I get quite a lot of attention from women and I'm sure it's more for what I'm associated with than who I am. I get a bit sick of the kind of birds who want you just because of what you're meant to have done. But you get women who are turned on by doctors and –" with a note of incredulity in his voice "– women who are turned on by press reporters. It's horses for courses. That's why we all look different, we've got different colour hair and different teeth and different fingerprints. I've had hundreds of women in my time so I know the score.

'Crime is very glamorous really. You see, if you want to get a lot of money from property deals you've got to have some money in the first place and the only way to get that is to take it. If you get a job these days for a salary of twenty grand – it costs twenty grand to live, doesn't it? So you're never going to have any spare money for property developments. The only way to get a leg up is take it – usually illegally, unfortunately.

'The Conservatives have forced the issue – own your own business, own your own home, own your own car. They've made the council house man sound like he's nothing so people trying to better themselves, get away from the social stigma of being a bum in a council house, have very few ways to do it and most of them are illegal.'

Pete Gillet is surrounded by Kray memorabilia: there is a picture of Reg with his late wife Frances Shea who killed herself with a drugs overdose; there is a copy of brother Charlie's book, though at this precise point Charlie is persona non grata due to a bit of a row with Ron; and, in that familiar unjoined scrawled handwriting, letters from Reg with words of advice and encouragement and 'God bless' sign offs.

'What they call "gangland slayings" – that's when someone's upset someone else and they've gone and taken their revenge, maybe they've double-crossed them on money. That doesn't mean it's a gang thing. It's a personal thing. If you robbed me and I came round and shot you in the legs, it wouldn't be gangland, it would be personal. But the press like to build it up.

'A lot of "protection" is mythology. You do get gangs of people going round intimidating certain people for money and you do get people with heavy reputations and clubs owners and pub owners and shopkeepers go to them. Reg says he has never gone up to anyone and said, "You need protection otherwise this place is going."

'People used to come to them and say, "How much money do you want so we can use your name? So that if we have trouble down the club we just say the Krays are protecting this place." I'm sure it was the same for the Richardsons. But it's not like people going in and throwing all the chairs about and saying, "Give us a thousand pound a month or this happens again." Usually the club owner is thinking in terms of getting the place minded and getting hold of people who specialise in that. I knew one guy who used to provide bouncers for every club in Birmingham but he wasn't in protection, it was just a service he provided.'

Pete Gillet's excursion onto the tropical island with Annabel Croft and the others gave him a bit of a taste for television. He is not impressed with what is on offer at the moment.

'Whenever I see a programme about crime I have a tendency to shoot them all down in flames because I think, "As if that would be said, or as if that would be done!" People don't act that way under arrest. *The Bill* is quite good but sometimes I can watch a very good programme and something muggy will happen in it and I know that in no way would that kind of conversation take place. They do have a tendency to portray the copper as the everyday hero and the villain as the real thickie – like Hale and Pace as the two Rons, right dummies, but if you ever met the twins you'd find that, especially Reggie, they are very articulate.

'I've watched *Crimewatch* and personally I have got the right hump with some of the things that people have done to other human beings. I think to myself, "I hope they catch them." There seems to be a deterioration in codes with some criminals. And when they go to jail I have to tell you they do get badly treated. You don't have to be a rapist these days to get badly treated – someone can go on a robbery and beat up an old man and people will think "dirty scumbag".

'I met one guy in jail who was the first ever person on *Crimewatch*. Him and his brother had gone into a house and killed the dog – they had real long sentences, twelve, fifteen something like that, aggravated burglary. The way they got caught was, they were in a pub and on comes this *Crimewatch* programme. Like a mug this bloke pipes up, "Hey, that's me and my brother!" Then he wondered why it was he got grassed up.

'The British public love to read about crime and watch crime movies. Bob Hoskins is the best criminal actor, best we've ever seen. Reg wanted him to portray him – but he's too old now. If people come across some boring story about Sunday school teachers they skip the page but the moment they get a bit of villainy they read it. They like to see the daring in other people because some people lead such mundane lives – nine to five, come home, put the slippers on, the wife makes the tea, they might go down the pub on a Sunday dinner-time and that's their life so they like to read about the intrigue in other people's. People love to talk about crime.

'I'm in the position, being Reggie's adopted son, of never being able to put crime and prison behind me because people come to talk to me about what they did in the past. People trust me with their thoughts.'

Pete Gillet says he is still followed occasionally by the police and sometimes takes odd routes home to throw them off. 'I have met some very straightforward, nice coppers in my time. The majority are right slags but I've met some gentlemen amongst them. In all the dealings I've had with the Old Bill, I would say fifty per cent were absolutely devious bastards and haven't liked it that when it comes to being devious I can match them. But on the other hand I've also had some straightforward nice guys. I spoke to a copper one day when I was nicked and I was in the interview room and I was leading them up the garden path. They were trying to get me to inform on people. Some coppers would make top class villains if they wanted to step across the border. The Old Bill are getting more sophisticated. I'm not sure who's ahead at the moment but I would say the Old Bill were.'

Like most people who have stood trial, Gillet has theories about the twelve people whose duty it was to decide his fate.

'When it gets to court, I prefer women on the jury although I like a mixture of both because men are more practical. I prefer women because, being a good looking fella, it helps. I don't discriminate on age unless she's a real old fuddy duddy, old Victorian type, looks like she's law and order, an old stick. I like the housewife. The majority of people have had a bad experience with the Old Bill, if you get working-class people. I try to cut out the toffs and your sergeant-major types – to get yourself off you've got to weigh up all these things. Criminal people aren't stupid, you've got to be a bit of a psychologist. Sometimes I like a nervy type so I can play on it a bit. But I talk to the jurors as though they were friends – I've had juries giggling. If you get up and act the hard man – "I'll take whatever I've got coming to me" – it's no good, you've got to get the juries on your side.

'A good prosecution barrister could make Jesus Christ look like Satan. It's their job to make you look guilty and I dare say if they thought you were rank innocent they would still steam into you as though you are a guilty man.

'Defence barristers – I don't care what they say, you do get some that trade with the Old Bill. They reckon, "I haven't got much of a case here, I'll give that one across and next time round I want my man to get off." You'll never get a barrister to admit it but I've had the feeling before that I've been sold down the river. It's very important to get a barrister that has the attitude that all Old Bills are liars. You will get lots who will tell you that, whether or not they mean that in their heart. What really is the pig of it all is that at the end of the day the battle of wits can lie between the two barristers. You can get barristers who knew you're double guilty but can still get you off.

'What pisses criminals off is the inconsistency with judges. There seem to be no guidelines. When I was down for sentencing we were hoping for one they called Father Christmas. There's some you don't want – Gower. They say "Don't cower in front of Gower" because he's very strict and he'll weigh you in for a load of bird. For the most trivial thing, he'll give you a five stretch. For my particular crime I could have got half the sentence that I ended up getting. One judge you could always guarantee a result with – he thought we weren't bad people, just another way of making a living – unless he came across a dirty stinking rapist. He had the right attitude. I think there should be a mandatory death sentence for all rapists.

'The speeches that judges make, every criminal is just thinking, "Oh, shut up and give it to me." They have the cheek to give you a lecture and then sentence you. I have seen judges give them a real lecture and frighten the life out of them and then give a suspended sentence and they walk away thinking, "My God, I got an ear-battering there, I won't do that again."

'I went as a character witness once and because of what I said this guy got off. The screws were already booked up for overtime to take him off because he was the only customer of the day and I said he was in business with me, blah, blah. Because I went suited up and told the judge I was in business with him the judge gave him a right old lecture and told him how lucky he was that I was there and gave him fines and suspended sentences. I admired the judge for the way he handled it. Other times they give you a right old lecture and then have the cheek to weigh you off for ten years. They've got a big front some of them. I've always been very arrogant with judges and been threatened with contempt.'

Then comes the jail sentence and the long journey in the big van with the wired up windows.

'Some screws ... they don't want you going off your head after getting sentences so they pacify you by saying how out of order was your sentence. They say, "That was a bit strong, blah blah blah." That's a very tricky period of time. Some screws don't have a clue but in general you will get ones that try and put you at ease. They've got to take you from the court to the prison so they'll say anything to keep you quiet. It is a very stressful time and they know that.

'There was a screw at Coldingley and he acted like a social worker with me, forever getting me telephone calls because I had domestic problems but at the end of it he nicked me for possession of dope. I thought, 'You two-faced bastard!'

'You'll get a good screw that when you go through after a visit and have a fag tucked behind your ear, they won't do anything and you can get another one, a dog, who'll take it off you. You can't get packs of ten or twenty past because that's just taking the piss.

'There are blind eyes turned because if they came down heavy on everything they'd have a riot. Cannabis is not really a serious drug, more like having a drink, but if they catch you with it they'll nick you. It's like here if you walk down the street with a big spliff in our hand a copper's going to nick you for it but if you do it in privacy chances are you'll get away with it.

'I was dealing in it in Coldingley. I was the main man but I lost six months remission because I wouldn't name the screw that was giving it to me. They tried to blame my family. I still won't say who it is, I'll take it to my grave. He was making a lot of money out of me.

'The visits are not nice for the wives and girlfriends. I suppose a lot are quite pleased they can't visit more often because they only have to come once a fortnight and it's a long way to travel sometimes. But two hours once a fortnight is not enough to keep families together. A lot of people come out and the wife's off with someone else because it's been a strain on them. You can't blame them, what would a guy do? Most guys if their wife leaves town for the night are off fucking someone else, aren't they?

'The majority of guys try to kid themselves that nothing's going down. My wife left me. One mate in prison used to say it would never happen to him and I used to sing to him "Oh no, not my baby". But I knew his wife was at it just from the way when she would visit him she would put her tongue down his neck. And when he got out he phoned up and told me. He said, "The dirty slag, she's been with every man in Burnley." She used to come down and visit him and pretend she was so innocent and when he went back on his home leave everyone was telling him all the blokes she had been sleeping with.

'There are a lot of wives who will patiently wait but a lot don't. You've only got to think about it in terms of what would the guy do in the circumstances. I think it's very indiscreet to do it in their own manor. I would say to a wife that she could go off the manor and get sex but that she shouldn't go with the same guy more than half-a-dozen times. They should have conjugal visits. More marriages would stay together and it would be easier when you come out.'

Coming out is the Big Day, even if at first it is only on weekend leave, through which prisoners are supposedly gradually rehabilitated into society. There may be a reception party, waiting with a bottle of something in the back of the car, and a pub full of friends at night with people squeezing some ten-pound notes into the hand so that the man who has just paid his debt to society can pay for his round at the bar. But they are not all misty-eyed knees-ups.

'It was quite an anticlimax when I came out. I expected all my family to be there when I came home but there were only a couple and the others came in dribs and drabs afterwards. But in your mind you do think there's going to be this big welcome. I drank a whole bottle of brandy and I came out in the most dreadful boil-type spots, ruined my whole weekend out that did. But it may have been the brandy, I wasn't used to having that in my system. I was used to prison booze but that's two different things. Prison booze you need only a couple of glasses and you're on your back. Fortunately Reg was there when I went back to prison after the weekend out because I was in bits and I hated my family for not turning up, but life's all about disappointments.' There were other disappointments inside.

'Most priests inside are hypocrites and I say that as a God-fearing man. They can see someone being beaten up by the screws and swear they saw nothing. A lot of people go to church because they think it helps with parole. It used to be the thing: if you want parole – go to church. There was one really lovely old boy, Catholic priest, but the others were two-faced gits. One was always drunk and with a betting paper.'

The pecking order inside, as rigid in its way as any sanctioned by Debrett's on the other side of the walls, persists even for the younger offenders like Gillet.

'Robbers do tend to think that other criminals aren't as equal as them because they haven't done the severity of crime that they have but I don't agree with that at all. You don't have to be a heavy dude to do armed robbery. It's a bit like a Rolls Royce mechanic turning up his nose at someone who works at Ford, the same sort of snobbery goes on and there is this class distinction. The bigger the amount of money the more respect they should have, is how they see it.'

Least respect, of course, goes to the informer. Which Pete Gillet feels is right and proper: 'My co-defendant grassed me up. I don't think they should get light sentences. If someone goes out and shoots someone in the leg then just because they've been weak and spilled the beans on someone doesn't mean that they're not responsible. I would understand if they got an eight instead of a ten for being helpful but getting half the sentence is bollocks.

'There is not much honour among thieves any more. My mates know where I'm coming from but there are an awful lot of criminals who are horrible slag people and I hate them. People think because I am associated with who I am I'll like criminals. But I only like staunch people, people who don't trade bodies with the Old Bill. It's morally wrong to grass your mates up. I hate that attitude, they should be put up against a wall and shot. The days when you could go and work firm-handed, five or six-handed are slowly dying because if you can go through life and count your true friends on one hand you've had a result. And the only way you can be sure you're not going to be grassed is to be with true friends.

'Some criminals get caught because they don't know when to stop. They have a lucky tickle here so they carry on and then it all comes on top. Some get off on the adrenalin, just enjoy the buzz. It's nice for them to go out, rob someone and get money for twenty minutes of work, then have a flash car, eat in a flash restaurant and not have to lose face by signing on. I met another fellow who didn't like signing on – he had had a good job, got made redundant – went out kiting, rather than lose face by signing on.'

Not that Pete Gillet seems of a mind to return to crime. He passes me a copy of his latest single, the cover shows him in dungarees, tattoo, ear-ring, chain, smiling sweetly at the camera.

'I know if I got involved with a gun I would get a life sentence. My life now is showbusiness and watching out for Reg's best interests out here.' However, the other side is always lurking.

'No criminal really becomes a non-criminal. They might not be an active one but they still think like one. If you're a straight person and you see a crime you think, "That's terrible." But a criminally-minded person sees a bank job, thinks, "Good luck to them, fair play. Fair play."

'People say that criminals don't deserve fair treatment but I've met people who go out thieving who don't know any other way to support their family. I spoke to one drug smuggler, a right well-spoken fellow, a jock. I said why did you do that then? He was into china pottery and wanted to start his own business, but the bank refused him a loan. He thought the only way I can do this is get the money from smuggling and he got caught in the airport.'

23

The Cocaine Man

There isn't another commodity in the
world today that leaves as large a margin
of profit for the little guy as coca or, in
coca's pressed form, cocaine. In economic
terms its rationality is overwhelming.

Alexander Cockburn, *New Statesman and Society*

It started like this: 'This guy was a nutcase, a real pest, giving us a lot of aggravation and he knew a lot about what was going on, our operation. If we had been a heavy mob we would have shot him but we drew the line at violence. So we gave him £15,000 and told him to go down there and see what he could do. We thought – ninety-nine per cent he's going to get robbed, he's going to disappear. But he came back super-successful. We didn't know what to do with it at first, it was a whole new area of expertise and a different strata of society. What you can buy there for £5,000 is worth £500,000 wholesale here. A good half of the first lot got wasted because everyone tried it out at parties. My partner got into it disgustingly and was written off for about six months.'

'Down there' was Bolivia. 'It' was cocaine. And the 'pest' helped to add Steve to a long, long line of cocaine smugglers at a boom time for the drug.

Until the 'pest' discovered Bolivia, Steve had made a discreet but lucrative living as a hashish smuggler, driving the routes from the east and bringing in mighty quantities hidden in buses. It had enabled him to move into property, provide for his young wife and children and contemplate settling in New Zealand. But drug smugglers, like any old paunchy bank robber, have a way of wanting to do one last Big One before they put their scales in the attic and stop bulk-ordering cling-film.

He had bumped into his partner after a lying-low period and found out that he was short of hard cash because everything was tied up in bricks and mortar. 'He said the obvious thing was to move into cocaine because we still had the contacts through this guy who had given us trouble. He had pulled a right flanker on us – it was peanuts to us, £20,000 or something – but when we found him we said, "You've been right out of order, you're going to have to sort out this run." So I became the main person down there getting it back as far as Europe.'

The life of the cocaine smuggler began.

'What you need is a lot of front, because you've got to be almost crazy to do it. I took the guy down with me to be a runner and got him to introduce me to everyone he had met. Through them knowing I was a friend of a friend the word went round that I was all right and people approached me.'

He had no Spanish but by chance found himself doing business with a Bolivian family who had connections with Southampton through the rubber trade.

'The mother of the two guys I worked with spoke fluent English. When it went wrong one time and one of the guys disappeared his mother got hold of me and said it was very embarrassing for the family so it's got to be sorted out. She'd seen how we operated over the last year or so and she said she'd like to work with us and keep us supplied. We were the only people who dealt with this family, which was nice because that meant there wasn't a lot of heat.'

At this stage the cocaine was being moved as accompanied baggage, in false-sided cases and in the heels of shoes. Business was brisk. 'There were people moving 150 kilos a week. It was very ugly and very, very heavy.

'The DEA [the Drugs Enforcement Agency] were all over the place. They were fairly obvious and not very efficient. There was a classic case of this lady we dealt with at the Holiday Inn and some guy didn't turn up for his room for a few days and when they went into his room to check they found drugs and suitcases half-packed. She got on the phone to the local DEA guy. They said, "Sorry he's very drunk, he won't talk to anyone." She said, "We've got a guy here who's a drug smuggler," but it was no use. And anyone who was anyone knew who they were.'

Bribes were the oil that lubricated the smooth-running machinery.

'A friend of mine was a pilot who used to fly into Cochabamba in a Piper Cherokee every week and pick up 150 kilos. He said, "You have to pay the man $10,000 and if you don't they arrest you." Then his plane crashed – three hundred hours on the engine and the fuel line blocked. He ran into the side of a mountain. The people he was working with were very good. They buried all the stuff before they called in the emergency teams and insisted on paying for medical treatment, even though they'd lost a lot of money. They even paid for a specialist who'd been trained in Switzerland in putting steel pins in smashed-up bones so now he's back playing football again. But it meant that they needed a new pilot. And on this occasion they only gave him $5,000, even though our pilot said it was crazy. So when he gave the police just the $5,000 they arrested him. They've got to crack a certain number of people to show the Americans they're doing their bit.'

Discretion rather than ostentation was essential: 'I had a flat in Brixton which cost £16 pound a week and my car cost me £200. Under the floorboards I would have anywhere between £100,000 and £200,000. When I moved out to the West Country, I said I was a property developer and bought a house for £15,000. I did all the work on it myself – that way the locals see what you're doing. You can't go to college and study what to do with that amount of dough, you have to feel your way along. As far as the tax man was concerned, I didn't exist.'

The currency in Bolivia was American dollars. To get it into the country Steve would wear a blouson with plenty of zips and stuff it full of money. If he needed help in getting the money, or the paraphernalia for hiding the cocaine, into

Bolivia he would hire an assistant. 'You've got to be a little careful about taking in superglue and stuff like that, but you can't be sure of buying it down there. So if you want to move stuff in, you just send someone down with them and then send them out again.'

To start with they used just shoes and briefcases. 'Three of us going down, business-suited up, very tidy, three pairs of shoes and a briefcase. A kilo and bit each. At that time it was £70,000 a kilo. It cost £3,000 to buy, £1,500 for the air fare, so you came out at a fair old profit. Even so we never got the prices that you see quoted in the papers as "street value" – they're just propaganda really.' The cocaine, thanks to the technical expertise of one of their suppliers, could come in a variety of colours. 'Customs are looking for white powder – you bring in bright pink powder in sachets that say "Mouthwash" on them. In America, pink was popular – it was a designer drug – but here they didn't trust that it was the real thing.

'You get to a point when there's so much money about that you think that there's not really very much point in doing any more of this. So you withdraw, go your separate ways for a few years. This is very good from a security aspect because if they've got a hint of what you're up to there's this two years when you're not involved in anything at all except socially. They can't keep tabs on you for that long, from a financial point of view. Even when you're active they can only keep tabs on you for a very limited amount of time. They have to justify everything they spend so they have to be sure something's going to happen. We used to cut away from it completely and go our separate ways and then meet up again.'

Steve was born in south London, and lived there until the age of six, when the family moved to the West Country, which is where he finished off his school education in a secondary modern. He describes himself as lower middle-class. His parents had met during the war, divorcing twenty-five years later when his mother returned to her native South Africa. His father was a 'jack of all trades, he never quite cracked it, a bit like me'.

The teenage Steve trained in hotel management and catering, spending two years at college. He ended up running the kitchens of a 350-bed hotel in Bloomsbury.

'I joined as a third chef, then the second chef had a nervous breakdown, the first one just about cut his hand off with a carving knife so I did all three jobs, working sixteen hours a day. Kenco took over the hotel and they offered me a good job. But they were going to do microwave food – quite nice food but already prepared – so all I would have to do was slide it in the microwave, press the button and serve. I said, "I haven't spent three year's training just to serve microwave food . . ."'

He became a chef at a Pizza Palace in the Kings Road, Chelsea, but when his relationship of the time broke up and he got his pay cheque he decided to abandon the lure of sliced olives and grated cheese and hitch-hike to South Africa. He got as far as Syria, bumped into a war there and had to return to base. He saw an advertisement in *Private Eye* for drivers to take buses to Greece. That led to similar trips to India and in a short while he was bringing back a twelve-kilo load hidden expertly in the bus.

The hiding of the drugs was a speciality of his which he prefers to keep to himself.

He was a good driver and mechanic and those skills allowed him to travel Europe and Asia, legally at first. On one occasion he had to travel to Turkey to rescue a broken-down bus.

'I was offered about £2,000 for going. So we shot down, found the bus on the border of Turkey and towed it through to Iran overnight – 1,000 miles in fourteen hours, one bus towing another one, then we fixed the bus. Got it into Teheran where there was a whole street of workshops where we got it rebuilt. So we followed it down, made our way back, picked up some people in Kabul. Unbeknown to me the bus that I went down to rescue had some gear in it. Then it was a snowball effect, getting more and more involved, more and more responsibility and then pretty well running the whole show.'

He became a successful dealer, bringing in much of the hashish that was to percolate round London in the seventies.

'At that stage it was all hash, commercial Afghani. We hired a German guy to run the whole area. He oversaw the preparation, the packing, the pressing and everything. We gave him a nice four-wheel drive vehicle to run around in – he was dedicated to good smoking gear so he would stay in the village, make sure it was done properly, not too much dust and chicken shit. So we ended up with a good product, pressed the shape we wanted it so that we could pack it efficiently. We used to bring 125 kilos in each bus.'

The bribes required then were more modest and were usually just to speed up a border crossing, a bottle of Scotch slipped into the palm of the immigration man.

He had the one essential requirement of the profession: 'I didn't get nervous. Even when it came right on top I would just think – this is part of the deal. I got a very good reputation for being very, very cool under pressure – I've even surprised myself.'

On one occasion he brought his kilos of hashish in at Ramsgate, unaware of the fact that Customs had a training school there. 'Thirteen-handed they were, from ten at night till six in the morning: mirrors, lights, everything. The vehicle was loaded and they still didn't find it. You're talking a lump the size of this table in one block.' He gestures at the three foot by four foot table in the Chinese restaurant where we're eating at the time. 'I thought it was all over. They had sniffer dogs in Germany – they were very, very hot – but they wouldn't have found it. They had them in England but they didn't use them much. The stuff has to have access to air and it was sealed, totally sealed.' (One popular piece of dealers' apocrypha is that some customs services turn their dogs into junkies to make them more desperate to locate drugs.)

There were other rules in the operation, which was run with a cell-like structure, rather like an efficient intelligence service.

'You would never put the drug and the money in the same place. We got to the point where we would have 125 kilos and have it gone in two hours. From us to one person, from that person to three, from the three to six. The six would know one of the three and one of the three would know the one but it only goes one stage back. None of them knew me at all. I knew some of them and socialised with them but none of them had any idea of my role. It was all sectioned off for security reasons.'

However, he had had his share of nervous nights: 'In Kandahar, in the early days, they used to clear out the hotel so that we could work in the courtyard packing the stuff. One night we were in there just rabbitting away and all of a sudden this massive army comes in and starts smashing down doors. We thought, "Here we go, end of the road." We're going to get banged up in an Afghan jail, which is a pig of a place. The guy who owned the hotel was rushing round trying to stop them getting to us and eventually he manages to stop the soldiers and find out what it's all about. It turned out that there were two buses of people going to Mecca on their pilgrimage and all the other hotels were full. So they asked in our hotel, were told there was no room, looked at the register and said, "Bullshit!" The soldiers had gone raving mad and starting smashing down doors, proving that the rooms were empty. Eventually it all quietened down. There were a few of those.'

His success led to promotion.

'What my partner did was lift me up to the same level so that there was no jealousy and he had someone he could relate to. The others in the operation would work, say, four times a year. The rest of the time they would buy and sell cars or run a business, all the time working dead normal. When you've got money like that floating about you can't help but make a profit. You buy a shop – fruit and veg is the easiest, it's very cheap and your stock goes in two or three days. You can't help but make money and if you don't it doesn't really matter anyway. Some people were subtle and maintained a front, others were just outrageous.

'Some people didn't want to get heavily involved so they didn't make a fantastic amount of money and the deal was if the shit hit the fan you would say that guy didn't have anything to do with it, he's just the mechanic.' He avoided employing people who enjoyed the merchandise too much: 'There is a saying that users are losers.' And he drew the line at heroin.

'There were a few times we chucked in a couple of hand guns on top of a load, which I wasn't very comfortable about. It's stupid to have one in London; in other parts of the world you can carry one and you don't get aggravation for having it. There was no involvement with any terrorist organisation amongst us, though it did happen.

'You could actually buy dope, the confiscated stuff, off a couple of police officers in London. They sold a bit of everything. I was brought up to believe that the police were there for the greater good of the common herd. I think they do an incredible job and are a very necessary part of society but I do feel great unease about the way they operate, because they feel they are an élite above the normal law and they justify the means by the ends.'

He had little respect for some of the people he sold to: 'A lot of the buyers are wallies really. They don't really understand the market because a lot of coke that comes in has been adulterated in a big way with speed because speed is obviously much cheaper; they get so used to buying it like that and getting a big buzz that they think that's it. In fact, it's the speed making them feel like that. Now good stuff is eighty per cent pure, and now and again we got even better than that. The uncle in the family we dealt with could produce blinding quality. One time we had a few pure ounces and we were punching them out. These two right sharp characters came round and they said they wanted to try it. So I did them a line. They said, "Naw, naw, naw, we're used to liiiiinnnnnes," so they did a long one. I said, "This is the real McCoy," and they said, "We're used to it." I didn't see them for forty-eight hours. They came back and said, "We'll buy that." I said, "Too late, it's all gone. You've got no idea what you're dealing with."'

Early retirement was planned, then a deal came unstuck when some of his colleagues broke one of the rules.

'They put a big lump of dope and the money in the room at the same time. They got raided by the police – then it turned out it wasn't the police at all. It was a mob – two were really police and the rest were dressed up as policemen. They steamed in and one of our guys jumped straight out of a second storey window, leaving the gear behind him. We lost about £70,000 and a big lump of dope.'

Steve was called in to tidy up, destroy all evidence of contacts, since at the early stage they genuinely believed that the police had carried out the raid. It was agreed that everyone would lob in enough to finance one more run.

'We knew we were coming to the end of the line and we thought we were pushing our luck so it was a farewell gesture. We had got away with it so many many times.'

When he decided to pack it all in he told his girlfriend how he had been making his money for the last few years. She had had no idea. 'She just said, "Fucking hell," and was glad it was all over.'

But it wasn't. It ended like this: 'I got caught because of stupidity. It was being Mr Nice Guy and going against my better judgement.' He was in Latin America with his partner's girlfriend en route back to Europe with the cocaine.

'We got to Rio and were told that the plane to Lisbon, where we were meeting my partner, was full, so they told us we would have to go on a different flight. I thought this was great – they (the authorities) wouldn't have us on the computer and wouldn't have enough time to arrange anything; most of the cock-ups have happened because people have been traced through tickets. I was very happy to fly to, say, Geneva and then meet up with my partner in Portugal. But she started screaming and saying, "He's going to be waiting for me." He was married and so they didn't have that much time together.'

The upshot was that Steve went to the airline, told them that he spent a lot of money with them and asked them to contact an airline official who had helped him out before quite legally. They were duly given tickets. It was just before Christmas so they had had to book the flight some time in advance, giving the authorities plenty of time to see where this couple who interested them and whose names were already on file were travelling. 'They could see the whole flow of ticketing. London – Madrid – Lisbon – London on one ticket and on another Lisbon – Rio – Bolivia – Rio – Lisbon. The foolish thing was I should have made the ticket go to London and then got off in Lisbon.'

The alarm bells rang with Customs and a telegram – which Steve saw after he was arrested – was despatched to Lisbon.

'When I came off the plane they were waiting. Had we done it the other way it would have been sweet. I was a mug. I said to the Customs guy there, "You and I are not very different, similar backgrounds, similar education. You work on one side and I work on another. There's no way you would give away your best friend and there's no way I would either. You wouldn't respect me. It would make your job easier but you wouldn't respect me." So he said, "Yeah, yeah," and took me away and locked me up.'

He was unimpressed with the Portuguese lawyers: 'The biggest crowd of thieving, robbing bastards I have ever met – far more immoral than anyone in jail. All they wanted to do was take money and do nothing in return.' And he received a stern lecture from the bench: 'The judge looks at you and talks about murdering babies and all this harm you are doing. They put all drugs in the same category as heroin but to me it's not the same.'

His former colleagues planned an escape route, but not just so that Steve could breathe the sweet, soft air of freedom: 'They had another one planned and no one had the arsehole to go and do it. So for that reason they were willing to pay a lot of money to get me out and back to work again.'

This was the proposed scam: 'There was a section in the penal code that says you're not allowed to stay in jail if it's endangering your physical health so you get a bent specialist to come in and say, "Yes, his health is being seriously endangered." All I needed was to get bail and then I could get down to the south of Portugal where there was a boat waiting. I could have got a new passport and my fingerprints changed. But by the time they organised it I had got a date for my court hearing, so there was no way I was going to be allowed bail for such a brief period.' He was sentenced to eight years.

'I had a strange night when I sat on my bunk in that cell with ninety people and I thought – can I handle this for eight years? And a little voice said to me if you make a commitment to have nothing more to do with drugs then you'll get help, but if you carry on it's going to get worse. I'm not sure where the voice came from.'

With eighty-nine other people in the cell, which measured twenty metres by ten metres, there was no shortage of other voices.

'It was three storeys underground, with walls three metres thick and windows opening out onto a moat. It had been used for storing munitions and explosions.

You had a nail on the wall; your stuff in a plastic bag. You left the room and someone stole your gear. You stayed in your cell all day. There were only fifty-three bunks for ninety people so a lot of people had to roll their mattresses up and slide them under the bunks during the day, which meant they had nowhere to sit. It was mind boggling.

'I arranged my own protection: I lent the guy that ran the cell some money for his daughter to get married and an unwritten part of that agreement was that he gave me protection.'

He studied Portuguese with a language course sent in to him and wrote long letters every day.

'I went through comparative religion, Buddhism. Then a book called *The Magic of Findhorn* turned up. It was a magic book, not very well written and published in 1967, about this community in the north of Scotland which sounded terrific. So I wrote to it, not knowing if it still existed about twenty years later and a lady replied.'

In the world outside his wife divorced him, sold the house and left for New Zealand with their son and daughter. He had no visitors during his time inside.

'I bribed the prison authorities to send me to a prison near a guy that I had been inside with because he could mind my stuff and I could get some decent food. But I had only been there a few months when he got arrested and went back inside himself. The place I had bribed my way into was for young offenders and it was noisy and horrific. They allowed me to set up furniture because I was getting a computer sent down and the day I did get it all set up they moved me to a different prison. I was very worried because it was a high security prison and they had had a lot of riots and had shot two thousand rounds off in an afternoon; there were bullet marks everywhere. But when I got there it was marvellous: older, more mature people, not like the crazy kids, not bad food. If someone was killed it was usually for a very good reason, whereas at the other place there was aggravation for nothing because they were manic kids. The biggest problem with health was teeth – they had to pull them out.'

He became the prison computer whizz: 'I would do the end of year report, complete with graphics, the prison newspaper and so on. It gave me a chance to get to know them and be useful.'

His partner had previously wound up in Fort prison near Chichester, where white collar offenders, non-violent types, ex-policemen and the like go. 'It was like holiday camp. I used to go down and visit him. He was working on a marina – technically he was doing up a barge. Eventually the screw told him he couldn't take him down for the work every week because the prison would no longer pay his overtime, so my partner asked him how much he was paid for it and arranged for him to get the money. I used to drive down and see him every Saturday, take some fruit and some wine. Everything he needed was buried by the goal posts in the football field. One time a guy had a birthday party inside the prison with thirty bottles of wine, but the screws who didn't know what the score was came down and blew the whistle.

'There was a time in the seventies when it looked as though cannabis would become, if not legal, then decriminalised. We used to think how ironic it would be for us to become respected members of society and it could so easily have happened. That's the sort of division between being legal and illegal. It would be very sensible because there is this mass of people who like trying things because they're wrong and illegal and that gives it its added spice. I wouldn't care if I never had a drug in my life. From a purely medicinal point of view, late at night, if you want to slow down and sleep well, you could have a joint but I've never bought it in my life.

'Part of the problem is the information people get about drugs. There's an irresponsibility there which is quite damaging. It started off when they started writing about marijuana and said it's going to make you a different person, lethargic, not able to work, accelerate the destruction of brain cells. And when we tried it out we found it was bullshit. There is still that gap between what the government says about drugs and what the actual truth is. Lots of people have the poster showing what you look like if you take heroin on their wall! If only it could come from the direction of truth it would be much more helpful.'

The life of the dealer has changed dramatically.

'The information technology has developed so much that you don't have the same freedom of movement. The small dealers are disappearing and it's either big or nothing. And very, very heavy. One faction controls for a while, then another. My ground rule was if there's violence involved, I'm going, but now if someone messes around they're going to at least lose an arm or a leg or possibly their life. The Colombians started it off and then when the East Enders got involved their philosophy was that they can't be seen to be done down because then the next one will put one over on them.'

He still gets good offers to move back into the mainstream of the dealing world: 'I get offered crazy things: drive a car up to Scotland, don't have to know what's in it, twenty-four hours, park it, leave the keys and walk away, £5,000. But if you do that you can't say no to anything else. They offer that because they know I need the money and they want to get me started.' He is aware that his movements are still observed, Customs men can be very persistent. 'I get nervous because they've just rounded up several people I know.'

We met up again a few weeks later in the high-rise council flat where he now lives. He was anxious that the picture that emerged of him should not paint him as 'a cockney thug. I see myself a little bit more subtle than that.' He has decided to abandon the criminal life and do something 'useful' though many of his former colleagues have not.

'A lot of people talk to me about computer fraud because I got heavily involved with computers but I said no. Most of it is done from inside; you can have outside money and outside equipment but you need inside information. You never hear about it because the banks are too embarrassed to admit that it has happened.'

He wondered what the next generation of criminals would move to, if they sought fresh markets beyond cocaine.

'There are many ways now to rob with the pen rather than the sword that are perfectly legal – there's almost no point in being criminals. Everyone seems to be able to sleep at night doing it, so – God bless.'

Select Bibliography

Box, Steven, *Power, Crime and Mystification*, Tavistock, 1983

Clarens, Carlos, *Crime Movies*, Secker & Warburg, 1980

Chibnall, Steve, *Law and Order News*, Tavistock, 1977

Cox, Barry, Shirley, John and Short, Martin, *The Fall of Scotland Yard*, Penguin, 1977

Dickson, John, *Murder Without Conviction*, Sphere, 1988

Eddy, Paul, Walden, Sarah and Sabogal, Hugo, *The Cocaine Wars*, Arrow, 1989

Green, Jonathan, *Says Who?*, Longman, 1989

Greene, Graham, *Brighton Rock*, Penguin, 1943

Hercules, Trevor, *Labelled a Black Villain*, Fourth Estate, 1989

High Times Encyclopaedia of Recreational Drugs, Stonehill, 1976

Hughes, Robert, *The Fatal Shore*, Pan, 1988

Kelland, Gilbert, *Crime in London*, Grafton, 1987

Kray, Charles, with McGibbon, Robin, *Me and My Brothers*, Grafton, 1988

Kray, Reg and Kray, Ron, with Fred Dineage, *Our Story*, Sidgwick & Jackson, 1988

Nown, Graham, *The English Godfather*, Headline, 1987

Orwell, George, *An Age Like This: Collected Essays, Journalism and Letters*, Penguin, 1970

Parker, Tony and Allerton, Robert, *The Courage of his Convictions*, Hutchinson, 1962

Pearson, John, *The Profession of Violence*, Granada, 1985

Read, Piers Paul, *The Train Robbers*, Coronet, 1986

Samuel, Raphael, *East End Underworld*, Routledge & Kegan Paul, 1981

Stern, Vivien, *Bricks of Shame*, Pelican, 1987

Tremlett, George, *Little Legs*, Unwin Hyman, 1989

Woffinden, Bob, *Miscarriages of Justice*, Coronet, 1987